AF605914

Law as Metaphor

Law as Metaphor

From Islamic Courts to the Palace of Justice

June Starr

State University of New York Press

Published by
State University of New York Press, Albany

Printed in the United States of America

For information, address State University of New York
Press, State University Plaza, Albany, N.Y. 12246

Production by M. R. Mulholland
Marketing by Fran Keneston

Library of Congress Cataloging-in-Publication Data

Starr, June.
Law as metaphor : from Islamic courts to the Palace of Justice/
June Starr.
p. cm.
Includes bibliographical references and index.
ISBN 0-7914-0781-0 (CH : acid-free). — ISBN 0-7914-0782-9 (PB : acid-free)
1. Law—Turkey—History and criticism. 2. Islamic law—Turkey.
3. Law and anthropology. I. Title.
KKX120.S73 1992
349.561—dc20
[345.61] 90-49066
CIP

10 9 8 7 6 5 4 3 2 1

For Laura Nader, my teacher and friend,
a pioneer in the anthropology of law.

On Nation-Building:
But how can one characterize what it was that was being built, if the thing was changing character all the time?

—Katherine Verdery (1983:4)

Was there a culture or rather several cultures that carried on beside the official one we knew and studied, and that at some point gave up or were integrated with the larger whole? If so, how did this happen?

—Eugen Weber (1976:xii)

On Social Anthropology:
I . . . believe that anthropology has a distinctive and essential contribution to make to the larger enterprise of understanding social phenomena. Macrosociologists and historians, political scientists, and economists may give us the broad sweep, but anthropologists and local historians are the ones best equipped to demonstrate that sweep's particular, "on-the-ground" manifestations, and to show how events at the level of the particular often serve not just to reproduce but also to constrain the general processes of development and social change. It is our documentation of the specifics that verifies, amends or invalidates larger theories about social process. . . .

—Katherine Verdery (1983:17)

Contents

Maps xi

Figures xiii

Tables xv

Preface xvii

Acknowledgments xxvii

A Note on Orthography xxxi

Introduction xxxiii

I. The Historical Context: From *Kadı* Courts to the Palace of Justice

1. The Search for a New Society 3
2. *Şeriat* and *Kanun*: Islamic Law and Secular State Law 21

II. From Ottoman to Modern Times: The Restructuring of Social Space and Social Relations

3. Land Transformations 45
4. Bodrum—One Hundred Years of Solitude 69
5. Gender and Family Transformations 89

III. The Development of Secular Law

6. Managing Disputes at the Village Level: Cultural and Legal Forms 119
7. Judicial Decision-Making in District Courts 149
8. The Continuing Dialectic 173

Appendix I.	Chronology of Uprisings Against the Ottoman Empire and Significant Events in the Formation of the New Republic	187
Appendix II.	Turkish Rural Law Enforcement Agents	195

Selected Glossary 199

Laws, Statutes, and Codes 205

Bibliography 207

Index 231

Maps

Map 1. Bodrum District in Relation to the Major Cities in Western and Central Turkey 4

Map 2. Bodrum District, 1968 46

Map 3. Bodrum Town: Names and Locations of Bodrum's Neighborhoods in the 1960s 78

Map 4. Mandalinci Village: A Dispersed Settlement......... 120

Maps

Figures

Figure 1. Chain of Jurisdiction Pertaining to Civil and Criminal Cases 135

Tables

Table 1. Land Cases in the Civil Courts of Bodrum, Turkey, 1965–1967 62
Table 2. Land Cases in Bodrum's Criminal Courts, 1965 through 1967 63
Table 3. Population by Religion and Ethnicity for the Years 1894, 1912, 1927, 1946, 1965, and 1980 in Bodrum Town and Bodrum District 71
Table 4. Bodrum District, 1927 Census, Population by Religion 75
Table 5. Boats in Bodrum, 1940 76
Table 6. Outcomes for Divorce Cases Initiated by Men and Women 99
Table 7. Gender of Principal Complainant and Principal Defendant in Middle Criminal Court Cases 102
Table 8. Population by Village and Household Size for 1946 and 1965 Census 104
Table 9. Population of Bodrum District, 1946 and 1965, by Villages, Towns, and Total 105
Table 10. Average Number of People per Household in the Years 1946 and 1965 by Certain Villages 106
Table 11. Out-of-Court Disputing Strategies by Grievance, Status Relationships of Disputants, and Category of Disputes 139

Tables

Table 1. [illegible]

Table 2. [illegible]

Table 3. [illegible]

Table 4. [illegible]

Table 5. [illegible]

Table 6. [illegible]

Table 7. [illegible]

Table 8. [illegible]

Table 9. [illegible]

Table 10. [illegible]

Table 11. [illegible]

Preface

> Our concepts structure what we perceive, how we get around the world, and how we relate to other people. Our conceptual system thus plays a central role in defining our everyday realities. If we are right in suggesting that our conceptual system is largely metaphorical, then the way we think, what we experience, and what we do every day is very much a matter of metaphor.
>
> Lakoff and Johnson (1980:3)

Words, like land, are often appropriated by small groups of users for their particular purposes, and words, like land, sometimes can be restored to their former usages through purposefully reclaiming them. I use the word *metaphor* as Lakoff and Johnson (1980) do, not in its narrow, semiotic meaning, but as a popular figure of speech in which one thing is likened to another. I appreciate the ability of a metaphor to startle by suggesting that dissimilar things may have some qualities in common. I love its "as if" dimension, its ability to allow a reader, for a moment, to suspend disbelief.

I chose the title *Law as Metaphor* for two reasons.[1] First, I hoped my book would relate to two monographs in the anthropology of law that over the last decade have greatly influenced my thinking. Sally Falk Moore's book *Law as Process* (1978) was an affirmation that law changes in expected and unexpected ways,[2] through many small institutional changes and through people interacting at the borders of law who create new normative patterns, that she called "semi-autonomous fields" (p. 55).[3] Comaroff and Roberts's *Rules and Processes* (1981) followed. They accepted Moore's conceptualization that law had to be viewed as many events in a process happening through time, and they emphasized the effect that legal *rules*, as well as norms, had in defining, shaping, and limiting legal processes.

I thought to add to this emerging anthropological, empirically valid formulation of law by suggesting that, in national capitals, elites competed over legal rules and the legal system's structures, and that many decades later the results of this competition among elites would be apparent in "the legal" and extralegal forums that rural villagers use. I agree with those anthropologists who suggest that the actions that agents take reveal their mental maps and "cognitive frameworks". That is what I understand rural legal consciousness to be.

I agreed that law is a process and that it is shaped by rules and a cultural logic, and here I add that it is also a *discourse* fought over by very real agents with different political agendas. The outcomes of earlier struggles over state law may have consequences for officials and ordinary people many decades and even centuries later. Yes, law matters, which law matters, and especially *whose law* matters. Thus, the first meaning of the title *Law as Metaphor* is to highlight the comparison between this book and two important texts in the development of anthropological legal theory.

The second meaning of the title *Law as Metaphor* is to suggest that a subject as complex as nation-state law[4] can be compared through metaphor to a subject as complex as group competition for control over the law of the nation. Law is multilayered, with meanings that sometimes are clear, yet often obscure. New meanings may be discovered (or developed, or read into the law) in different historical times, as the gestalt of the times changes. As groups holding different cultural values obtain power, they find new meanings in existing laws. Sometimes a law, or *the law*, is infused with class meanings and content (Thompson 1975:260–61); at other times a law mediates between conflicting class values; at still other times a law (or *the law*) is the resolution of competing social views or the starting point for the articulation of a different set of values (Tigar and Levy 1977).[5]

Law exists at every level of society, sometimes as state law, sometimes as norms or "rules" of conduct,[6] and law usually conveys historical meaning. Said differently, the enactment of every written law (or authoritative pronouncement) has its own history of supporters and opponents. Among social anthropologists, "felt" norms in small interacting groups and rules generated at the margins of interacting social groups[7] are considered law also, although unwritten. Pospisil conceptualizes this as the multiplicity of legal systems within one society (1971:100–102).

Like law, power relations among classes or status groups are also variably textured, sometimes clear and obvious, yet often masked and hidden through the unifying symbols of a society. At times unifying symbols of a society become the focus of conflicting values. (During the 1970s, mustaches in Turkey became a symbolic badge of political identity. After the army took control of the state in 1980, to wear a political mustache brought strong negative sanctions against its wearer.)

Power relations among social groups are usually hierarchically structured, although in a particular historical moment different social classes may have interests in common. Like a society's law, a society's power relations are always infused with cultural and historical meanings. Dominant groups may interact across a number of different national borders, amassing resources in one place to be used in another. That is how I understand the actions of elite actors in Wallerstein's core and periphery regions (1980). Such behavior characterizes the ways in which state agents and entrepreneurs in empires exploit their colonies and the ways dominant groups exploit subservient ones.

My own research and writing about law in Turkey has been less involved with exploitation made possible through law than with how state law became a resource for groups previously lacking power (Starr 1984, 1985b, 1989b), and this book, especially in the ethnographic chapters, continues that theme.

Implicit throughout the discussion is the assumption of the modern Turkish Constitution that Islam in today's Turkey does not offer a competing legal sensibility to secular law as it does in contemporary Iran and in much of the Arab Middle East today. Islamic law in Turkey has not been the established legal ideology of the ruling bureaucracy since the second half of the nineteenth-century Ottoman Empire, even though Islamic law persisted in the area of family relations until Ataturk's reforms in the early 1920s. This continues to be the situation in Turkey despite the fact that some Turkish groups actively organize for more Islamic structures and sentiment, and Islamic practices in Turkey are increasing.

The subtitle of this book's title refers to historical change, the movement from Islamic *Kadı* courts to secular ones based on European models. Just a hint of the reification of law is apparent in the term *the palace of justice*. The Bodrum courts I studied in the 1960s were called simply *Adliye,* which depending on the circumstances connoted either "law court" or "justice." In moving the Bodrum courts to a new building in the 1980s, the national hierarchy of courts grandly renamed them. Now these courts are *Adliye Sarayı*, the Palace of Justice, like their counterparts in Izmir, Ankara, Istanbul, and Europe.

The Relationship of This Book to My Earlier Book, *Dispute and Settlement in Rural Turkey* (Starr 1978a)

My earlier book focused on conflict and disputes, collected in an

Anatolian farming village by the sea in rural southwestern Turkey. It showed what kinds of problems caused rural Turkish villagers to argue and fight, what dispute-handling institutions existed in the village (whether informal or formal, legal or extralegal), and how sometimes kinship, patron-client relationships, and neighborhood ties provided the informal structures useful in resolving conflict before it escalated or before a party became less flexible in accepting a solution. I also discussed the types of disputes villagers took to local district courts in Bodrum, the region's provincial town. A dominant theme was how much secular national law affected rural Islamic villagers, both in the village and at the district level. I had followed village disputes taken to the Bodrum district courts and so spent nearly a year and a half studying Bodrum's four civil and criminal courts, which were the lowest level of the national legal system. With Jon Pool, a political scientist, I published in 1974 an overview of the work of that court.

Even in the 1960s when it was chic for an anthropologist to glamorize the exotic in native life, portraying natives as free of the repressive obsessions of urban society, I conceptualized my project not as the study of an isolated community close to "the natural," but as a unit participating within a national culture. This earlier monograph, an ethnography of local disputes, conceptualized the village in relation to the national and the national in relation to the region. The first five chapters encompassed the traditional subject matter to which every anthropologist attends: descriptions of place, kinship and marriage, the household unit, the work routine, the ceremonies, the political structure, the informal networks and power structure, and the limits of local authority.

The last three chapters considered disputing processes of self-help, self-help with a negotiator, with a mediator, with formal officials, and at court. It moved on to analyze violent as well as peaceable action, and ways the local law enforcement officials and the court intervened in the disputing processes, often settling, and sometimes confounding local disputes. Conclusions drawn from that study are found in chapter 6 here, along with new insights created by looking back at earlier work *through a different lens.*

This current book presents a more complex view of state-local relations, a more complex sense of historical time, and a more complex sense of how society changed. I attempt to describe how Ottoman civil servants made a revolution from above[8] by creating parallel, secular legal institutions at the national level that existed alongside Islamic ones in the later nineteenth-century Ottoman Empire. I trace aspects of these parallel systems in law and in education in the nineteenth-century

Ottoman state, and later during Ataturk's reform period of the early 1920s. This allows me to ask in later ethnographic chapters, based on my own field research, how much of the secular reforms of the 1920s reached rural Islamic farmers by the 1960s. I discuss changes in institutional forms in the law, in the courts, in the landholding system, and in village legal consciousness.

Empirical social science literature on law and conflict resolution has few studies of national law's effects on rural areas, and in the Middle East this lack is even more in evidence. Most Middle Eastern research on law has been in Arab Islamic countries and concerns "tribal" (Kennett 1925; Stewart n.d.) and village conflict resolution (e.g., Nader 1965b; Rothenberger 1978; Witty 1978, 1980; Dwyer in press). Geertz's anthropological studies (1968, 1983) are more general, while other anthropologists have studied Arab Islamic local courts (Rosen 1980–81, 1984, 1989a, 1989b; Messick 1983(a), 1983(b), 1986, 1990); Antoun 1979, 1990; Dwyer 1979, in press).

Empirical studies of law and disputes in Turkey, with the exception of my own work, number less than six (Stirling 1957, 1960; Yalman 1979; Magnarella 1988; Zwalen 1981.) (See also the nonempirical but noteworthy Mardin 1961.)

National Events Shaping the Anthropological Perception of a Project

Some of the complex events taking place in the Turkish nation influenced my thinking as I worked, for many years, in different places and libraries on this book.

In the summer of 1980, as I began writing a book about the rural Turkish trial courts that I'd studied in Bodrum, Muğla Province, from 1966 to autumn 1968, the decade of violence and unrest in Turkish cities continually intruded on my consciousness. By September 1980 the Turkish military, in a bloodless coup, had taken over national television and radio, dismissed parliament, and established military rule. This occurred to stop a decade of increasing violence between rival political groups in Turkish cities and on university campuses. At the time, and even later, it was reported that most Turkish citizens, exhausted by civil unrest and public terrorism, were relieved that martial law had ended the crisis of anarchy.

These events created a dilemma for me, as a social anthropologist. How could I write a book about ordinary times and everyday processes of the 1960s as if September 1980 had not taken place? To do so would imply that the Turkish Constitution of 1961 was still in effect when, in fact, all members of parliament and all leading politicians had been arrested and sequestered in Canakkale, a small seaport on the eastern Dardenelles.

The Turkish military, which considered itself the bastion of Ataturkian principles, had intervened in affairs of state twice before, in 1960 and again in 1971. Yet at those times control of the state had been quickly handed back to the civilian politicians. The uprising of 1980 marked a different time. Many of the rivals for state power had used violence, terrorism, and assassination to gain their ends, and they would do so again unless a different kind of social order was created. Moving toward a new social order would take more time than had earlier military interventions, and would necessitate the creation of new political arrangements. Meanwhile the military, as reluctant leaders, would keep control of the state for a longer time.

In Bodrum in the 1960s I had worked under the theoretical paradigm then dominating social anthropology; structural functionalism.[9] In 1980, I realized there was no way this theoretical orientation could encompass the events that had just occurred in Turkey. Everything I knew about Bodrum, her people, her law courts, her administrative structures, and her villages implied stable times, both in the region and in the nation. Rural Bodrum's townspeople and villagers dwelt in comparatively *secular* communities in a stable, comparatively *democratic* nation. The view from 1980 made the society I had studied in the 1960s one which could not just be *described*, but needed to be *understood*.

Like other social anthropologists writing books twenty years later and attempting to understand how the world was affecting their villages, small towns, or ethnic groups of study, I turned to history.[10]

I began to conceive of writing an anthropology book that would use some historical events and structures to discuss the development of Turkish society and law. I would treat law as discourse. The law and the legal structures in place when Islamic groups governed the state had promoted a legal culture different from those structures created by secularizing elites. Turkish law was an arena in which rival visions of the social and political world could be located. In defining and creating Turkish legal structures, elites carried out a power struggle for control of the state. The legal discourses, espoused by Islamic and secular law practitioners and users, projected two different visions of the world and the place of Islam in people's lives.

Contextualized in the power struggle for control of the Turkish nation, my data might be used to show how much the secular elites had won by the mid-1960s in a rural region. As a social anthropologist, I had valuable and unique knowledge of a particular region at a particular point in time. My field research of the 1960s might provide baseline data to illuminate what had changed and what structures had endured. People may be born into a culture and be socialized by those values, but in the process of interacting in structures, they both create and continue those structures and are constituted by them (Giddens 1983).

In the 1960s, Bodrum's people were governed by secular law, dwelled in secular communities, and used secular courts in ways that suggested their acceptance of the system. There was little to suggest in their behavior that they felt a conflict between their religious identities as Muslims and their secular identities as Turkish citizens. Bodrum townspeople and villagers both celebrated Islamic holidays and participated in secular law courts. The Bodrum district, similar to many regions in Anatolia, was a good place to study the ways national Turkish culture was affecting a whole region, because it was as typical as most small towns (*kaza*s) of western rural Anatolia. By the 1980s Bodrum town had become an international tourist center, filled with yachts and tourists in summer, with urban Turks and Turkish retirees in winter. Bodrum district had time-sharing condominiums in the small villages I had known and loved, and as an area it was no longer typical of many small towns and villages of Anatolian Turkey. Thus, a restudy of the region did not excite my anthropological imagination.

This book is based on field research in Turkey in the following years: winter 1966 to fall 1968, summers of 1985 and 1987, and spring semester 1989 when I held a visiting Fulbright research professorship to Ankara Law Faculty, Ankara University.

Influenced by the conceptualization of the state as an arena where power struggles among groups are mediated, an idea developed by Tigar and Levy (1977), Skocpol (1979), and Thompson (1975), I hope to bring to this study of Turkey the idea that its law developed in the same way. That is, that the growth of Turkish law and legal structures comes not as the logical evolution of ideas, but rather, as metaphor, that it represents the embodiment of struggles between groups that were worked out in compromises within the legal system.

Notes

1. In this book, law is conceived as state law, as regional law, as local-level law, and authoritative rules of conduct. It is embodied in written codes, judicial decisions, and those by administrative boards, by the legislature, by village councils, and often by other law-enforcement officials. Law like behavior or social control is also embodied in extralegal processes that human actors de-

velop to resolve conflict and disputes. A minimal definition of law was developed by Llewellyn and Hoebel (1941:20–21) as the regularized processes people follow to resolve cases of trouble. Malinowski (1942:1246) pointed the way towards empirical study of law by suggesting the ethnographer should not take too narrow a view, so that law is only equated with "law breaking"; instead he or she must be "primarily interested in the working of social control, that is the maintenance of order." He concludes a list of things to study by saying "the maintenance of law is never a matter of *yes* or *no*, that is an *all* or *none* reaction. It is a dynamic process of constant struggle and readjustment" (p. 1249).

2. Moore states: "The same social processes that prevent the total regulation of a society also reshape and transform efforts at partial regulation. The making of rules and social and symbolic order is a human industry matched only by the manipulation, circumvention, remaking, replacing and unmaking of rules and symbols in which people seem almost equally engaged" (1978:1).

3. Moore proposes that a "small field observable to an anthropologist be chosen and studied in terms of its semi-autonomy—the fact that it can generate rules and customs and symbols internally, but that it is also vulnerable to rules and decisions and other forces emanating from the larger world by which it is surrounded" (1978:55).

4. State law holds two meanings to a social scientist. It is the law of a nation-state, and it is the law of a particular province or regional division, like the law of New York state or, in the United States, the law of state courts as opposed to federal courts. In this passage I mean nation-state law.

5. Tigar and Levy argue that legal change is the product of conflict between social groups and classes seeking to turn the institutions of social control and law to their own purposes, and that each group wishes to assure that the legal system establishes a specific system of law and social relations that favors them (1977:xiii). Any group aspiring to state power attacks the old social order, using its own systems of legal rules and principles first. In thinking about the use of legal rules and ideology of the old order to create a new one, Tigar and Levy coin the suggestive phrase, the *jurisprudence of insurgency.*

6. Also see ft. 1 for additional definitions and discussions of *law.*

7. See Moore (1973).

8. Trimberger's book *Revolution From Above* (1978), a comparative historical study of Japan, Turkey, Egypt, and Peru, came to my attention after my book was fully written. Hers is interesting and well worth reading. It focuses on military bureaucrats, giving less weight to Islamic structures and culture than I do. She is little interested in legal change, she has not conducted intensive field research in Turkey, and as a comparative historical sociologist she did not feel compelled to study the Turkish language.

9. For classic anthropology of law studies written under this paradigm, see Bohannan (1957), Engel (1978), Epstein (1954), Gluckman (1955), Gulliver (1963, 1969, 1971), Llewellyn and Hoebel (1941), Malinowski (1926), Nader (1969b), Nader and Todd (1978), Pospisil (1958), Starr (1978a), Turner (1957), Van Velsen (1964).

10. See Moore (1986), Verdery (1983), Weber (1976).

Acknowledgments

Writing a book discontinuously over ten years and talking with friends, colleagues, and acquaintances about it means I accumulated a number of debts which I am glad to now acknowledge.

I am grateful to the following institutions for financial support, release time from teaching, and/or office space: the Socio-Legal Centre at Oxford University 1981–82, the Law Faculty of Erasmus University Rotterdam 1981–82, and SUNY Stony Brook. Wenner-Gren Foundation for Anthropological Research provided a grant in December 1988 that allowed me to return to Turkey for the spring term of 1989 to study the Turkish judiciary and appellate court structure. Fulbright Foundation, the Council for Exchange of Scholars, and the Institute of Turkish studies gave small grants when I was a visiting Fulbright research scholar at Ankara Law Faculty that same term, and SUNY Stony Brook provided matching funds. The Institute of Turkish Studies provided some funds in 1989–90 for xeroxing, typing, and editing of the manuscript; also an Institute of Turkish Studies travel grant in 1987 allowed me to present parts of chapter six in Zagreb at the International Congress of Anthropological and Ethnological Sciences, to the Commission of Folk Law and Legal Pluralism.

The *Law and Society Review* has graciously allowed me to reprint here much of an article I published in their journal, "The Role of the Courts in Changing the Lives of Rural Turkish Women, 1950–1970" (Starr 1989b). E. J. Brill has allowed me to reproduce three maps from the book I published with them, *Dispute and Settlement in Rural Turkey: An Ethnography of Law* (1978). These appear here as Maps I, II, and IV.

A number of people have commented on parts of this work, and Jane Collier deserves special mention for talking over many of these ideas with me and reading the whole manuscript several times. Jeremy Boissevain and William Arens's comments were useful on the first draft. Other colleagues at SUNY Stony Brook who encouraged this work were Beverly Birns, Rose Coser, Rhoda Selvin, Said Arjomand, and Dick Taatgen.

Anthropologists to be thanked for specific comments on chapter 6 or 7 are Carol Greenhouse, Robert Hayden, Sally Merry, and Clark Sorensen. Paul Stirling, professor emeritus of Kent University, and İbrahim Yasa have been in the forefront of anthropological studies in Turkey. Both are to be thanked for friendship and encouragement over the years.

At Oxford's Socio-Legal Centre, prolonged discussions of law and social science occurred, and I thank Donald Harris, Richard Markovits, Inga Markovits, Max Atkinson, Richard Lempert, and Mac O'Barr for those experiences. Helen Calloway, Renée Hirschon, and Shirley Ardener of the Oxford Women's Anthropology Committee provided stimulating discussions and critiques of my work on Turkish women. Rafeala Lewis and Geoffrey Lewis of St. Anthony's College, Oxford, and the Oxford Middle East Institute opened all sorts of unexplored pathways of Turkish studies for me; their hospitality and stories of Turkey enlivened many evenings.

Professor Burrill, Rhodes Murphy, Pierre Oberling, and others in the Columbia University Seminar, "The History and Culture of the Turks" provided a continuing classroom of Ottoman History. Heath Lowry, director of the Institute of Turkish Studies, Washington, D.C. made useful comments on a paper I gave on married women, reduction of household size, and Turkish village population (incorporated in chapter 6 here). Kathleen Burrill, Pierre Oberling, and especially Geoffrey Lewis puzzled with me over the last twenty-five Turkish law court case names that I had been unable to translate. I thank them as well as my first cotranslator of Bodrum law court case names, Jon Pool. Also, Carter Findley for legal information, and Cornell H. Fleischer for historical information. Thanks also to Ciğdem Kâğıtçıbaşı and İlkay Sunar, fellow students at the University of California, Berkeley, who as my first Turkish teachers, started my understanding and speaking of Turkish.

Law and Society colleagues also deserve thanks, including Richard Abel, Shari Diamond, Marc Galanter, John Griffiths, Robert Kidder, Frank Munger, Carol Seron, Susan Silbey, Keebet von Benda Beckman, and Franz von Benda Beckman. I am also grateful to Christine Harrington and other colleagues in the continuing seminar in Law and Society at New York University Law School.

In Turkey, in the spring term of 1989, at the Law Faculty of Ankara University, many people answered my naive questions and were generally helpful. A special thank you goes to Özcan Celebican, professor and dean of the Law Faculty, İlhan Akipek, professor of international law and my sponsor, Oya Araslı, professor of constitutional law, Ülker

Gürkan, professor of sociology of law, Adnan Güriz, professor of philosophy of law, and Serap Telli, Docent of international law. Also, Tuğrul Ansay, former dean of Ankara Law Faculty, now living in Germany, has been a continuing source of information and encouragement since my first publications on Turkish law and society. Ersin Onulduran, executive director of Fulbright association in Ankara, and his cheerful staff likewise deserve a resounding thank you.

At the department of sociology/anthropology at Middle East Technical University, in spring 1989, colleagues were helpful, and especially noteworthy were Kayhan Mutlu, chair of the sociology/anthropology department, Bahattin Akşit, Sencer Ayata, and Aşye Ayata. Besides many wide-ranging discussions, Yildiz Ecevit and Mehmet Ecevit went out of their way to help solve problems of daily living in Ankara, and I am truly grateful. At Boğazici University in Istanbul, I want to thank Asye Üncu, chair of the sociology department, Faruk Birtek, Binnaz Toprak, and Cigdem Kâğıtçıbaşı. Mübeccel Kiray, dean of Marmara University, has been a wondeful friend to me through the years; I thank Mehmet Turhan, a political scientist and law professor at Dilçe University in Dıyarbakır, for wide-ranging conversations. Finally, I thank Dursun Mutlu, his mother, and his sister, Jâle, and all the wonderful people of Bodrum who have continued to live in my imagination, in part compelling me to write this book.

I also thank the unsung heroes behind academic books—the tactful and patient librarians of this world. In my case the search for elusive volumes was carried out by librarians of SUNY Stony Brook, The Bodelean Library at Oxford University, The British Museum in London, and Yale University's law library, Stirling Library, and International Law Library. I also thank my research assistants Ricardo Senno, who helped prepare the tables on household size in chapter 6, and Selma Denize, who helped translate Bodrum proverbs, some of which appear here. Evin Clermont did admirable editing; Linda Reilly and Robert Reilly have provided unceasing help with typing and production of the manuscript. Roselie Robertson has provided unceasing support at SUNY Press, and Gordon Hartig did fine copy editing.

I thank my son, Stephen Starr, who sacrificed some of his childhood and adolescence to my closed study door, and who sacrificed all of the brownies he wished I had baked for his homeroom classes. He accompanied my first field trip to Turkey and subsequently went back with me as a college student in 1985, 1987, and briefly in 1989.

And last I thank Laura Nader, who initiated me into the study of disputes, who broadened my focus from the study of feuding among the patrilineal Albanians and bilateral Ifugao to the study of disputes and dispute resolution, both in and outside of law courts. Her empiricism and ability to leap from the specific to the general have made her an inspiring teacher. Her wide-ranging interests, incisive intellect, and moral commitments have made her a prominent scholar. It is to her this book is dedicated.

For mistakes in the volume I take responsibility.

A Note on Orthography

In general Modern Turkish orthography has been used for words that are now an accepted part of the Turkish vocabulary, irrespective of their origin in Arabic, Persian or Ottoman Turkish. Thus, *Sharīʿa* (Arabic) has been written *Şeriat*, and *Şeyhülislâm* has been used instead of *Şhaykh ül-Islâm*. Arabic words have been given in parenthesis where this would be helpful to the reader.

In regard to Ottoman Turkish words, I use uniform spelling throughout the text based on the *New Redhouse Turkish-English Dictionary* (ninth edition, 1987), despite slight differences in renderings among Ottoman scholars. I only deviate from this practice when the word or phrase is in a direct quote.

The following letters in modern Turkish are pronounced as indicated: "c" like the English "j"; "ç" like the English "ch"; "ğ" close to the English "y"; "ö" like the German "ö"; "ü" like the German "ü"; "ş" like English "sh"; and "ı" like the "i" sound in the English phrase "ion" in action. The symbol "^" indicates a syllable containing a long vowel.

Introduction

In today's world we are continuingly exposed to political groups expressing extremist philosophies. This makes the task of writing a book on the opposing ideologies of secularism and Islam in Turkey easier than it was fifteen years ago, when the differences between these two opposing views were less obvious to western scholars. Then the social anthropologist Lloyd Fallers could write: "Turks will continue their project of constructing a national reality as both Muslims and secular republicans" (1974:105). Political upheavals in Middle Eastern countries and the growth of Islamic fundamentalism as a worldwide movement have made the once-envisioned rapprochement between Islam and republicanism in Turkey seem less of a possibility.

In this book, I treat secularism and Islam in Turkey as two opposing ideologies used by competing elites for control of the nation. Each ideology has a different discourse, each espouses a different vision of the world as it should be. Secular ideologies recognize the legitimacy of the Enlightenment, which marked a major break with thought that was dominated by religion. To accept the Enlightenment is to recognize the validity of scientific explanations of the world and to recognize the need for secular educational institutions. Islamic ideologies (I use the plural because there are many different kinds of Islam represented in Turkey today) recognize a state constituted by Islamic religious traditions and culture.

In Turkey today, far fewer people believe that one can be a good Muslim and still be a good Turkish republican citizen. Those who follow Islam are demanding more Islamic structures of learning and wish to create a society in which the cultural values are expressly Islamic. Civilian politicians and elites who dominate the state still attempt to follow a middle-road policy. They assert the nation is a secular republic, yet for the last twenty-five years the state bureaucracy has been involved in extensive programs of mosque-building and of creating state-sponsored Islamic educational institutions, meeting the requirements of an increasingly devout minority.

The lessons I have learned from studying Turkey's past suggest that law became a metaphor for the struggle between coalitions vying for control of the Ottoman-Turkish state in the nineteenth and twentieth centuries. Islam as a religion and as an ideology favors male control of females and male control of state structures, including the legal system. In its ideal form, Islam posits Islamic institutions of state and of law and links its adherents to Muslims throughout the world. Secularism, on the other hand, in its ideal form suggests a society of free and independent equals. It posits gender equality and Western institutions of state and of law.

In Turkey, like many other Middle Eastern countries entering the world system as nation-states, these opposing ideologies have been expressed in differing degrees in different times by particular groups seeking state power. When learning modern Turkish history, I saw that the power at the center of state politics was precarious, consisting of shifting coalitions. Sometimes these coalitions were challenged by some of their own state bureaucracies. Thus, the Turkish state could not be treated as a given but needed to be analyzed in terms of the competition among political parties, government bureaus, and of groups outside of legitimate state power who also vied for political supremacy (Skocpol 1979:xiii).

In trying to understand contemporary Turkish political processes I was confounded by a spectrum of political groups: right, left, center, as well as Turkish Islamic parties. From 1973 on, any party wishing to rule needed to form coalition governments to gain a majority of seats in Turkish parliament. Between 1973 and the military takeover in 1980, an Islamic party became a major player in parliamentary politics. As significant as the entry of Islam into party politics was the willingness of more radical parties on the left and right to use violence as a political weapon. Ideological conflict led to violent clashes beginning in 1974. Partisan politics had left the debating forums and moved onto university campuses and the streets in most Turkish cities.

As I pondered the events that had changed the course of Turkish history, paralleling them to the data I had collected in Bodrum, I realized something so obvious I had taken it for granted, namely, how important secular law and a generally secular outlook had been in Bodrum town and in the village I had studied (Starr 1978a). In Bodrum district of those years, although the people practiced Islam, there was little interest in pursuing Islamic solutions to conflicts. Conflict resolution in and outside of government institutions was characteristically secular. This strikingly simple but profound finding indicated to me that, in the discourse among groups competing for power, a dialectical relationship had emerged between Islam and secularism at that time—that is, a relationship in which seemingly antagonistic processes or forces are fundamentally entwined.

The word *discourse*, according to Webster's dictionary, means the formal and orderly expression of thought on a subject. In conceptualizing law as discourse, I was influenced by Robert Gordon, a law professor; "Legal discourses are important because they rationalize and justify in myriad subtle ways the existing social order as natural, necessary and just" (1988:16). Indeed, legal discourses confer legitimacy on elites that espouse them because they "sketch pictures of widely shared, wistful, inchoate visions of an ideal" (p. 16).

Anthropology and History

Anthropologists have under-studied the relationship between elites and law.[1] It became clear to me in this study that I had to look at the early competition between elites over the form the *emerging* Turkish state would take. That consideration, and a search for the beginning of secular Turkish law courts, led me back into nineteenth-century Ottoman society.

Although I draw heavily on the scholarship of Ottoman historians, anthropological uses of history are very different from the historian's. Without venturing too far into the epistemology of the two disciplines, historians study "documents to construct for themselves a true or real account of what 'actually happened' " (Cohn 1981:241). Anthropologists sometimes use documents, but mostly they use texts, written by historians, to illuminate long-term processes of change. Historians learn languages in order to use texts and documents of the period they wish to study. Anthropologists learn languages to communicate with living actors in the group or community of study. In my case I needed to learn the rural Turkish spoken in Bodrum's villages, the Turkish spoken by judges and litigants in court, and Turkish legal terms used in naming cases and processes that occurred in court, the court docket, and the dossiers.[2]

In the past, historians and anthropologists did very different kinds of research. Historians searched documents for monumental events in world history—how the battle was lost, what life at court was like in the age of Napoleon. Today, social historians and social anthropologists are doing work more closely related because, like anthropologists, historians have become concerned with the life of ordinary people.

There are other reasons why today the work of social historians and cultural anthropologists converge. Historians' sense of rigidity of structures has receded under the impact of challenges to their earlier understandings of world order. Many feel new methods and approaches are needed to study decaying colonial institutions within the same frameworks as newly constituted societies and developing nations. The new feminist scholarship is challenging the received wisdom of the discipline and suggesting historical interpretations need to be totally reworked and rewritten, if women's contribution to and places in history are to be understood. These questions have led some historians to turn to anthropology and social linguistics as sources for new ideas of how to reconstitute the discipline of history (Ermarth 1985:507). Others have looked to anthropology to offer a pathway into the meaning systems of earlier societies, and the cognitive processes of another culture through seemingly incomprehensible "opaque" rites, texts, or actions. Still others sought a research agenda for the study of ordinary lives—the attempt to see things from the natives' point of view (Chartier 1985:683). Some look to cultural anthropology for ways to study social processes, the development of hierarchies, and for a guide to what to study when one studied a culture. (The study of culture used to be the unique domain of the anthropologist.) Like cultural anthropologists, many historians today use Geetz's definition of culture as "an historically transmitted pattern of meanings embodied in symbols, a system of inherited conceptions expressed in symbolic form by means of which men [sic] communicate, perpetuate and develop their knowledge about and attitudes toward life" (1973:89). In fact, that is the definition of culture used throughout this text. With both anthropologists and historians using the same definitions, looking at processes not rigidity of forms, and reading much of the same post-structuralist writing of French literary scholars and philosophers, the boundaries of the disciplines seemingly have disappeared. Thus the historian, Joan Scott (1988:4) writes: "Perhaps the most dramatic shift in my own thinking came through asking questions about how hierarchies such as those of gender are constructed or legitimized. The emphasis on "how" suggests a study of processes, not of origins—(a tenet of anthropological theory is that origins can never be known)—"of multiple rather than single causes, of rhetoric or discourse rather than ideology or consciousness." She continues by suggesting that attention to the meaning of institutions and structures has become more important than attention to structures qua structures. Later, she suggests that politics raises the question of causality, which leads her to ask the very question that has been paramount in current anthropological studies of social conflict: "In whose interest is it to control or contest meanings? What is the nature of that interest?" Asserting another tenet of cultural anthropology, she states that interests do not inhere in actors or their structural positions: "The objects of study are then epistemological phenomena, which include economics, industrialization, relations of production, factories, families, classes, genders, collective action, and political ideas, as well as one's own interpretive categories" (p. 5). To raise to a level of study one's own interpretive categories (the last item on her list) has become an increasing preoccupation in cultural anthropology as self-awareness of how the social scientist constructs the other and the genre of story-telling within ethnographic studies itself has come under scrutiny. Whether the similarity of interests among historians and cultural anthropologists will continue after the early fascination with postmodern thought of French philosophy and literature abates or becomes integrated into the main stream of the disciplines remains to be seen. Meanwhile, some differences between anthropology and history remain, stemming from their separate and unique historical developments.

In the past, social anthropologists rarely studied documents, but as we increasingly use historical analysis in our work, more of us are making use of essays and books by historians that shed light on how contemporary structures came to assume their present form. The more usual focus of cultural anthropological research is a living social group for the touchstone of our trade has been empirical research in the field—long-term, direct observations of native groups.

I began reading the work of Ottoman historians to understand the hegemonic system of politics that had created the particular forms of "expressive, secular, legal culture" I had witnessed day after day in the Bodrum courts. That a secular, European legal culture (with all its implied meanings of "the rule of law") could appear so firmly rooted in the countryside, and yet two years later the democratic processes of the Turkish state could be called into question with the military takeover of the parliament, evokes Plato's cautionary "things are not usually what they seem."[3]

Recent critiques of legal anthropology (Starr and Collier 1987, 1989a; Fitzpatrick 1985; Chanock 1983; Roberts 1979) have suggested that anthropology of law, to remain viable, must return to major themes in social anthropology. Returning to my roots in anthropological historical studies, I have contextualized empirical field research on law within a theory of cultural, societal, and legal change.

In developing the argument for this book, I chose to analyze the development of two nineteenth-century institutions central to my problem; education and law. Since I am not a historian, I have not analyzed the military and economic institutions of the nineteenth-century Ottoman Empire that contributed to the emergence of the Ataturkian state since they were less close to the modes of social control I sought to understand. As an anthropologist who worked in the countryside, I have intimate knowledge of a region and of local district courts over a seventeen-year period that a historian usually does not have. I draw on the work of historians in the first chapters, using the methods of historical sociology, because historical analysis provides ways of understanding how secular law became entrenched in Islamic Turkey.

An Overview of the Book

The Islamic fundamentalist revolution in Iran has placed Turkey in a unique position. Unlike legally pluralistic India, which even today recognizes Hindu, Sikh, Islamic, and all Indian secular law, the official law of the Turkish republic was wholly secular after 1926. The return of Islamic law in Iran, the creation of a *Shi'ite* Islamic constitution, and the Islamization of much that had been secular in Iranian life raises questions about Iran's relationship to secular ideologies. (Of course, much of commercial law in Iran and in other Islamic countries remains European and secular in content.) Unlike Iran, where secularism appears far more problematic, the reforms of Kemal Ataturk and his coterie have been consequential. Secular law and a secular legal system under a nonreligious constitution have endured in Turkey, despite disruptions and challenges. Constitutionalism, elections of national officials, a secular, hierarchical system of courts, a parliamentary form of government, clear division of state powers among a number of functioning bureaus, a multiparty system, and *laique*, in which Islam is a religion under the control of the state—all continue despite three (comparatively bloodless) military interventions in Turkey since the creation of the republic. Secular Turkish law, like British law in India, has had some integrative effects on society, even though by creating secular state legal forums, other legal forums and some informal types of social control have been diminished or destroyed.

The central question is, therefore, that given the successes of the Islamic elites in creating Islam as one of the pervasive ideologies in Ottoman and later Turkish society; given the richness of Islam's contribution to the history of the Ottoman Empire and of Asia Minor and the wholeness of Islamic penetration into corners of daily consciousness and daily life; given the staying power of Islamic law in countries like Egypt, Pakistan, Libya, Iran, Afghanistan, Soviet Central Asia, and Muslim India; how did secular elites in Turkey manage to supercede Islamic law? Furthermore, as Islamic fundamentalism has gained in strength in the second half of the twentieth century, why have Islamic groups in Turkey been unable to mobilize for a restoration of Islamic law?

In my search for an explanation, I have used this book to place my field research in Turkish trial courts between 1966 and 1968 within a broader historical perspective. Going back a century, I found that education was the arena for power struggles between competing elites. In the initial chapter I describe how secularizing elites of the *Tanzimat* period developed a secular educational system first to parallel, and then to rival, the nineteenth-century Ottoman Islamic tradition.

By the mid-nineteenth and early twentieth centuries law became the metaphor in the competition for state control between secular and Islamic elites. In this context, in chapter 2 I examine the nineteenth-century origins of Ottoman secular law courts and trace their development during the reformist Tanzimat period to the enactment of the *Mecelle* of 1876—which, in fact, was a partial digest of *Şeriat* Law of the *Hanefi* School. I briefly describe the enactment of the first Ottoman constitution of 1876 and the end of the reformist Tanzimat period.

The restoration of the constitution during the Young Turk period (roughly 1908 to 1918) is next discussed. The reform of Islamic family law during the Young Turk period in 1915 and 1917 and historical events leading up to the establishment of a secular legal system under a new constitution then follow.

The Young Turk period provided the sources of some of Ataturk's ideas when he created the new Turkish Republic in 1923. A discussion of the interrelationships among national identity, law, historical events, and Ataturk's modernizing goals facilitates an understanding of the transformation of Asia Minor from a faltering empire to a modern, complex participant in today's global economy.

Chapter 3 shows how land/people relationships changed from Ottoman to contemporary times and the role that secular district courts and other governmental administrative agencies played in easing this transition.

Chapter 4 places the seaside town of Bodrum and the Bodrum region, the *place fixée* for my study, in the richness of her history. It was in Bodrum district in an isolated village without electricity, and later in Bodrum town itself, that I first learned Turkish and studied the effect of Turkish national law at the local level. The story of Bodrum town's incarnations—from rural nineteenth-century Ottoman town to authentic rural town of the new republic to international tourist spot in the 1980s—and some of the different legal problems encountered in this transformation are essential to anchor this study in the tangible.

In chapter 5 I address the domestic aspect of historical transition, examining how family relationships were changed by the movement from Islamic to secular Turkish civil law. I pay particular attention to how women, the most oppressed group under Islamic law, are faring under the modern secular legal system.

The results in the legal arena between Islamic and secular groups after the secularists won control of the state are shown in chapter 6. By examining forms of dispute resolution in a Turkish village, I demonstrate that Islam plays no obvious role, while national secular law has both defined existing relations and reinterpreted disputes taken to district-level courts. The inescapable conclusion is that Islamic law is not invoked, and villagers have no conscious knowledge of Islamic solutions to problems. Islam in the 1960s in western Anatolia had been relegated to the religious sphere only.

Chapter 7 moves inside the district-level courtroom to examine the decision-making powers of Turkish judges and the restraints placed on them, both by the structure of Turkish law and the way the law court hierarchy is organized. I begin by describing specific differences between the Turkish civil law tradition and the common law tradition, then focus on several cases to demonstrate how evidence is processed and the negotiating and adjudicative roles judges play.

In the concluding chapter I bring together the dominant themes of the book, moving toward a theory of the role of elites in state formation. Norbert Elias, a European historian, has suggested that to comprehend long term processes of state formation, we need a restructuring of the sociological imagination. We should not reduce the flow of time to static chunks, but ask how "relatively large 'systems' *became* and *become*, in these cases, *more* highly integrated and their 'parts' functionally more interdependent," a process that takes place through "integrative and disintegrative spurts" (1972:278).

Stimulated by Elias, I took as my project the attempt to discover how Turkey could appear so secular and integrated as a society in its uses of law in a rural region in the 1960s, yet experience disruptive urban upheavals and the recurrence of Islamic groups emerging as a national political force during the 1970s.

This study neither exhausts my data from the 1960s nor the ideas I wanted to explore in explaining the interaction of local legal practices and national culture in Turkish society prior to the events of 1980. But a small book on the interrelations between law and Turkish society, easily read in several evenings, perhaps is more useful to the modern reader. With the revival of Islamic fundamentalist movements in Middle Eastern, African and Asian countries, an account of the success of the Turks in developing a legal system that is secular and separate from the religion of Islam is a story well worth telling. With the disintegration of the "iron curtain" between western Europe and the Soviet bloc countries, and the return of eastern Europe and Russia to a market economy and more democratic structures, the Turkish experience with ways the legal system both shaped, and in turn was shaped, by rural actors and institutions of government has instructive lessons.[4] It reminds us of the possibilities and limitations of attempting to restructure society by restructuring her legal institutions. This study is part of the larger story of Turkey, of how her many peoples, through various difficult and troubled times, worked together to build a nation based on democratic institutions.

Notes

1. But see Barnes (1961), Cohen (1969, 1981), Cohn (1983, 1989), Marcus, ed. (1983), Nader (1974), Rudolph and Rudolph (1983), Schneider and Schneider (1983), Schneider, Schneider, and Hansen (1972), and Wolf (1966).

2. The court docket is the daily record of cases scheduled to be heard that day and their disposition. A dossier is the file kept by the court on each case.

3. In Plato's *Republic* there is a description of images on the cave wall that men, chained for their whole lives in the cave, take for real. Yet these are merely shadows of the real world of sunlight, darkness, shade, grass, and trees. The metaphor is about being blinded by partial knowledge.

4. For studies of cultural practices shaping legal practices, see Friedman (1990: 4–5, 43–4), Greenhouse (1986), Hayden (1987), Kidder (1979), Merry (1990), Moore (1986), Nader (1990), O'Barr (1982), Rosen (1989a), Starr (1991), and Yngvesson (1988).

I

The Historical Context: From *Kadı* Courts to the Palace of Justice

Chapter One

The Search for a New Society

> For much of the population [in the Ottoman Empire], nomad or settled, rural or urban, . . . cultural separation was the most striking feature of its existence on the periphery.
>
> Şerif Mardin (1973:173)

At its zenith in the sixteenth century, the Ottoman Empire embraced within its boundaries different countries, many ethnic groups, cultural divisions, religious denominations, and language groups, each related to the empire through their local communities and taxable statuses (Inalcık 1964:44). For example, the empire continued the Islamic system of taxation. Each religious group (called a *millet*), was allowed to govern itself as long as it paid taxes to the state. *Zimmi*, who were non-Muslims possessing sacred texts, for example, the Christians and Jews, had a higher tax status than Muslims. *Zimmi* were allowed to live in their denominational groups and practice self-government, but they did not share all the rights and privileges of Muslim citizens, their taxes were higher, and their status carried a number of other prohibitions. Townspeople, peasants, tribespeople, landlords, and soldiers each belonged to a particular taxable status.

Islam

Despite the multiethnic empire, from its beginnings in the fourteenth century until its demise in the twentieth, the Ottoman Empire was committed to the advancement and defense of the Islam faith. For six centuries the Ottomans were "almost at constant war with the Christian West, first in the attempt—mainly successful—to impose Islamic rule on a large part of Europe, then in the long, drawn-out rear guard action to halt or delay the relentless counter-attack of the West."[1] At the heart of this centuries-long struggle was the preservation of Islam. Until the second half of the nineteenth century, Islam affected all the cultural institutions of the Turkish state.

MAP 1

Bodrum District in Relation to the Major Cities in Western and Central Turkey

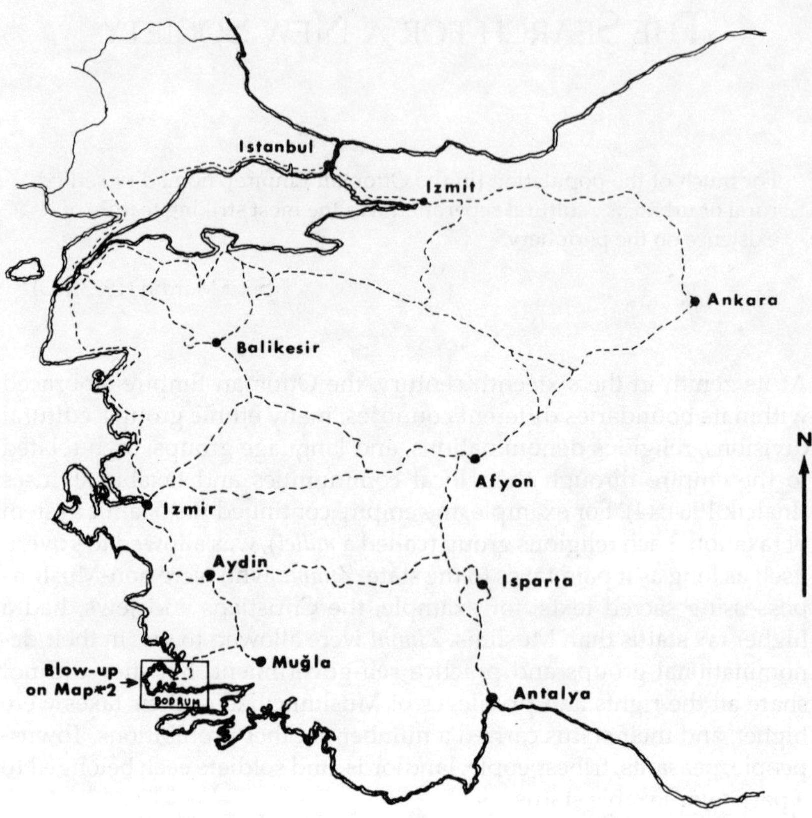

E. Velis

To the Ottoman Turk, the empire was Islam itself. It contained all the sacred places of Islam, and Ottoman chronicles referred to its territories as "the lands of Islam," its sovereign as "the Padishah of Islam," its armies as "the soldiers of Islam," its religious head as "the *şeyh* of Islam, and its "people thought of themselves first and foremost as Muslims." This empire was the center of the Islamic world, housing its fundamental institutions, the *caliphate* and the *Şeyhülislâm*.

In classical Islamic theory, law is the revealed will of God, "a divinely ordained system preceding and not preceded by the Muslim state, controlling and not controlled by Muslim society" (Coulson 1964: 1–2), and for over six hundred years Islamic law was the fabric that held the Ottoman Empire together. The Ottoman sultans sought to make the *Şeriat* (*Şhari'a* in Arabic) the basis of private and public life. Joseph Schacht, an authority on Islamic law, says the Ottoman Empire gave the *Şeriat* "the highest degree of actual efficiency . . . it had ever possessed in a society of high material civilization since early 'Abbasid' times" (1964:84). Islamic leaders, or *ulema*s, gained significant power at that time and for the next three centuries, during the gradual decline of the empire, fulfilled important functions in both the empire's capital city, Constantinople, and throughout its dominions. *Kadı*s (Islamic judges) and *Kadı* courts were the official Ottoman courts.

The official state religion of Islam and the "popular Islam" of the Anatolian tribespeople and villagers differed considerably in the Ottoman Empire. Popular religious practices had become institutionalized in the form of dervish orders and other mystic sects. As the many parts of the empire were settled, the leaders of these orders linked ordinary Ottoman subjects to the Ottoman administrators and rulers.[2] (Only men belonged to these "secret societies"; women expressed their belief in visits to local shrines, saints' tombs, and in mourning rituals.)

By the nineteenth century, the dervish orders provided a number of important social functions. They were centers of cultural and educational training for minor state positions and for the religious establishment, and they partly controlled charitable foundations, holding in their possession vast agricultural lands and religious shrines (pious endowments known as *evkaf*), given to them as gifts. Thus, Islamic brotherhoods and the monasteries of the Turkish mystic orders controlled part (or all) of the income of hundreds of villages, mostly through ownership of village lands. Islamic values and practices, entrenched as they were in the Ottoman administrative system, reinforced Islam as the symbolic ideology of Ottoman society. Islam was the mediating link between local-level society and the political structure: Locals shared religion with the Ottoman ruling elites, and religion provided the cultural fund that shaped ideals of political legitimacy. Thus, a universe of discourse was established through Islam, but affiliation and, of course, Islamic practices differed for the ruling elites and for the masses. A common saying, according to Mardin, was "religion and the state are twins."

Stanford Shaw, however, suggests further reasons for the continued importance of Islam in nineteenth-century Ottoman life. Instead of viewing Islam as a mode of discourse between the rulers and the ruled, Shaw suggests that, with the decay of the Ottoman Empire during the seventeenth and eighteenth centuries, the local Islamic clergy assumed administrative tasks that were neglected by state officials. *Kadı*s, *müftü*s, and *hoca*s (Islamic judges and teachers) were also local administrators. *Kadı*s were heads of *Kaza*s (districts), and they assessed and collected taxes, regulated markets, organized local security, and even maintained irrigation systems and roads. Thus, in the absence of all-powerful governors, the functions of "moral and spiritual guidance long exercised by the *ulema*s were developed into the kind of political influence sought after, but rarely achieved, by civil authorities" (1971:195).

In Mardin's view, local Islamic structures gained control of the countryside not because they were so powerful, but because the Ottoman administration viewed them as allies. He argues that because the Ottoman Empire protected crafts guilds (unlike feudal Europe) against the monopolistic practices of the merchants and denied independent government to towns, it "blocked the formation of oligarchies of merchant capitalists" (1969:261).

Evidence is accumulating, however, that by the nineteenth century, lively export economy from the Turkish hinterland was carried out through the ports of Constantinople and Smyrna in western Turkey, and traders had become independent of the state. Governors of *vilayet*s (Veinstein 1976; Inalcık 1984) and rural notables (*ayan*s) extracted large surpluses from the peasants for this trade, oppressing the peasants, which explained why the peasants would not support governors and *ayan*s against the state.

In Europe, by contrast, landed gentry developed in the countryside centuries earlier (when feudalism ended), and a merchant class had evolved in the free towns and cities. Strong alliances were formed between the new merchant class and landowners as they organized to make European state institutions responsive to the needs of a growing urban/rural middle class (Tigar and Levy 1977). Landed European gentry, in their struggle for legal reform, also gained strong support from the peasantry.

In Turkey the group who finally challenged the existing central government in the nineteenth century were high-ranking Ottoman administrators, men of the ruling elites. Unlike the Islamic clerical *ulemas*, these administrators had received a practical education. Because of their service in diplomacy and finance, the bureaucrats gained an increasing influence in the administration from the eighteenth century on. Devoted exclusively to the secular interests of the state and free from formalism and the bonds of tradition, they were ready to become faithful agents of radical administrative reform in the nineteenth century (Inalcık 1964:55).

Ottoman Administration and the "Ottoman Way"

The Ottoman ruling elites belonged to four administrative institutions: the Imperial Office (*Mülkiye*), the Military (*Askeriye*), the Bureau of Finance (*Maliye*), and the cultural/religious institution (*İlmiye*) (Shaw 1970:51, fn. 2). The Ottoman administration affected the Anatolian countryside in three ways: (1) through the Ottoman civil administration, (2) through the tax-farming system, and (3) through Islam in its official and popular forms (discussed above). To understand the structure and ideology of Ottoman society is to understand why much of the route to change came through European law instead of through reform of the existing Ottoman institutions.

At the beginning of the nineteenth century, even the most liberal members of the Ottoman ruling class believed that Ottoman governing institutions had been perfected four centuries earlier.[3] Believing their ways far superior to what could be achieved in the infidel West, Ottomans saw no reason to learn anything about European culture. The more educated an Ottoman official was, the more he was convinced of Ottoman superiority. Decline or loss of territory was attributed to a failure to apply and use the institutions, techniques, and weapons that had brought Ottomans greatness in the past. As a result, in the beginning of the nineteenth century, there was strong bias against learning from the West.

By the nineteenth century, the ideology of this administrative system was committed to what has been called "the Ottoman way." Administrators obtained their privileges directly from the sultan, and he was directly responsible for the welfare of his peasants (Mardin 1969:259). The state did not consist of tiers of responsibility, making this system of government patrimonial rather than feudal. Combined with this patrimonial principle of government was the traditional Ottoman concept of *had* (literally: boundary. But this was a cultural concept that suggested no one could invade or critique the way another person did his job). *Had*s were inviolate, making it impossible for any official or independent commission to investigate affairs under the jurisdiction of another. Any intervention inevitably caused a loss of status and prestige on the part of the individual concerned (Shaw 1970:52).

Given the ossification of the administrative system, with the power of the *ayan*s limited by their inability to attract peasant support, with independent burghers in free towns nonexistent, with peasants too downtrodden to envision a different world, and a complacent clergy sharing power in the countryside, the only Ottoman institution where a wider vision was possible was the military.

Educational Reform

It was via the military that European ideas of education first entered the Ottoman Empire (Lewis 1966:38–39). France became the country to which the Ottomans looked in search of models of change and reform (Berkes 1964:25–26). Sultan Selim III (reign: 1789–1807) hired several French instructors for the newly reorganized military and naval academies.

Yet the basic problems of Ottoman education remained for Sultan Mahmud II (reign: 1808–39) to define and solve. The traditional system of education was controlled by the *millet*s, Muslim and non-Muslim denominational groups recognized by the *Kur'an*. Islamic education was ruled over by the *ulema*s in *mektep* schools, and Mahmud II did not want to oppose them (Shaw and Shaw 1977:47). What he did instead was to bifurcate Ottoman education by leaving the Muslim schools alone and building up, alongside them, a new secular educational system (ibid.:47–48, 106).

Two technical schools already existed when Mahmud II began educational reforms: the naval academy, dating from 1773, and a military engineering school, founded in 1793. In the early nineteenth century, Mahmud II took the radical step of sending four male youths to Paris to study; they would become teachers in the new schools. Other students were to follow, and a large group went in 1826 (Lewis 1966:82). The outbreak of the Greek revolution in 1821 meant the Ottoman government had to replace Greek interpreters with Turks at the "Sublime *Porte*" (the central headquarters of civil/bureaucratic government). At this time a translation office to teach foreign languages was opened at the *Porte*. Like the Ottoman embassies established in Western capitals earlier, this became an educational center for a new generation of "Westernized" administrators (Inalcık 1964:55; Findley 1980:124). By 1827 a new medical school was opened in Constantinople to train doctors for the new army (Lewis 1966:82). Thus, by the end of Mahmud II's reign and the beginning of the Tanzimat, there were several advanced technical schools in operation with one thousand students enrolled at a time, a mere shadow of what was to come (Shaw and Shaw 1977:48).

Parallel secular education became the solution to avoiding direct challenges to the *ulemas*' authority over primary education. By circumventing this opposition, new secular schools for male students were developed beyond the elementary level (Shaw and Shaw 1977:47–48; Lewis 1966:83). Developed in Constantinople, they were later established in the provinces, and attracted students who did not choose a career in the Ottoman religious administrative arm, the *İlmiye*. The *mektep* system of education was very much concerned with Islamic teaching and, because of the past prominence of Islamic doctrine, very conservative. By 1838 young males between the ages of twelve and sixteen were able to attend new, essentially secular *rüşdiye* (adolescent) schools, located at two mosques in Constantinople, the Süleymaniye and the Sultan Ahmet (Lewis 1966:83). From here they could enter military academies, which were technical schools providing training for the civil service, or they could enter schools for literary education that provided studies in Arabic and French, the latter being the first European language intensively taught in Ottoman Turkey. *Rüşdiye* schools were opened for girls about 1858.

With the penetration of foreign commerce by mid-nineteenth century, and with increasing Christian missionary activity in Constantinople (which became the eastern capital of the Holy Roman Empire after Rome fell in A.D. 410 to the Visigoths), a number of foreign schools were established. These included the American secular school Robert College, established in 1863, and other denominational schools opened by French, Austrian, English, German, and Italian missionaries (Shaw and Shaw 1977:110).[4] Some were only elementary, others secondary:

> But their teachers, curriculums, lessons, and textbooks had to be certified by the Ministry of Education so that they would not teach anything that would violate Ottoman morals or politics. . . . The *millet* schools, especially after their curriculums were modernized late in the century, and the foreign schools provided a superior education to that offered in the still-developing state schools, but the general feeling of scorn for Muslims that they fostered among their students deepened the social divisions and mutual hatred that were already threatening to break up the Ottoman society and the empire. (Shaw and Shaw 1977:110)

The educational system was reformed, first at the top and then downward. The graduates of the new technical schools, referred to later as "Men of the Tanzimat," "were created by and for the new governing order. Their graduates formed a new elite of relatively well-educated and highly motivated individuals whose main desire was to modernize the state and bring the *Tanzimat* plans to fruition" (Shaw 1968:36). Many were children of the older elites, which acted as a brake on their reformist ideas, as they themselves would be economically bankrupt if all their reforms were carried out. Their education was in the values and ideology of Europe. Thus, the "Men of the Tanzimat" dwelled in a contemporary, symbolic world vastly different from most of those they ruled, and they were much farther removed from Muslim subjects than former Ottoman administrators had been.

The Young Ottomans and the Young Turks

The existence of two separate educational systems, one Islamic, the other more secular and European, each adhering to different philosophies, textbooks, and courses of study, created a situation that divided Ottoman society and also stimulated dissent.

Western ideas of nationhood, parliament, and constitution began to spread through the Turkish intelligentsia (Ramsaur 1957:34). By the 1860s, many ideas of the newly organized groups of Ottoman youths were too radical for the central government, and outspoken critics were forced into exile in London and Paris. The Egyptian prince Mustafa Fazil, an exile in Paris, named this movement in a letter to the Belgian newspaper *Nord* when he referred to the Ottoman youth as the *jeunes Turcs* (Lewis 1966:149–50). The name was picked up and translated into Turkish in a reformist journal, the *Muhbir.* Editors tried various Turkish phrases, and finally decided on *Yeni Osmanlılar*—the Young Ottomans (p. 150).

When the first Ottoman constitution of 1876 was suspended in 1878, members of the Young Ottomans, worried about repressive measures to follow, dispersed to Paris, Cairo, London, Cyprus, and Salonika. Their criticisms of the empire were expressed mostly through literature—in newspapers, journals, plays, and poetry. For example, the idea of a *Turkish*, as distinct from an Islamic or an Ottoman, loyalty was first voiced by Ali Suavi in his journal *Ulûm* (Science), published in Paris and later in Lyons during the Franco-Prussian War (1870–71) (p. 151–2).

The Young Ottomans put forth three demands: (1) a return to a constitutional empire, instead of the growing autocracy of the sultan and his ministers; (2) less censorship of their newspapers, journals, and books (pp. 184–85); and (3) an outlet for their patriotism, in the form of a renewed sense of Ottoman homeland. Their loyalty was to an Ottoman and Turkish society, and not to the multiethnic empire. Schoolboys at the Imperial Lycée of Galatasaray (subject to direct control by the Imperial Palace) by the 1880s were reading French and dreaming of freedom from the sultan's control. They now had a concept of fatherland, of how progressive reforms of society might take place, and what more humane governmental institutions would be like (p. 191).

A descendant of the Young Ottomans, some three decades later, were the Young Turks, first organized in 1889 by four students in the military medical college as a secret patriotic society (Ramsaur 1957:14). Their goal was to overthrow the sultan, Abdülhamid II, who was also the Caliph, the spiritual head of Sunni Islam. The Young Turks movement grew so rapidly that in 1896 their first attempt at a coup d'etat occurred, although it was discovered and crushed (pp. 19–20). Nevertheless, the ranks of the opposition continued to grow, both in Constantinople and among exiles in Paris (p. 22). By 1906 revolutionary cells among serving officers in the military were formed, the first being *Vatan* (fatherland), established by a small group of officers in Damascus, among them Mustafa Kemal (later known as Ataturk) (p. 95; see also footnote 2). Branches were also initiated in Jaffa and Jerusalem, among officers of the Fifth Army Corps, and among officers of the Third Army in Salonika (Lewis 1966:201). In 1906, Mustafa Kemal went to Salonika (considered the most advanced city in the empire because of its cosmopolitan population) to organize another cell of his revolutionary group (Ramsaur 1957:96). Here the name of the organization was expanded to *Vatan ve Hürriyet* (fatherland and liberty).

As revolutionary cadets became captains and majors, they joined members of a "ruling elite, prepared by education to command and to govern; their complaint was that they were not permitted to do so effectively" (Lewis 1966:201). By 1907 the center of the conspiracy had moved to the Turkish mainland, where new revolutionary groups were being formed in Macedonia and Anatolia under the Committee of Union and Progress that had originated and developed in Paris. Mustafa Kemal's revolutionary cadets "fused" with the Committee of Union and Progress in September 1907 (Ramsaur 1957:123).

In 1908, the British and the Russian sovereigns met to demand more concessions from the Ottoman Empire, as a wave of strikes spread from Anatolia to Rumelia. Soldiers—unpaid, underfed, and underclothed—were refusing to fight (Lewis 1966:202). By mid-summer the mutiny had spread among Third Army units in Macedonia, and the Second Army Corps in Edirne. The Committee of Union and Progress sent a telegram to the *Yıldız* Palace on July 21, 1908, demanding an immediate restoration of the constitution (p. 204). If the sultan refused, the heir-apparent would be proclaimed as sultan in Rumelia, and an army of 100,000 men would march on Constantinople. The sultan capitulated, and on July 24 announced that the constitution was again in force: "The mutiny had become a revolution, and the revolution had achieved its goal" (p. 205).

But although the second Turkish constitutional regime lasted longer than the first, it too ended in "failure, bitterness, and disappointment, because the government degenerated into a kind of military oligarchy of Young Turk leaders" (p. 207). With the defeat of the Ottoman Empire in 1918, this regime ended.

The Young Turk revolution was extremely nationalistic, and secret organizations, such as Freemason Lodges in Italy and the Bektashi dervish orders in Anatolia, had played some part in it (Ramsaur 1957:107–110). Little consideration had been given to how the non-Turkish ethnic groups in the empire would fit into the Ottoman constitutional state other than the need to become Ottomans in "a revived and powerful empire capable of holding up its head among the European nations" (p. 147). During the brief period of 1908 to 1918 when religion and nationality, freedom and loyalty, Islam and secularism were debated in books and periodicals, intellectuals and revolutionaries alike expected that Islam would remain the predominant force in the empire.

Thus Islam, as "a mental moral map" and as practice, was still an integral part of the Ottoman state and Ottoman consciousness at the start of the twentieth century, although a tremendous intellectual fervor now existed among all young urban intellectuals. Many "longed for a new life without knowing, however, what it was they wanted or how it would be realized. . . . It was a time when the empire had to exert enormous effort to recover, not only from the effects of corruption, tyranny, and economic bankruptcy, but also from moral and intellectual confusion" (Berkes 1959:20–21).

Ataturk

A complete reconstruction of the empire was considered by most intellectuals to be of the utmost urgency. During the period 1906 to 1917, when the Young Turks came to power, intense disagreement still existed among various groups concerning how the country should be reconstructed. The most conservative elites wanted to return to a total system of Islamic law within an Islamic nation. The second group, the Turkists, longed for the romantic ideal of ethnic unity of all Turks and, therefore, called for a return to the pre-Islamic past of Turkic groups (Berkes 1959:18–22). The third group, the Young Turks who had seized power, were intensely nationalistic. Some leaders among the Young Turks began to talk about relinquishing the empire and creating a Turkish nation, and some among these began to dream that it would be secular. In contrast to the Young Ottomans' motto of "preservation of religion and state," the Young Turks' motto was "union and progress" (Mardin 1973:181).

With the treachery and then capitulation of the Ottoman leaders at the Armistice of Mondros in 1918 and the subsequent Allied occupation of the straits, the Ottoman Empire was left leaderless and defenseless. At Versailles in 1919, the greedy European nations divided up all of the former empire, including Asia Minor, the homeland of the Ottomans.

Out of the ashes arose Ataturk, the most distinguished Ottoman general and a recognized military hero. He had led Turkish troops to victory against the British at Gallipoli in 1915, had skillfully defended the Russian front in eastern Anatolia against the Western Allied forces, and also had wisely retreated from Palestine in 1918. His landing at Samsun on May 19, 1919, "ostensibly to supervise the disarming of Ottoman forces in the area, but in reality to rally and organize national resistance against occupation, marks the real beginning of Turkey's War of Independence" (Reed 1980:321). He rallied an army from the Anatolian Turkish peasantry and reconquered the Turkish homeland from the French, English, and Greeks, in part because the former were tired of war. Rather than fight, the British and French withdrew, and Ataturk and his army were free to drive the invading Greek army from Izmir and Anatolia by 1922. Turkey's new frontiers and status as a nation-state were recognized in the Treaty of Lausanne in July 1923, thus confirming international recognition of the end of the Ottoman Empire.

Ataturk now faced an even more immense task—the creation of national institutions that would bring the Ottoman homeland into the twentieth century. The betrayal by the Islamic caliph and the Ottoman sultan at the 1915 armistice made his task easier, for now Islamic leaders were unable to gain popular support and could not rally Islamic followers to oppose him. In creating new symbols and institutions for the republic, Ataturk drew on the ideas, programs, and leaders of the Young Turk period. Joseph Szyliowicz, a political scientist, found a remarkable degree of continuity (1971) existed in both the core members of bureaucracies and in the political elites surrounding Ataturk during the creation of the Turkish Republic.

The New Turkish Nationalism

Since Turkish Islam had a seriousness of purpose and a "sense of devotion to duty and of mission, in the best days of the empire, that is unparalleled in Islamic history" (Lewis 1966:13–14), the transformation to a secular nation between 1922 and 1926 created, for many Ottoman subjects, a problem of national identity.

In Asia Minor until then, there had been no established *Turkish* identity. Until 1897 the ruling elites had been Osmanli, and "Turkishness" was despised, associated with the illiterate and ill-bred culture of Anatolian peasants (Kushner 1977:20–21). A person was an Ottoman diplomat, an Ottoman gentleman, an Ottoman soldier, a Turkoman, Yürük or Kurdish tribesman, an Arab, a "Laz," a Greek Orthodox trader, a Jewish or Armenian merchant, or a Turkish peasant (see Ramsay 1916:410–412; Mardin 1973:176). To be called a Turk was an expression of contempt. In 1908 an English observer could remark, "If you ask a Muslim in Turkey 'Are you a Turk?' he is offended and probably answers 'I am Osmanlı,' meaning 'I am an Ottoman' " (Kushner 1977:20). It was Ataturk who taught his citizens to say, "How lucky I am to be a Turk!"[5]

Under the impact of the Ataturk-led revolution, every aspect of Turkish life began anew. Language changed—a pure, genuine Turkish (*Öz Türkçe*) was distilled from the Ottoman model, and the written word was brought as close as "possible to the spoken languages of the people . . . [so that it could] serve as an efficient medium of instruction in schools" (Heyd 1954:20). A committee was charged with the preparation of a new script, composed of Latin characters instead of the Arabic calligraphy. In November 1928, the new alphabet was adopted by parliament. Modern Turkish, the official language of the republic, was based on phonetic spelling, which meant it would be easier for everyone to learn (Heyd 1954:22–23). A new spelling dictionary was published in the same year, and many Arabic and Persian words were excluded. Those that remained were either Turkicized or now appeared peculiarly foreign because they lacked the characteristic Turkish vowel harmony (pp. 23–24). Western numerals replaced Arabic ones.

Symbolic aspects of Ottoman culture were disparaged in dress. Western-style hats with brims were substituted for the red Moroccan fez, the distinctive mark of the nineteenth-century Ottoman man. This particular change was significant: Muslim men do not remove headgear when praying; a hat with a brim prevents a forehead from touching the ground, an essential act in the Islamic ritual of prayer (Yalman 1973:153). In some places Islamic women covered their faces with veils or long head scarves, which was now strongly discouraged.

The Islamic educational system was suppressed. Now public education was secular and open to everyone, female as well as male. European languages were taught in the newly secularized Turkish universities. In 1922, the sultanate and caliphate were separated and the sultanate abolished. By 1926 the caliphate was abrogated as well.

Under the guidance of the League of Nations, huge population exchanges were undertaken. Greek-speaking, Christian Orthodox peoples were returned to Greece. Turkish-speaking, Islamic peoples from the Balkans, Greece, and Egypt—in fact, from all corners of the dismantled Ottoman Empire—were transported to Turkey.[6]

Ataturk also began introducing more egalitarian gender relationships. His reforms were so revolutionary that hearth, home, the business firm, and public spaces were virtually reconstructed from the bottom.

As for Islam, a secular Directorate of Religious Affairs was established, and all Sunni Muslim activities were placed under the auspices of this bureau, with the prime minister of Turkey in "firm control." Islam was now supposed to fulfill the same marginal role in public life that Christian religious practices had been reduced to in a country like France. In Europe, the Roman Catholic Church is an institution separate from the individual states. It is autonomous, owning its own institutions in the Vatican. Under Ataturk's reforms, and continuing to the present day, all Turkish Islamic institutions were excluded from ecclesiastical control to come under the control of the government of the Turkish Republic. Indeed, the concept of "laicism" was developed to describe the relationship between Islam and the state in Turkey.

Metin Heper (1985) interprets Ataturk's emphasis on Turkish republican identity as an effort to replace Ottoman "mentalities" and "representations" by a new symbolic system. It embodied some indigenous Turkic elements, but drew more directly on progressive movements that flourished in the empire in the tumultuous years after 1908. Once new values and routines were established, strong state control could loosen and be replaced with democratic practices (Heper 1985:9, 17–20). Heper acknowledges that what happened differed from Ataturk's vision and has been aptly characterized as "cyclical democracy" (Heper 1985:19, quoting Turan 1984).

Ataturk's success in establishing a secular government and legal system in Turkey in 1926 does not rest merely on force or coercion. Rather it accrued from the long and uneven participation of some elite groups (and their children) in structures that promoted non-Islamic values. The tradition of non-Islamic education that began in the 1850s, and the values promoted by secular education have had a longer history in Turkey than among comparable Islamic neighbors (Iran, Iraq, and Syria). Over five generations of families of elite reformers had experienced (in their daily and ceremonial life) some of the structures and symbols of secularism, each generation moving slightly farther from immersion in Ottoman Islamic symbols, rituals, and practices, and closer to the symbolic patterning of the world of secularism.

The Secular Legal System

When the new Turkish Republic abolished *Kadı* courts in 1924 and set up an entirely secular system of courts, administrative bodies, and a professional, secular judiciary, it was striking at the very foundations of Ottoman society and culture.

Like the secular system of education that began under the Ottoman Empire, Ataturk's secular system of government was firmly based on the European tradition. For his minister of justice, Ataturk chose Mahmut Es'ad Bey, who had been trained in law at Lausanne, Switzerland. He became chair of the committee that would overturn Islamic family law and create a new civil family law. The European model was essential to Bey's thinking:

> We are badly in want of a good scientific Code. Why waste our time trying to produce something new when quite good Codes are to be found ready made? Moreover, what is the use of a Code without good commentaries to guide in the application of it? Are we in a position to write such commentaries for a new Code? We dispose neither of the necessary time nor of the necessary precedents in practice. The only thing to do is to take a good ready-made Code to which good commentaries exist, and to translate them wholesale. The Swiss Code is a good Code; I am going to have it adopted, and I shall ask the Assembly to proceed to a vote *en bloc*, as Napoleon had his Code voted. If it had to be discussed article by article, we should never get through. (Ostrorog 1927: 87–88)

A new law school (the second in Turkey) was opened in Ankara in 1925 to train judges and lawyers in the new secular law. Ataturk himself became the first dean of the law faculty, and at the opening ceremony remarked: "The greatest and at the same time the most insidious enemies of the revolutionaries are unjust laws and their decrepit upholders. . . . It is our purpose to create completely new laws and thus to tear up the very foundations of the old legal system" (Lewis 1966:269).

By 1926 an entirely secular legal system was in place. If secular law was an alien notion for Turkish citizens of the Islamic faith, it was just as alien for Christian and Jewish subjects. Under Ottoman rule, the denominational groups called *millets* had the right to choose their own leader, practice their own religion, and follow their own laws. Now they would lose their separate *millet* status and become individual citizens of the Turkish nation. Their leaders would be religious leaders only; their religious courts would be replaced by secular ones.

Designated secular courts had existed since the 1840s to decide some commercial disputes and, a decade and a half later, to make decisions in criminal cases. But Islamic family law, embodied in the *Şeriat*, had remained unchanged. By 1926, judges were working in the new secular courts, and the decisions they made were supposed to promote the new values—Turkish nationalism, Turkish populism, and Turkish secularism.

The groups most displaced by the new legal system and its ideology were Islamic judges, Islamic clergy, and members of the "outlawed" Islamic brotherhoods (*tarikats*). All religious orders, endowments, and brotherhoods were disenfranchised and ordered to disband. The religious endowments became state-owned land.

Much of the rural Ottoman countryside can be characterized as ethnically parochial and conservative, with loyalties to local notables, religious leaders, tribal *şeyhs*, and household heads. Now the Turkish state under Ataturk planned to bring the values of the ruling elites to the periphery. Its new values for new citizens were populism, individualism, and equality of gender. These are profoundly different ideas of justice than can be found in Islamic law or under Islamic sensibilities. My research in Bodrum's villages and law courts demonstrates that these goals were mostly achieved in western Anatolia by the mid-1960s.[7]

Islamic Revival

Much of the work in reconstructing Turkish society was accomplished by Ataturk and his coterie in a period of one-party rule that in part repressed, and certainly ignored, Islamic sentiments among many groups of citizens. With his death in 1938, a transitional phase began, and by the early 1940s an interest grew among national elites to allow more democratic practices. In this period, roughly 1945 to 1960, multiparty competition began, and the first two-party elections took place in 1950. It was also in this period—twenty to thirty years after the secular state was established—that Turkey experienced a surge of renewed Islamic sentiment, a sentiment wholly or in part stimulated by political party competition to gain what they perceived as the "religious vote."[8]

Competitive political parties meant different interests could be represented in national and local elections. It also meant concessions to what politicians perceived as "Islamic values" among the lower classes in cities and among rural peasants. Politicians in power began an extensive government-financed mosque-building program, and state-supported programs in religious instruction.[9] Although the training of religious functionaries had almost stopped for a generation during Ataturk's control, in the early 1950s it began again in special middle and secondary schools, called the *İmam Hatip* schools. Founded in many Turkish cities by the Ministry of Education, over 40 percent of the curriculum was devoted to the *Kur'an*. This included studying the sayings of the prophet, Islamic law, theology, and the Arabic and Persian languages. After the 1950s, European languages were barely taught in *İmam Hatip* schools, which as educational institutions were widely accepted—not just as institutions for professional religious training (as they were meant to be), but as alternatives to the state-financed, secular educational system (Heyd 1968:16).

It is still unclear if *İmam Hatip* schools have succeeded in producing graduates who are both "good Muslims" and "enlightened modern men" loyal to both the precepts of religion and the secular principles of the Turkish Republic. Graduates of these schools consider the Ankara Faculty of Theology neither traditional enough nor sufficiently religious to warrant enrollment. The demand was for traditional Islamic learning, and special advanced Islamic institutes (*Yüksek Islam Enstitüleri*) were established in Istanbul and Konya. Much more traditional, these institutes have become important in training a new generation of religious *imams*, whose outlook is more Islamic than Western. (ibid.; See also Reed 1986).

In addition to the Islamic schools, private instruction in religion (disapproved of in Ataturk's time) increased, often with the support of the authorities. By the 1950s the local *İmam* of a town or village had resumed teaching children (both boys and girls) the rudiments of Islam, the Arabic script, and the traditional recitation of the *Kur'an* in Arabic, often without translation into Turkish.

The heightened interest in Islam and the training of new generations in Islamic thought appear to indicate that Islam will play an increasingly important role in Turkey's cultural development. Yet it is important to recognize that Ataturk's success in establishing a secular government and legal system accrued from the long-time participation of some elite groups (and their children) in structures that promoted non-Islamic values. The tradition of non-Islamic education that began in the military academies in the early eighteenth century and the values such education promoted has had a longer history in Turkey than in other Middle Eastern Islamic countries.

The paradox cannot be ignored that secular law and courts represent a configuration of cultural ideas in opposition to Islamic culture. A secular legal system represents in theory, if not always in practice, access to state law for all citizens, not just one dominant group. It symbolizes a fundamental reorientation of values and a dissociation or disavowal of values inherent in Islam, such as male superiority and male control of the lives of females and younger males. Turkey's secular court system asserts universal legal norms of individuality and equality and, like other civil law countries, uses established norms of proof and systematic legal procedures, required by the rule of law.

Notes

1. The discussion in this and the following paragraph is based on Lewis (1966:13).

2. The discussion about dervish orders and Ottoman society is from Mardin (1971:201–206).

3. The discussion in this paragraph is based on Shaw (1968:30).

4. See also Kazamias (1966).

5. For further discussion of Turkish nationalism, see Kuran (1968) and Kushner (1977).

6. See Nansen (1922a, 1922b, 1923), Ladas (1932), and Refugee Commission Reports.

7. See Starr (1978a, 1978c, 1984, 1985) and Starr and Pool (1974).

8. See Toprak (1981) and Landau (1974).

9. The discussion in this section is based on Heyd (1968:16–18).

Chapter Two

Şeriat and *Kanun:* Islamic Law and Secular State Law

In the *Tanzimat* period the traditional Islamic concept of "justice" (*adalet*) was reinterpreted. It no longer meant "securing to each category of the ruled no less and no more than it deserved according to its function or state in society." It now meant promulgation of secular legislation outside the jurisdiction of the Islamic traditions and autonomous from them.

(Berkes 1964:94–95)

The development of state law and secular courts in the nineteenth century reflected, in part, a struggle for state power between Islamic and civil bureaucratic reformers at the *Porte* (the seat of the central government). For nearly three centuries the Islamic clergy and the holy law of the *Şeriat* were more important than state law, which was issued in the form of *kanun* by the sultan, but written by the civil administrators. By the middle of the nineteenth century, the balance had begun to tip toward the civil bureaucracy (see Findley 1986:6).

This chapter surveys the ground-breaking effects of that struggle and how Ottoman-Turkish law and legal institutions slowly evolved into a secular nation-state. The cultural attitudes of nineteenth-century status groups required massive changes in perception, in power relations among groups, and in the ideas and behavior of administrators. To realize this required the restructuring of much of a multiethnic society's ways of behaving, of conceptualizing events, even of musing about the future. Abrupt, violent revolutionary change happens quickly; gradual change requires a slow restructuring of social structures and social practices. If social scientists can recognize that a longer temporal dimension is necessary to bring a nation-state from Islamic feudal relationships to modern ones, we will have moved closer to understanding how to study why Islam—as religion, law, and a total prescription for life—is once again exerting a strong emotional pull in many Near Eastern and Central Asian communities today.

The Tanzimat Period

In classical Islamic thought, no principles of law could exist apart from the *Şeriat*, but under Ottoman rule a new relationship developed between the supreme position of the caliph in the Islamic community (and therefore in the Ottoman Empire) and the power of the Ottoman sultan. Scholars commonly refer to this as "the circle of justice" (Heper 1985:25–26), based on an old Oriental maxim: "A ruler can have no power without soldiers, no soldiers without money, no money without the well-being of his subjects, and no popular well-being without justice" (Inalcık 1964:43). References to the circle of justice—the absolute power of the Ottoman sultan—are found in the famous Turkish political writing of the eleventh century, the *Kutadgu Bilik*, the books of the seventeenth-century Turkish traveler Katib Celebi, and in the *Gülhane* Rescript of 1839, the document that initiated the major liberalizing reforms of the Tanzimat period. It was then that justice was redefined—not as a circle of power, but as rules existing in secular legislation that represented a legal tradition separate from Islamic law.

In the centuries of Ottoman rule "an independent category of law, called imperial laws or *kanun*s developed, which were derived directly from the sovereign will of the ruler" (Inalcık 1964:57). Ottoman sultans issued these directives, which were not a legislative enactment but rather a codification of existing law—a tabulation of legal rules (Lewis 1966:107). *Kanun*s were justified because they covered areas of life not mentioned in the holy *Şeriat*. In earlier periods, secular law came from the pronouncements of the sultan. By the mid-nineteenth century, sections of the Ottoman bureaucracy were generating legal procedures and institutions (e.g., the Trader Courts) without sultanic pronouncements being necessary.

Reform Beginnings: 1839

After the Janissaries (the reactionary army loyal to the sultan) had been destroyed in 1826, it was possible to contemplate change. The period of the Tanzimat, literally "beneficial reforms" (Redhouse 1968:1095), or *Tanzimat Hayriye*, "auspicious reorderings," began in 1839 with the proclamation of the reform edict, the *Hatt-i Hümayun*. This period, which brought fresh ideas, new concepts of work, and new bureaucratic structures, lasted thirty years. It ended when the first Ottoman-Turkish constitution was adopted in 1876 by the pronouncement of the conservative sultan Abdulhamid II who had assumed the throne. Within two years, he had dismissed parliament, reinstated authoritarian rule, and suspended the constitution.

In *The Genesis of Young Ottoman Thought* (1962), Serif Mardin argues convincingly that the ideas of the nineteenth-century Ottoman reformers arose from the genius of certain Ottoman statesmen and were not (as many scholars had previously thought) *only* European-inspired, or *only* resulting from a series of Ottoman capitulations to European powers. Mardin suggests that before the 1830s, political ideas of the European Enlightenment had been unknown in the Ottoman Empire; Ottoman values, standards, culture, and hierarchically stratified society had developed independently (p. 8). In addition, Turkish writers throughout the nineteenth century did not cite European writers, statesmen, or philosophers when advocating new ideas, a fact that supports the first assertion (p. 7).[1]

Stanford Shaw (1970) also argues that the Ottomans had experience with representative government at many levels of society beginning in 1854. Although reforming Ottoman bureaucrats did borrow European legal and political models for the structural changes they sought, there was a genuine Ottoman liberalizing spirit at work. New political philosophy, contributed by successive generations of Ottoman bureaucratic reformers, sprang from complex interactions of events, actions, ideas, and subterranean processes that created the structure for change, first in ideology, and then in institutional structures in the empire.

It was not the intention of the early Tanzimat reformers to undermine the Islamic state. Rather, advisors to the sultans and each cohort of reformers were responding to specific problems and designing institutions to handle increasingly complex situations. As the Ottoman Empire moved into the world economy, it was also experiencing local rebellions within its ranks and external wars that threatened its downfall (see appendix I). Political actions and reorganization in one year led to further elaborations in the next.

The legislation introducing the reforms was the *Hatt-i Hümayun*, or Imperial Rescript.[2] The brilliant statesman Mustafa Resid Pasa, then foreign minister in Constantinople, was responsible. He had received both Islamic training from the *İlmiye* and secular education in the *Porte*'s scribal service[3] (Shaw and Shaw 1977:58) and, previous to heading the Foreign Ministry, had been an ambassador in Paris and in London, where he mingled with great European statesmen and became fluent in French. His knowledge of Europeans and their institutions, combined with his uncanny ability to analyze administrative problems, partly accounts for his genius in devising new institutions of state to deal with the almost insurmountable problems of the empire (Mardin 1962:15–32).

Rebellion in the Ottoman province of Egypt led Resid Pasa to ask support from Britain and France. The threat of losing Egypt helped gain acceptance for his reforms by conservative ministers anxious to protect the empire. The Imperial Rescript was issued when the new young sultan, Abdülmecid, a youth sixteen years of age, took the Ottoman throne at the death of Mahmud II in 1839.

The *Hatt* was Janus-faced. It looks backward toward the classical period of the Ottoman monarchy, blaming the empire's decline for a century and a half on non-observance of the "precepts of the glorious *Kur'an*." However, in the statement "glory cannot be accomplished by returning to Islamic principles," the *Hatt* also faces the future. Only through creating new state institutions could the empire become a significant force among the world's powers.

The *Hatt* departs from Islamic tradition by calling for the "absolute equality" of all subjects and the protection of all property of Ottoman subjects.[4] Under Islamic law, the *Zimmis* or "people of the book"—the Christians, Jews, Greeks, and Armenians—were allowed to govern themselves and practice their customs as long as these were not offensive to Islamic cultures, but they paid more taxes than Muslim subjects (a fixed poll tax and a land tax), had to wear distinctive clothing, mark their homes, and were forbidden to marry Muslims. Restrictions also included not building their houses higher than Muslim homes, not riding horses or bearing arms, and not building any new synagogues, churches, or hermitages (Schacht 1964:130–31).

Although Roderic Davison interprets the dualistic character of all Tanzimat reforms as representing conflicting desires—the need to create new institutions in response to changing times and the wish to preserve traditional institutions of Islamic faith and statehood—alternative readings of the proclamation are possible. Traditional rhetoric became the discourse of innovative reforms. It was a strategy to disarm the powerful Islamic groups, who were still very much in charge of many sections of the government and its administration. Support to this suggestion is given by the ways Ottoman reformers dealt with education (discussed in Chapter 1). They built parallel educational institutions as a way to avoid direct confrontation with the Islamic clergy over their traditional right to control education. The reformers dealt with quasi-legal institutions in the same way, creating parallel institutions. As trade and commerce increased in the nineteenth century, and as ethnic groups rebelled, new governmental councils and new laws were devised. The older Islamic institutions had to adapt by expanding or, as happened later on, became so bogged down with work that after they were divided into several component parts, the more secular institutional framework took precedence. The one exception was that the holy law regulating family life, inheritance, adoption, marriage, and divorce remained in full force.

Thus, reference to the *Kur'an* and the glorious Ottoman past in the *Hatt* was in part a mask of the *affirmation* or *equality* of life and property now to be extended to all Ottoman subjects. The implication was clear: All subjects in the multiethnic, multinational empire would be on more equal footing. The affirmation of equality, whether meant or not, was to reassure Europeans who had expressed concern for Christian subjects. The proclamation of equal rights for all subjects was immediately noticed, and objected to by the Islamic clergy, the *ulema*.

The *Hatt* also reasserted the importance of earlier attempts at reform. No longer would property be confiscated. Trials must be public and in accord with recognized procedures. An orderly system of fixed taxes would be created to replace tax-farming. A regular system of military conscription would be established instead of lifetime service; conscription would be limited to four or five years. Adequate salaries would be paid to provincial officials to eliminate bribery, and finally, a penal code would be compiled that would apply to *ulema*s, *vezir*s (ministers), and other civil servants, including those of high as well as low rank.

The reforms of this period were undertaken to revitalize and preserve the empire in a world increasingly ordered by European power and civilization. Although these two needs were interdependent and entwined with each other, most important was the need to reform the government. "The fish begins to stink at the head" was a popular Ottoman proverb of this time (Davison 1963:6–7).

Legislative Councils: The *Meclis-i Vâlâ-yı Ahkâm-ı Adliye*

The *Hatt* of 1839 gave the *Meclis-i Vâlâ-yı Ahkâm-ı Adliye* (the Supreme Council of Judicial Ordinances) (hereafter Meclis-i Vâlâ) the impetus it needed to become a serious and effective legislative council. Begun in the reign of Mahmud II, its mandate was to meet at the palace of Topkapi Saray to advise the sultan on "beneficent reorderings" of state and society.[5] Another council, the *Dar-ı Şurayı Bab-ı Âli*, had also been created then to perform the same function for the foreign minister and his staff, for other ministers, and for the members of the administrative councils who met at the *Porte*.

Since both councils advised the foreign minister and sultan on the same problems, over the years confusion over goals and functions arose. The *Hatt* declared that the *Meclis-i Vâlâ* should be increased in size and made more representative; the sultan promised to accept its recommendations if a majority vote of its members concurred.

When the *Dar-ı Şurayı Bab-ı Âli* was abolished as a separate institution, its staff and function were united with those of the *Meclis-i Vâlâ*, which assumed a dual name, *Encümen-i Âli*. Charged with the responsibility of discussing important matters requiring legislation, the newly constituted council investigated the basic facts involving cases of high officials, regardless of the prohibition against invading individual *had*s (personal boundaries of responsibility) and presented proposals for legislation. New legislation was to be recommended to the sultan by a specific council, the *Meclis-i Hass-ı Umumi*, composed of senior ministers, retired officials, and the members of the *Meclis-i Vâlâ*. Thus, the special council gained a far more influential voice in the process of ratifying its own decisions than had been possible when the Council of Ministers (the earlier group) had sole authority to ratify legislation. The new special council's scope has been restricted to considering legislation referred to it by other executive bodies. Yet the vagueness of this requirement meant that in practice the *Meclis-i Hass-ı Umumi* discussed whatever issues it wanted, since almost everything was relevant to problems referred to it.

In this period the *Meclis-i Vâlâ* was enlarged to ten permanent members, all chosen from senior officials from the four institutions of the Ottoman ruling class—the administration, the military, the financial, and the cultural/religious. The actual choice of members was made by the same *Meclis-i Hass-ı Umumi* that ratified its decisions, but they still had to be sanctioned by a statement issued by the sultan. Two scribes were attached to the *Meclis-i Vâlâ*, who were in charge of drawing up its deliberations and ideas and presenting them to a higher authority.

A new headquarters was constructed in the compound of the *Porte*, which signified that its decisions arose from the leadership of Mustafa Resid Pasa and other Tanzimat reformers. Within a short time the *Meclis-i Vâlâ* set to work with an intensity rarely seen in Ottoman administrative circles. Originally the council met only four days a week, but the press of business soon led it to limit its day off to Thursdays, the same day taken off by the remainder of the *Porte*. Despite numerous problems, the *Meclis-i Vâlâ* successfully operated as the principal Ottoman legislative organ for fifteen years. Its very success assured its ultimate doom as it became overwhelmed by the sheer bulk of work, falling drastically behind.

In the years immediately preceding the Crimean War of 1853–56, the burdens of the *Meclis-i Vâlâ*'s work contributed to the increasingly severe administrative injustices that came to be inflicted upon the populations of the empire by the autocratic Tanzimat bureaucracy. A new generation of Ottoman reformers wished to weaken the power of the older generation, and so a political decision was made to separate the two major functions of the *Meclis-i Vâlâ*, leaving it with largely judicial tasks, and to create a new council to deal with legislation.

In 1854 the more specialized *Meclis-i Vâlâ* drew up legislation to create an entirely new legislative body called the High Council of the Tanzimat. Made up of the second generation of reformers, all experienced Tanzimat administrators, it took up headquarters in the former Council of Education at the *Porte*. The High Council was placed above all other executive councils in rank and authority and was separate from and equal to the Council of Ministers (i.e. the cabinet that advised the sultan, called (*Meclis-i Vükelâ*) and, like it, had direct access to the sultan.

The High Council's main objective was "to complete and extend the reforms of the Tanzimat"; therefore, it immediately set to work to process the almost two years' backlog of legislation that had built up during the last years of the *Meclis-i Vâlâ*. It was also mandated to study all existing regulations for all other state organizations, including other councils, ministries, departments, and schools. It was empowered to change these organizations to meet new conditions and, if necessary, to draw up entirely new regulations for them. It could add new regulations to other state bureaus in order to expedite the flow of business or to free members from political pressures. A new law in 1854 declared it to become the *Meclis-i Tanzimat*, turning what previously was custom into a legal right to draw up all new laws and regulations for the increasingly centralized government.

The Evolution of Secular Courts: Commercial Courts

"In earlier centuries, the Ottomans had developed secular civil law (*kanun*) in terms of administrative categories and rules to an extent unmatched in other Islamic states" (Findley 1986:5). Now in the nineteenth century, the Ottomans were to develop a system of secular courts previously unknown in the world of Islam.[6]

Early forms of commercial law can be found in the special licenses granted to European traders (*Avrupa Tüccarı*), and later to non-Muslim Ottomans.[7] A person holding a license in commercial cases was exempt from the jurisdiction of *Şeriat* courts. One type of license specified that when disputes occurred, the central government, at the *Porte*, would hear disputes. Another type of license stated that commercial disputes would be settled by an employee of the Ministry of Commerce. Here judges were selected by the minister, along with the commercial counselor of the city (*Şeybender*), his assistants, and the parties to the dispute. When imprisonment was the penalty, the defendant was held in the Building of Commerce.

The licenses and the law used in the commercial dispute councils was "Traders' Law," not the *Şeriat*.[8] By referring to these as "councils" rather than courts, reformers hoped to offset objections by Islamic judges, on whose jurisdictional boundaries they were encroaching. The councils heard disputes between all types of merchants (based on the European Law Merchant), and over time they extended their jurisdiction to disputes between a Muslim and a non-Muslim, and between two Muslims. Muslim disputants could stipulate in advance that they wished to use Islamic law instead of the secular Traders' Law. For example, the *Müftü* of Public Utility (an Islamic office) also heard disputes in the Ministry of Commerce. After 1839 Muslims in cases against Muslims could appeal decisions from the commercial council or the courts of the *Müftü* to the *Şeyhülislâm* (the head of the Ottoman community of Islam), a type of appeal not open to non-Muslims.

By 1840 the Ministry of Commerce (*Ticaret Meclis-i*) was set up at the *Porte* to supervise traders and money lenders and to hear disputes arising between foreign merchants, between Muslim Ottoman merchants licensed to trade with Europeans, between non-Muslim Ottoman traders, and between purchasers and sellers of commercial notes. Both Muslim and Christian judges sat on the panel representing the Ottoman Empire, as did several foreign merchants, representing the interests of foreigners. The council met in the presence of the undersecretary of state for commerce and was chaired by the commercial counselor of Constantinople. In more important cases, members of the Council of Public Improvement (which included the Bureau of Agriculture in an advisory capacity) were present among the panel of judges. Like the earlier merchants' council, if the parties wished to be tried under the *Şeriat*, the case was referred to the *Müftü* of the Council of Public Utility.

In 1841, one year after the commercial legal forums had become secular, the *ulema*s won a major battle by defeating the commercial code proposed by the foreign minister, Mustafa Resid Pasa. Their grounds were it was too secular and it increasingly encroached into domains of Islamic law, the law that *ulema*s by tradition and custom controlled. Although the facade of non-encroachment was visibly strengthened, the values of trade and commerce had breached the powerful religious establishment.

The concept of secular legal forums to hear commercial disputes was expanded in 1847 when "mixed" civil and criminal courts were set up in Constantinople with a regularized system of selecting judges ("mixed" meaning European and Ottoman judges in equal numbers). Rules of evidence were taken from the European Law Merchant rather than Ottoman law.

Other Ottoman Secular Courts

The first Ottoman secular criminal courts were established in police headquarters in the 1840s. By 1858 they operated under a new secular penal code (Davison 1963:255) (discussed more fully below). A mixed Court of Maritime Commerce was also established in 1850 at the Port Authority in Constantinople , and between 1848 and 1850 special commissions were created throughout the empire to settle commercial conflicts arising between Ottoman subjects and between Ottomans and foreigners. Following the precedent set by the mixed commercial courts at the *Porte*, these courts followed European Traders' Law. Most of the sitting judges were civil servants employed by the Ministry of Commerce, sitting under the chairmanship of the governor of each province. The ministry itself served as a court of appeals for these cases. Further appeal existed to the *Şeyhülislâm*, but it was only open to Muslim disputants who had previously agreed to the case being tried under *Şeriat* law.[9]

This latest extension of the system of commercial courts, along with the secular police courts, was of great importance in establishing the legitimacy of extra-*Şeriat* courts. By sanctioning Traders' courts already in use, the central government thus circumvented Islamic Law and created a new system of secular commercial courts.

Equally important was the new chain of jurisdiction established by the central government, which extended upward through the secular provincial governor to the *Porte*, bypassing links with Islamic courts. In addition, the document announcing these courts did not resort to the face-saving device of pretending that they were established because of foreign pressures.

In 1850 an Ottoman commercial code was announced. It was translated and adapted from sections I and III of the French commercial code—the first clear example of transplanting European codes to Turkish soil.

From the 1860s on, Ottoman reformers engaged in stimulating trade and commerce all over Anatolia. Shaw tells how new secular commercial courts (*Mahkeme-i Ticaret*) were established to settle trade disputes in major centers throughout the empire and how a special police force to regulate trade and industry was developed (1970:71–72).

Thus, from a small, informal commercial court, which started in Constantinople in the Bureau of Commerce, the idea gained official sanction and spread in less than thirty years into all important centers of the empire as the first Ottoman secular courts.

Toward Centralization

A new system to centralize provincial administration had been proposed by Mustafa Resid Pasa in 1840. Modeled on the French system of prefectures and departments with salaried officials in charge, it was to replace the loose-knit, quasi-feudal association of pashas, derebeys, and tax-farming that had been abolished in 1839. Lewis, however, calls it "premature centralization" (1966:380), for when Mustafa Resid Pasa fell from power the following year it was not carried out.

The next attempt at centralization and uniform administration of the provinces came twelve years later, in 1852, when Resid Pasa was restored to power. By 1864 the tendency toward uniform centralization was clearly evident. A new provincial code had been drafted, derived from French provincial administration. A clear hierarchy was created from the provincial governor, down through districts, counties, and sub-counties to villages with an elected headman.

The Land Code: 1858

The Ottoman land code of 1858 represents a true evolution of Turkish law (Bracken 1954:26), not a transplanted code. Bernard Lewis considers it "more important than either the new commercial or the new criminal codes" (1966:117), and Kemal Karpat suggests the transition to a modern system of private property was the most difficult problem faced by the Tanzimat reformers (1968:85). Undoubtedly, the new land code was inspired by the freehold farming system in France. Many Ottoman reformers had viewed the beneficial effects of the post-feudal, post–tax-farming system in France and recognized that the prosperity of the family farming system in the French countryside grew out of private ownership of the homestead by the farming family.

The *timar*s (a form of tax-farming) had been abolished by Sultan Mahmud in 1831, but they continued on in other guises. All other types of tax-farming were made illegal in 1839, and the reformers were making gradual progress by "abrogating the earlier agrarian relationships and progressively extending and confirming the rights of use, possession, and ownership."[10] Under the new code of 1858, leaseholders and tax-farmers acquired freehold ownership with full rights of disposal and succession. Their rights would be confirmed by the possession of documents issued by a Cadestre Department.[11]

But the actual cultivators had their rights and statuses much diminished because, due to impoverishment, they were forced to become sharecroppers or hired laborers at the mercy of a reinforced landlord class, which was the principal beneficiary of the reform. In a pointed phrase, Lewis concludes (1966:117): "The harmful effects of the new law were modified only by the inefficiency of its application."

New Penal Codes: 1840, 1858

At first appearance not extraordinary, the 1840 penal code, *Ceza Kanunnamesi* (criminal law), placed it well within the tradition of sultan *kanun*-making. Lewis describes it as revealing influences of French criminal law, yet remaining within the framework of the penal code of the *Şeriat* (1966:107–108).

It possessed two remarkable differences from the *Şeriat*, however. One was the reaffirmation of the equality of *all* Ottoman subjects before the law, a statement first found in the *Hatt*. The other was its organization. For the first time in Ottoman history, a *kanun* assumed the form of a secular law code. It consisted of a preamble and fourteen articles, drawn up by a corporate body given that task. Though "the code was confused in thought and expression and ineffective in application," it marks the first tentative appearance in the Ottoman Empire of a group of persons given the right to draft new law. The innovative aspects of this document and the legislative committee that drafted it escaped the notice of the *ulemas*, who offered no resistance (p. 108).

The Ottoman criminal code, adopted in 1858, was based on the Napoleonic code of 1810. It put aside Islamic punishments such as "lapidation of adulterers, flogging for wine drinkers, mutilation of thieves, crucifixion of highwaymen" (Ostrorog 1927:49). It announced a system of courts, based on French models, with tribunals of first instance, courts of appeal, and a court of causation, where "Christians and Jews were to sit side by side with Muslims, and be judged according to Codes of Procedure translated from, or closely imitating, the Codes of France" (p. 49). These courts, called *nizamiye* courts, were an outgrowth of the police courts established in Constantinople for foreigners and non-Muslims accused of crimes (Davison 1963:255). They mark the first distinct hierarchy of a secular court system in the Ottoman-Turkish state (Heidborn 1908:216–224; Findley 1986:7).

The effectiveness of the new penal code was limited, because neither procedural nor enforcement machinery was provided to assure compliance. However, the next generation of young men trained as judges would view crime and punishment in broader societal terms. The French-modeled code of 1858 had adopted the principle: *Nullum delictum sine lege, nulla poena sine lege* (there is no crime without a law, and no punishment without a law [Heidborn 1908:368]).

With minor changes, the 1858 penal code constituted the basic criminal legislation of the Ottoman Empire and remained in effect until the beginning of the republic in 1923.

Growth of Secular Civil Courts

At the *Porte* in 1849, an institute to educate judges, called *dar-ul maarif*, was begun under the patronage of the sultan's mother. It included special classes in secular commercial law (Bracken 1954:47). These events demonstrated the government's commitment to using the secular Law Merchant and to creating legal institutions with functions and powers that paralleled those of Islamic law courts.

A pilot project of secular tribunals was launched in the Danube province in 1867, and later that same year secular tribunals were written into the laws for administering all provinces (Mardin 1961:277). This meant a *secular*, hierarchical court system was being established throughout the empire, an occurrence formerly unheard of in Islamic law countries, and especially noteworthy in the country hosting the Islamic caliph. Concessions were made to Islamic groups by not calling these "courts," but "assemblies" (*meclis*). Dispute assemblies (*Daavi Meclisi*) for lower administrative districts were created with Courts of Appeal (*Temyis Meclisi*) at the provincial level, and a Council of Appeal (*Divan-i Temyis*) for cases from the provincial capitals (Bracken 1954:40). Like the criminal courts, this system later was the civil appeal system under the *nizamiye* courts.

The Emergence of a Secular Legal System, May 1868

What is the essence of a secular legal system? First, it must endure through time; second, there need be ways to appeal decisions; and third, judging functions need be separated to a great extent from the legislative functions of councils or assemblies. Although secular commercial courts began earlier, we might place the true beginning of a secular legal *system* in Turkey at the division of the *Meclis-i Vâlâ* into two governmental institutions in 1868. One became the Council of State, a legislative body (the *Surayı Devlet*), the other a court of appeal (the *Di-*

van-i Ahkâm-ı Adliye) (Mardin 1961:277). The latter was divided into two sections, one for civil and the other for criminal cases. Later that year its name was changed to Ministry of Justice (from *Divan* to *Nezareti*) to mark the emergence of a separate Department of Justice. Its mandate was to look into appealed cases arising from the commercial and criminal codes. It is interesting to note that the first use of the modern term for court in Turkish, *mahkeme*, is attributed by Heidborn to the year 1868 (1908:226, fn. 57).

In 1869, when Ahmed Cevdet Pasa's position as president of the Judicial Council evolved to that of the minister of justice, a set of regulations to clarify the position of the *nizamiye* courts was prepared (Findley 1986:6–8). These courts were organized hierarchically. At the lowest level was the council of elders at the *nahiye* administrative unit. (Today, *nahiye* is a subdistrict embracing several villages, but smaller than a district town.) The council of elders worked through conciliatory remedies. Both parties needed to accept the decision to make it binding (Davison 1963:255). Courts in centers of larger administrative units, such as districts (*kaza*s), counties (*sancak*s), and provinces (*vilayet*s), had powers of adjudication, and the more inclusive levels heard more serious cases. Appeal procedures were explicitly stated. The *Divan-ı Ahkâm-ı Adliye*, established in 1868, was the highest court of appeal for all cases arising from civil and criminal *nizamiye* courts, yet all judges continued to be appointed by the *Şeyhülislâm*, as specified in the provincial (*vilayet*) law. The confusion between secular and religious courts was not yet entirely removed (pp. 255–56).

The Mecelle, 1867–1876

During the entire reform period of the Tanzimat, the *Mecelle* stands out as one of its most characteristic achievements.[12] It was the first time that part of the holy *Şeriat*, the part concerning transactions, was written in the format of a legal code. The *Şeriat* concerning family law was left unchanged. Thus, the *Mecelle* is viewed by many scholars as a rapprochement between the Islamic groups pressing for the return to an Islamic past (or at least a continuation of the status quo) and the third generation of reformers—known as the "Young Ottomans"—intent on bringing the empire into the modern world.

The full name is *Mecelle-ı Ahkâm-ı Adliye*, and it was developed between 1867 and 1876 (the actual laws were issued between 1869 and 1876). The penal code and the commercial code were its predecessors, but those two codifications had been largely based on European law, whereas the *Mecelle* represents an effort to codify that part of *Hanefi* school of Islamic law that deals with transactions (*muamalat*), contracts, and obligations.

The brilliant Ottoman statesman, Mustafa Resid Pasa, in the 1850s had the prescience to prepare for a rapprochement between the European-educated reformers and the powerful Islamic-trained *ulema*s. He had sought a young man of "superior intelligence and liberal bent," educated in Islamic theory and law from the office of the *Şeyhülislâm* to be trained by the secular bureaucracy. By the 1860s this candidate, Ahmed Cevdet Pasa, had risen in the bureaucracy to become the minister of justice. His dual training by both Islamic and secular institutions made him acceptable to both the *ulema*s and the reformers as chair of the committee that created the *Mecelle*.

Founded in 1867, the *Mecelle* Committee was recognized by Imperial edict in 1869. This royal document remarked on the importance of their task and mandated that the *ulema*s who made up the committee should remain. The committee consisted of seven jurists: Ahmed Cevdet, its chair, a member of the *ulema*s, and currently minister of justice; two jurists belonging to the Islamic High Court of Justice; two counselors of state; an inspector of Islamic Pious Foundations; and one identified only as "member."

In a preliminary report dated 1868, the committee explained why a codification of Islamic civil law had become necessary. The new secular tribunals often had to resolve conflicts by recourse to commercial law, but the judges were rarely knowledgeable about the practical propositions of the *Şeriat* known as *Fıkıh*, which is the science of understanding and interpreting the *Şeriat* (Coulson 1964:75). At first this problem was solved by the president of the religious courts becoming the president of the secular courts as well. But this soon proved unsatisfactory, and a decision was made to codify the main points of Islamic Law of Obligations in one volume that would be easy to consult (Tyser 1967:i–ii). The Introduction and Book I were submitted to the *Şeyhülislâm* and approved by him as well as by other prominent jurists (p. ii).

Though the different books were successively sanctioned by Imperial decree, the *Mecelle* was not considered the ultimate authority. Judges were left free to form their own opinions by study of the *Hanefi* law books. The *Mecelle* thus became a useful compilation of the Civil law of Obligation and a guide and reference on the existing rules. Even today it is used in countries governed by Islamic law. For example, Tyser's edition (1967) was recently reprinted in Pakistan.

The *Mecelle* is divided into two prefaces and sixteen books, the content of which is outlined below:

- Preface I explains the meanings of *Fıkıh;*
- Preface II provides the legal maxims from the *Fıkıh.*
- Book 1 considers contracts—things sold, their prices, right of disposition over the price and the thing sold after the contract, delivery and receipt, and options.
- Book 2 concerns "letting"—the contract of letting, the payment for hire, whether the person hired to do work may keep the thing delivered to him, the time of letting, options, the kinds of things given for hire and the effect, the duties and rights of the letter and the hirer after the contract has been made, liability to make compensation, etc.
- Book 3 considers suretyship;
- Book 4, the transfer of obligation;
- Book 5, the contractual nature of a pledge;
- Book 6, trusts, loans, and the safekeeping of something entrusted to your keep;
- Book 7, gifts;
- Book 8, wrongful taking and destruction;
- Book 9, prohibition, unlawful compulsion, and preemptions;
- Book 10, joint ownership, ownership servitudes, and partnerships;
- Book 11, acting as someone else's agent;
- Book 12, compromise and release;
- Book 13, evidence and admissions;
- Book 14, conditions and consequences of actions;
- Book 15, proofs and oaths; and
- Book 16, judges and their responsibilities, judgments, and arbitration.

As an Ottoman legal code, four aspects of the *Mecelle*'s significance dominate. First, it was an authentic Ottoman/Islamic legal code rather than an imported European code. The *Mecelle* was created to be applied in both *Şeriat* and secular (*nizamiye*) courts (Findley 1986:6). Second, it presented part of the *Şeriat* in the form of a modern law code for the first time in history. Third, its creation was a "joint venture" between Islamicists and Europeanized Ottoman reformers who, in other respects, had opposing interests. Fourth, it demonstrated that negotiation and compromise, rather than exclusion and repression, were still possible options for the Ottoman bureaucracy in dealing with Islamic groups who also, like the civil bureaucracy, had vested interests in the Ottoman state.

Subsequent events underscore the preeminence of the *Mecelle* as an authentic Ottoman legal code. When the *Mecelle* was completed, the committee drafted a code of procedure, which was duly sent to the Council of State (charged with drafting laws and reviewing cases of administrative law) for approval. The council amended so many provisions deriving from French law that the *Mecelle* Committee rejected the altered document. When the conservative Sultan Abdülhamid II came to power in 1876, he dismissed the committee because he "did not trust any corporate organization other than the state itself, especially one which to all appearances was [sic] now useless" (Mardin 1961:279).

The *Mecelle* did not touch the core of the *Şeriat*, which related to family matters. This meant the Islamic laws of marriage, divorce, inheritance of property, succession, and adoption were left unchanged (Ostrorog 1927:50).[13]

Constitution of 1876

The first Ottoman Constitution was the first constitution written for an Islamic state. It was enacted in a situation of crisis. Russia was threatening to invade Ottoman-controlled lands on the Black Sea, and the European powers were about to convene in Constantinople for a peace conference concerning the Ottoman Empire's Balkan holdings, the results of which would be unfavorable for the empire. Many Young Ottomans had been interested in drafting a constitution, and this crisis, like the one several years before, provided the opportunity for legal change.

The constitution (*Kanun-ı Esasî*) consisted of 119 articles, divided into 12 sections. Modeled on the Beligan Constitution of 1831, and written in French, it was considered liberal and monarchical (Lewis 1966:356). Although it did move further toward accepting Western principles of representation in government, it retained the sultanate and the caliphate.[14] The sultan insisted that he be named as sacred and responsible to no one in the constitution, and he demanded the sole right to appoint and dismiss ministers of state, to declare war and peace, to conclude treaties, and to convene and dissolve parliament. The constitution stipulated that there be an executive, the grand *vezir*, who performed functions of a prime minister (though some reformers preferred this Europeanized title, they lost the debate on it). There was also a parliament, which was divided into two houses, an elected Chamber of Deputies (*Meclis-i Meb' usan*) and a Chamber of Notables (*Meclis-i Âyan*), appointed directly by the sultan. Parliament was to convene annually from November to March. The Council of State (*Şurayı Devlet*) was retained as the Supreme Court of Appeal for administrative law cases and was to continue its original legislative function. A new

High Court (*Divan-ı Âli*) was created to hear cases against members of the government. This court consisted of ten members each from the Chamber of Notables, the Council of State, and the High Court of Appeals.

In the constitution, Islam remained the official state religion, and Ottoman remained the official language. But for the first time in history, all subjects were declared to be Ottomans regardless of their religion. All subjects were equal; this enactment opposed the ancient Islamic rights that followers of Mohammed would be taxed at a lesser rate than *Zimmis* or nonbelievers. All were to enjoy equal liberty; a person's home was declared inviolable.

Finally, the entire secular court system that has developed during the Tanzimat period was incorporated into the constitution, with judges appointed for life, courts organized by law, and no outside interference allowed. *Şeriat* courts were to be retained for Muslims in matters of religion, and non-Muslims in matters of religion were to use their own denominational *millet* courts.

An irony of history is that Turkish parliamentary democracy embodied in the new constitution was brought into existence by the conservative Sultan Abdülhamid II who, after signing the document in 1876, two years later suspended the constitution by formally closing parliament in 1878. Thirty years later, the Young Turk revolution of 1908 would restore the constitution fully and add new provisions.

The Ministry of Justice and the First Law School

Legal acts of 1879 established the *nizamıye* court system and the Ministry of Justice, essentially as they were to remain until the Young Turk era.[15] The Ministries of Justice and Religious Affairs were united in one bureau (*Adliye ve Medhahıb Nezareti*), which had the double mandate of jurisdiction over the *nizamıye* courts and all matters, legal or otherwise, of non-Muslim communities. Written laws now regulated the jurisdiction of the *nizamıye* courts, their organization, and the organization of the Ottoman judiciary. Written law created a system of public prosecutors and of judicial inspectors. New laws addressed issues of execution of judgments and judge's fees.

Attempts to regulate the Ottoman legal profession had begun in 1878, and in 1880 the first independent, secular law school in the Ottoman Empire was established when the Istanbul Law Faculty was opened. Cevdet Pasa said, in his opening address, "It is not that we did not try [before]. But, however we tried, the time was not suitable"

(Bracken 1954:48). Although secular legal training would be available for judges, lawyers, and public prosecutors from that time on in Constantinople, a number of Ottoman males seeking legal education went to study at European law facilities.[16]

Reform in Marriage and Divorce

Since the *Şeriat* remained as sacred law governing all matters of the family and inheritance after the *Mecelle* was adopted, the Islamic clergy were still the sole recourse for Muslims in family disputes. Reformers, however, took an interest in regulating aspects of marriage. In 1876 legislation was passed (in the one season that parliament functioned under the constitution) limiting the amount of expense and extravagance spent on betrothals and weddings. The new laws limited the amount of financial exchange at betrothal between the family of the bride and the family of the groom. For the wedding, a bride was supposed to pay for her own cosmetics and finery, and her betrothed was only to pay for the use of the public baths. No gifts were to be exchanged between relatives, nor were gifts to be given by guests (Young 1905–1906:ii, 210). Also, "les fêtes dans les noces de la première classe consistéront seulement en soupe, zerde pilaf, et cinq autres plats" (p. 210). But travelers' reports of the times, such as Lucy Garnett's (1909:241–42), suggest that these restrictions could not be enforced, and weddings continued to be extravaganzas.

Reform in Ottoman Family Law

Centuries of official sponsorship of *Hanefi* doctrine by the central Ottoman government resulted in establishing *Hanefi* courts in provinces of the empire, even where the population belonged to another school of Islamic law.[17] Seemingly, this situation should have created a conflict of allegiance for individuals, but in practice that was not the case. In matters of cult and rituals, Muslims identified with a particular Islamic school, but in legal matters they were prepared to accept the jurisdiction of tribunals of a different school.

When in 1915 the Sudanese Mohammedan law courts recognized the principle that "the *Shari'a* [*Şeriat*] courts might be ordered to apply, in all relevant cases, an opinion other than that of the school to which they were traditionally bound,"[18] the Grand *Kadı* issued a judicial circular saying that the application of rules other than the authoritative *Hanefi* doctrine could be used. In terms of family law in the Ottoman Empire, this meant that the courts might use one of several existing variant opinions instead of the conservative *Hanefi* law. A woman's petition to dissolve her marriage, for example, now could be interpreted under the more liberal Sudanese *Maliki* rule. This provided the groundwork for the revolutionary *Ottoman* Law of Family Rights, 1917.

Enacted by emergency order on 25 October 1917 (Lewis 1966:225, Allen 1935:137–39), the Law of Family Rights "constituted the first officially adopted codification of Muslim Family Law in the modern period" (Esposito 1982:53). The law gave marriage a more official character by declaring the male practice of simple renunciation in front of two witnesses insufficient grounds for divorce. Now the presence of a judge or deputy was required. Also, every marriage and every divorce had to follow state procedures, such as a preliminary publication of wedding banns and registering both marriage and divorce with the state (Allen 1935:137–39).

The law also granted a wife two grounds for divorce: first, from a husband who was suffering from a contagious disease (venereal or leprosy) that made conjugal life dangerous for her, and second, from a husband who had deserted her without providing for her maintenance. In the first case *Maliki* authority was cited, while in the second *Hambelî* doctrine was used.[19] Broader interpretation by Islamic courts also made divorce possible in two other instances. One was the instance of non-support by a non-absentee husband (using the wider *Maliki* rather than the *Hambelî* rules); the other was when the wife was deserted by the husband for a continuous period of one year. In both cases, courts were allowing divorce even though the husband's property might be available to provide maintenance.

Further provisions existed concerning a wife's divorce petition. If a wife could prove cruelty in the required fashion under the new law, the court would grant a decree of dissolution of the marriage. In cases where cruelty couldn't be established and yet discord obviously existed, two mediators (one from each family) would be appointed by a judge. If they failed to reconcile the couple, the judge could then grant the wife's petition for divorce. Or, if disagreement arose among these family mediators, new mediators might be appointed from outside the couples' families, and their recommendation would be followed (see also Allen 1935:137–39).

For the first time age limits were set: Females would not marry before the age of nine, males not before twelve, and girls between the age of nine and seventeen could only marry with the consent of their guardians. Males between twelve and eighteen needed judicial permission to marry. Perhaps most important, the new Family Law allowed women, at the time of betrothal, to write into the written marriage contract that should the husband take another wife, her marriage was immediately null and void.

Ottoman reformers had definitively moved into the arena previously controlled by Islamic law and Islamic custom. It was at this time, in 1917, that the *Şeriat* courts were placed under the authority of the Ministry of Justice. Findley has pointed to the paradox in Ottoman legal development, namely that "the same empire that had so impressed Schacht through its emphasis on the *şhari'a* [sic] ultimately evolved in such a way as to prepare the legal and judicial foundations for the most secular Islamic state of the twentieth century" (1986:5–6).

Conclusion

Although the nineteenth-century movement to secular law and secular institutions in the Ottoman Empire was uneven and sporadic, certain trends emerged. Legal change came not from a grass roots movement, nor was it born of reactionary fervor; it occurred at the top of the government. Secular legal practices came as a result of the problems the Ottoman reformers faced in protecting the empire. They needed to gain control of the state in order to safeguard its interests against Russia, the European powers, and revolution from within. From the mid-nineteenth century on, Ottoman armies had engaged in skirmishes and wars on two continents—in Asia against the Russians, and in the Balkans against the Europeans (see appendix I). They had lost Egypt to the French. They also had to contend with uprisings by minority populations within the empire and with European criticism and threatened intervention because of their treatment of Christian groups. It was in meeting these varied and complex challenges to the state that reformers developed plans to defend the empire through secularizing its legal system.

Other trends can be discerned when the large number of nineteenth-century legal reforms are considered. Ad hoc secular courts became recognized through *kanun* law. This is true of the secular police courts that became criminal courts, and of the secular commercial courts. New administrative law and provincial reorganization also were established under *kanun* law, as well as numerous secular law codes.

The third trend concerns the *Şeriat*, the Islamic holy law. The part that pertained to family relationships and inheritance of property remained wholly outside the scope of legal change until the twentieth century. And it continued to be used in *Şeriat* courts by Islamic judges.

However, the *Mecelle* of 1876, was the codification of the Islamic law of transactions. It had been a part of the holy law, but through codification became recognized as part of the official secular law[20] and was applied in secular courts, presided over by secular judges, during the last quarter of the nineteenth century.

All reforms were intertwined, however, each in turn changing the bureaucratic structures of state, because farsighted Ottoman reformers knew that all branches of government needed to be modernized in order to contend with increasingly complex problems. The reformers were well aware of the powerful interest groups who would oppose their reforms—the Janissaries, who were destroyed in 1826; the rural tax-farming groups, who stood to lose economic power; and the powerful Islamic clergy, with vested interests in education, land management, religious brotherhoods, and shrines, and who held the devotion of the Muslim populations. The reformers also recognized that the discourse of law needed to become transformed from that which favored Muslims over non-Muslims and Ottomans over Turks to more universal forms of justice if the empire was to stay together.

Looking to the future, radical Ottoman administrators attempted reform by creating parallel secular institutions, first in education and then in law. In the long nineteenth-century of change, the evolution of Ottoman law and the development of secular legal and administrative systems stand as remarkable and enduring achievements.

Notes

1. Şerif Mardin suggests that it was the Young Ottomans, a group attaining power between 1867 and 1878, who first introduced the ideas of the Enlightenment to the Turkish reading public. But even understanding the European idea of the separation of secular and religious power, they tried to work out a synthesis between the ideas of the Enlightenment and Islam (1962:3–4).

2. Here and the following from Shaw and Shaw (1977:60 ff.).

3. Scribal service was the official place in the *Porte* where male translators and secretaries worked in the Ottoman bureaucracy. They were educated there, taught European languages, and trained for their professions.

4. Except as otherwise noted, the discussion in the remainder of this section is based on Davison (1963:39–40).

5. The discussion in this section is based on Shaw (1970:54–69).

6. The best original sources for nineteenth-century Ottoman law are Heidborn (1908) and Young (1905–06). For excellent discussions, see Findley (1986) and Davison (1963).

7. Except as otherwise noted, the discussion in this section is based on Mardin (1961:190–193).

8. Known in Europe as the Law Merchant, for a more extensive discussion, see Starr 1991.

9. Except as otherwise noted, the discussion in this section is based on Mardin (1961:193).

10. The discussion in this and the following paragraph is based on Lewis (1966:117).

11. A new Law of Title Deeds of 1876 transferred the Office of Land Titles to the Ministry of the *Defterhane* of Constantinople.

12. The discussion in the first four paragraphs in this section is based on Mardin (1961:274–78).

13. For a more extended discussion of the *Mecelle*, see Onar 1955.

14. The discussion in the remainder of this section is based on Shaw and Shaw (1977:174–78).

15. Except as otherwise noted, the discussion in this section is based on Findley (1986:8).

16. The first woman to study law in Ottoman Turkey, Ms. Surreya Agaoğlu, gave this account. In 1920 she went to see Dean Selahattin Bey of the Istanbul law faculty who said, "You know, we don't accept girls yet, but if you can find two or three girls, maybe we'll let you in." She was twenty years old and so returned to her last school and found three women to join her in law school. For the first three months, the girls attended classes by themselves in the afternoon. The men studied the same courses in the morning. When the morning classes were over, the boys in law school, who were Ms. Agaoğlu's friends, waited to see her before she went to class. "The administration found out that it's stupid to have separated classes, and they stopped after three months" (Henry 1987).

17. Except as otherwise noted, the discussion in this section is based on Coulson (1964:182–87).

18. Section 53 of the Sudanese *Mohamedan Law Courts Organizations* and *Procedure Regulations.*

19. Here and the following based on Coulson (1964:186–87).

20. Findley (1986:6), has pointed to the ambiguity between *Şeriat* law and *kadı* courts, suggesting that when there were only *kadı* courts in the Islamic world and no *kanun*, then the holy law and the holy courts were synonymous. During the period of Ottoman control of the empire, the meaning of the *Şeriat*, the holy law, began to shift, and it was not until the *Mecelle* was written and used in *kadı* courts that one could really claim them again as *Şeriat* courts.

II

From Ottoman to Modern Times: The Restructuring of Social Space and Social Relations

II

Chapter Three

Land Transformations

Kemal Karpat, a Turkish historian, suggests that the nineteenth-century need for change in land use patterns was internally generated by groups of landed gentry and intermediate titleholders competing with the Ottoman state over control of productive farmland (1968:89). Huge revenue losses drained the state's economy to the extent that, under the existing semi-feudal conditions, forced the empire to borrow vast sums of money from European countries. These funds were used to wage wars against foreign powers encroaching on the Ottoman Empire and to put down internal uprisings by various ethnic liberation movements.

This chapter considers the ways nineteenth-century changes in agrarian society and land law paved the way for the reforms of the twentieth-century Turkish Republic.

Land and Landownership

As outlined by Tute (1927:1–3), land in the nineteenth-century Ottoman Empire was divided into five classes:

1. *Mülk* was land possessed in full ownership (known in Europe as freehold land).
2. *Mîrî* (or *araz-i memleket*) was agricultural land owned by the state and held in the *iltizam* tax-farming system (discussed in more detail below).
3. *Vakıf* (plural: *Evkaf*) (also known as *mevqufe*), was land held in a religious trust. Such land ordinarily could not be diverted from its original purpose.
4. *Metrouke* was a type of state land reserved for public or communal use, such as roads and pastures.
5. *Mevat*, a different type of state land, consisted of uncultivated areas lying outside the boundaries of existing communities, usually available for clearing and cultivation.

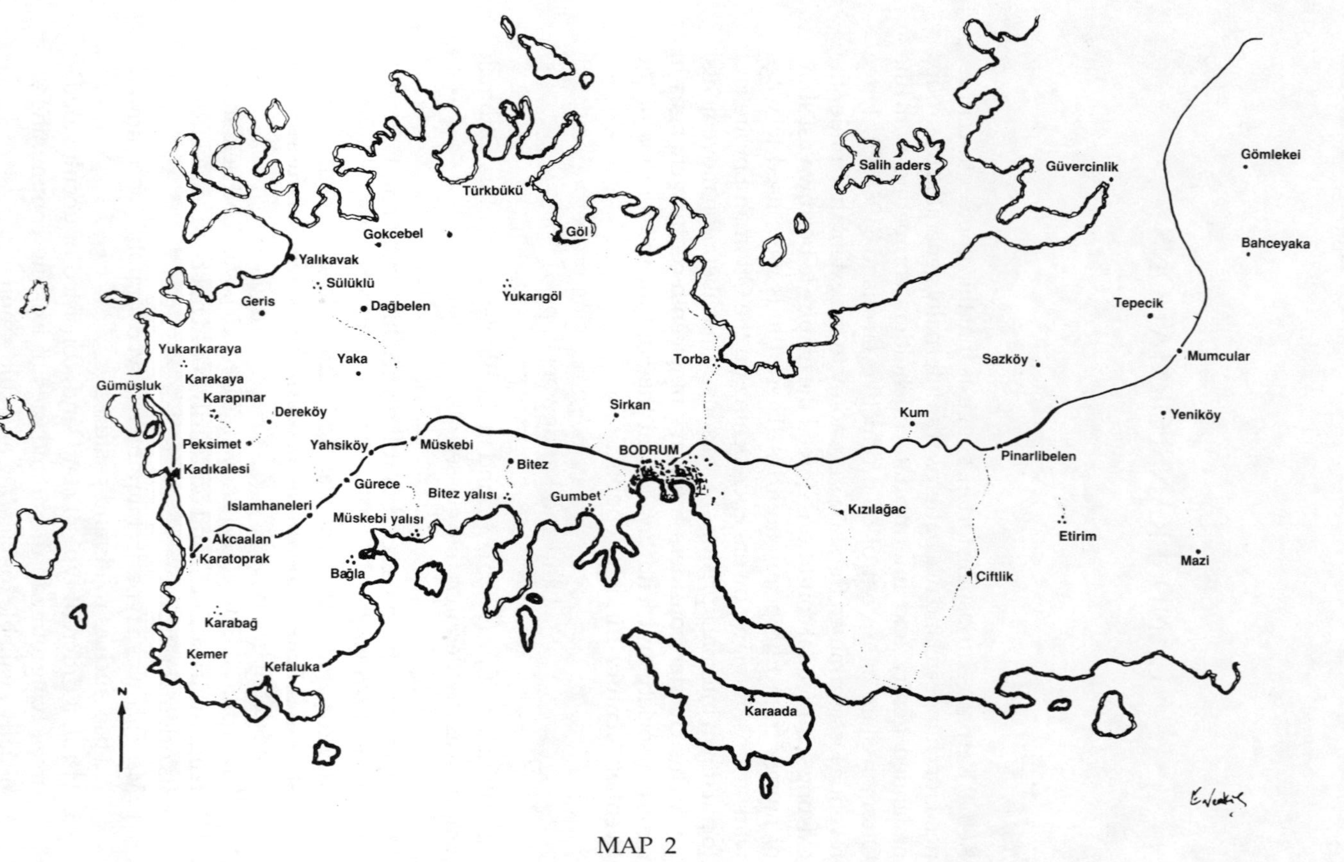

MAP 2

Bodrum District, 1968

Mülk lands were governed by the provisions of the *Mecelle*. *Mevqufe* or *evkaf* lands were governed generally by the *Şeriat*, and *mîrî* lands fell under the jurisdiction of the Ottoman Land Code. Persons holding *mülk* property had the most lasting control and rights to that land under Islamic law.

Land in private ownership, that is *mülk*, was of four kinds:

1. Sites for houses within towns or hamlets; i.e., land parcels not exceeding half a *dönüm*, situated within the confines of towns and villages, and considered appurtenant to dwelling houses.
2. Land separated from state land which became *mülk* land in a valid way.
3. Land on which a tithe was paid, distributed at the time of conquest among the victors and given to them in full ownership.
4. Tribute-paying land, which (as in #3 above) was confirmed in the possession of the non-Muslim inhabitants at the time of the conquests. The tribute imposed on these lands was of two kinds: (1) *kharaj-i-moukasseme*, which was proportional and levied to the amount of from one-tenth to one-half of the crop, according to the yield of the soil, and (2) *kharaj-i-mouvazzef*, which was fixed and appropriated to the land. Legal ownership remained with the titleholder of *mülk* land.

A *vakıf* was land or other revenue-producing property dedicated to pious purposes, a consequence of the Ottoman policy of confiscating estates upon the owner's death. In time the practice arose of establishing family *evkaf* which was land held in pious endowments for the benefit of the founder's family and descendants—a safeguard against the general insecurity of property rights in the empire (Lewis 1966:91). Only a sultan could turn *vakıf* land into *mülk*, or freely held property. A further drawback to the older system was the prohibition against pooling *evkaf*, so most were unavailable for commercial investment.

The Ottoman Tax-Farming System

New research in the Ottoman archives in the last three decades has provided more systematic knowledge of Ottoman tax-farming systems and the development of *ayan*s, rural notables, who began to appear in Asia Minor and Rumelia in the late eighteenth century. *Ayan*s developed through two basic Ottoman tax-farming systems that collectively were known was the *iltizam* landholding system (Rahman and Nagata 1977:179). This replaced the feudal *timar* system,[1] which had existed until the end of the sixteenth century and which, as a method of landholding, continued on some of the sultan's privately held lands.

The *iltizam* land system appeared in Egyptian records as early as 1658. It was a landholding system that regulated the relationship between peasant cultivators and the state by placing every village or group of villages in a unit, called *hissa*, that was sold at public auction to the highest bidder, called *multazim*. The *multazim* bought from the state the right to collect taxes from the peasants at a fixed amount. Some of this money he turned over to the Ottoman treasury, and the rest he kept for himself. This tax-farming system was called *mukâtaᶜat-i mîrî*.

In Anatolian Turkey, land auctions had become common by the middle of the seventeenth century: Whoever could pay the largest sum of money bought the right to be the *multazim* and collect taxes (Rahman and Nagata 1977:181). Peasants complained bitterly under this system, because unofficial taxation was excessive under these short term leases, as every titleholder sought to extract the maximum profit.

By the beginning of the eighteenth century, an attempt at reform was introduced (p. 182). Long term leases were auctioned off. Called *mâlikâme* (p. 181), these were for the life of the titleholder with fixed amounts of yearly tax payable to the state treasury, and often renewable (but at a higher rate) by the heir's male or female children. Because this new tax collector was allowed to develop a long term relationship with both the tillers of the soil and the land itself, it was thought he would be more interested in the peasants' economic well-being. An added incentive to take a longer view of productivity was that wealth in lands could be passed on to inheritors. Thus some titleholders began to acquire (in fact, though not in law) the rights and powers of freeholders.[2] But short term tax-farming was never abolished entirely because the central government feared the growing power of local notables (*ayan*s and *derebey*s).[3]

A third tax-farming system, the *esham*, was introduced in the middle of the eighteenth century. Profit by titleholder was fixed at 5 percent yearly for periods of eight to ten years. In a period of inflation, the central government found *eşham* more profitable than the *mâlikâme* system that allowed titleholders to profit from inflated prices of agriculture. Women, children, orphans, and the lower strata tended to purchase these (Rahman and Nagata 1977:182).

By the nineteenth century, some estates became full legal freehold, alienable and inheritable according to the *Şeriat* laws governing freehold property (see Tute 1927:1, 47). Sultans who had the right to grant *mîrî* land as *mülk* (freehold) sometimes had done so to favored people. But since this changed the tax status of the land, these grants were rare.

Under Sultan Mahmud II (reign 1808–39) and his successors, land auctions became even more frequent. The purchaser obtained a deed called *tapu temessükü*, which gave him only a lease of revenues. Legally, it conferred no right to freehold, yet such purchasers were steadily able to extend and confirm their ownership. The influence of the agrarian laws of the Tanzimat reform period (lasting from 1839 to 1876) was to transform these leases into something barely distinguishable from freehold. Changes in the rules concerning registration and transfers of land increased the value of such titles, which over time turned into a true deed of title (Lewis 1966:443).

The Big Farms

Ottoman scholars had known of plantation farming systems (*çiftliks*) in the Balkan areas of the empire, and new research, based on work by Veinstein (1976) and McGowan (1981:1–44), Nagata (1976), Inalcık (1984), and Rahman and Nagata (1977), suggests that Ottoman Turks also managed big farms in western Anatolia by the nineteenth century, producing cotton, rice, and maize for sale to European, primarily French, markets (Inalcık 1984:124–26, 120 ftn. 33). Founders of family fortunes might obtain their wealth through being a governor of a state or from various other sources: farm production, usury, tax-farming, and controlling the trade between European merchants and Turkish producers (Veinstein 1976, Inalcık 1984:124). Inalcık states, "It is safe to say that, in the eighteenth century, changes were definitely taking place, under the impact of Europe, in certain coastal areas of the Ottoman Empire, which ultimately led to the reorganization of agrarian production" (p. 125). Some *ayans* (plantation owners who were rural notables) were trying to maintain their control of the export trade of the principal staples—cotton and wheat—from western Anatolia, while French merchants were trying to break their monopoly (Veinstein 1976:138–42; Inalcık 1984:125). The Ottoman government allowed *ayans* to survive because they had a long term interest in protecting agriculture and trade in their areas, while governors and tax-farmers, with short term tax-farming leases, tried to maximize gains at the expense of the peasantry (Veinstein 1976; Inalcık 1984).

Types of lands held in western Anatolia by two great *ayans* at the time of their deaths in 1815 and 1816 are now known (Nagata 1976). Some of the fortunes of these powerful *ayans* came from collecting taxes for the *sancak* (governor) or performing other financial and administrative functions (Inalcık 1984:116). These lists of landholdings show that their fortunes also came from arable land, livestock, buildings, equipment, and crops (p. 117). The highest rate of profit came from the cash crops of cotton, rice, or wheat.[4]

There is a debate among Ottoman historians concerning the sources of *ayans'* wealth and power. For example, Nagata concluded from a study of records of productivity of six rural big farms (*çiftliks*): "It is a well known fact that the socio-economic influences of the notables (*A'yans*) [*sic*] in Anatolia and the Balkans in the eighteenth and nineteenth centuries were based on their Big Farms [*sic*] which had developed in these areas through the seventeenth century (1976:1).

Veinstein (1976), Wallerstein (1980), Inalcık (1977), and McGowan (1981:171–72) refine this idea further and demote the theory that these big farms (resembling plantations) were created for an export trade. They suggest, instead, that the *ayan* as a rural class developed primarily through their abilities to extract *surpluses* from the peasantry. Wallerstein (1980:120) quotes Lewis (1966:31): "The shrinking economy of the empire after the sixteenth century led to an acute increase in the amount of surplus extraction from the direct producers."[5]

The role of the Ottoman legal system in this restructuring of the rural economy is also noted by McGowan:

> The Ottoman judicial system of the seventeenth and eighteenth centuries worked both for and against preservation of the old order [the *timar system*], but seemingly mostly against it, owing to the deliberate neglect of key norms of the classical land regime. The transformation thus countenanced by territorial courts became inevitable after the central government itself lost interest in defending the old regime. (1981:171)

Inalcık by 1984 had partially revised his earlier position, saying the *çiftlik* system (or big farms) was a market-oriented farming system. It coincided with a parallel expansion of land reclamation and improvement of marginal lands, especially in the pastoral and flooded lowlands. This market-oriented farming system developed on lands, beyond the old *mîrî* lands, that traditionally had small-sized peasant farming households (*çifthane*) units (1984:116; see also Starr 1991).

Furthermore, the Ottoman land law of 1858 prohibited the acquisition of a whole village as one estate to be owned by one person,[6] suggesting that large estates had grown in number and that the Tanzimat reformers were attempting to restrict these practices. These new laws seemed to have had little practical effect, however. The expansion of commerce and the development of Turkish agricultural exports had brought a flow of money into Asia Minor and created a class of persons with cash to bid for leases, to buy estates, and to lend money on land. The new laws gave them legal powers to enforce contracts of debt and sale; the reorganization of the provinces and the introduction of a system of gendarmerie to serve as rural police, first in Macedonia and then elsewhere, kept the violence usually attendant to such enforcements to a minimum.

The position of the peasant deteriorated considerably under these changes. As a titleholder became a freeholder, the peasant became a hired laborer or sharecropping tenant with no rights at all. His emancipation left him worse off than before: In addition to government taxes, he now had to pay part of his crop as rent, and sometimes render personal services in addition. Folk tales from the nineteenth century reveal a bitter struggle between the impoverished and unhappy peasants and the landlords who dominated and exploited them.

As the rural notables were becoming a social group with special features of its own, it became clear that the Ottoman state needed to break the power base of these *ayan*s and of the new social order that was developing under them (Karpat 1968:85). This order, represented first by the *ayan*s and later by a variety of entrepreneurial, agrarian, and commercial groups in the nineteenth century, demanded a rational legal system capable of meeting the needs of the increasingly differentiated system in which they acted. By 1847 the Ottoman state was preparing a new land law (p. 87), which was embodied in the land code of 1858.

Western Anatolia in the Nineteenth Century

A multiethnic society existed in Anatolia in the nineteenth century. In addition to Muslims, other groups, such as Christians and Jews, lived in towns but were divided from the sultan by religion rather than by nationalism or ethnicity (Miller 1966:30). When people converted from Christianity to Islam, they joined the dominant social rank, regardless of whether they considered themselves as Osmanlı, a Turk, or the descendants of Bulgarians, Bosnians, Albanians, or Cretan Muslims. Christians, with few exceptions, were classified with the Greeks and were thought to belong to the Greek Orthodox Church (p. 30), although now we know that diverse Christian sects inhabited the empire at that time.

Smyrna[7] (Izmir today) was an urban seaport, with a population of about 100,000 in the late eighteenth century; it had a large Greek, Jewish, Ottoman, Armenian, and foreign population (Ramsay 1916:366–67). By the century's end, it had become the most important Ottoman port in trade with Europe[8] and the main exporter of Persian silk to Europe, even surpassing the Ottoman port of Aleppo (now in Syria). Marseilles had dominated the export/import commerce from Smyrna, but during the French Revolution French trade declined, and British and Dutch merchants became first and second in importance.

When the travel writer Henry Field (1885:52–53) visited Smyrna in 1831 after a terrible cholera and plague epidemic, he described it as "a city of the dead." Nevertheless, it recovered from this (last) episode of the plague and resumed eminence as the major Ottoman trading port for European commerce.

An English National residency has existed at Smyrna since 1646; English landed estates there dated from that time (p. 30). By the nineteenth century, English-owned plantations were found as far south as Myndos and Halicarnassus (now Bodrum), two small Ottoman seaports on the southwestern Aegean coast.

Trading Concessions and Religion

In the sixteenth-century florescence of the Ottoman Empire, Jewish groups had played important roles as merchants, diplomats, and bankers. But by the eighteenth century, Armenians and Greeks had become the most important merchants, profiting commercially and culturally from their ties with European Christian communities.[9] Even though supplanted as a merchant class, a large Jewish community continued late into the nineteenth century at Smyrna, and forty-five people of Jewish faith lived in Halicarnassus at the end of the century.[10]

A class of foreign-protected merchants (*Avrupa Tüccarı*) with special rights and privileges had grown up in Constantinople, Smyrna, and Salonika by the end of the eighteenth century. In return for a fee of 1,500 piastres, foreign traders could purchase certificates called *berat*s, which allowed them to trade with Europe and which thereby conferred a number of important legal, economic, and commercial advantages. A second set of privileges was granted to locally recruited interpreters and consular agents. Over time these *berat*s or licenses were given to European embassies and consulates who sold them to Greek and Armenian merchants, thus extending privileges and "protected status" to these groups as well. Protected foreign merchants had gained rights through a series of Ottoman "capitulations" to western European powers. The mercantile skills of Greek merchants allowed them to prosper, and a large community lived in Smyrna and farther south, in the sea town of Halicarnassus.

To remove the disadvantages of Muslim merchants in relation to the privileged status of European traders, the Ottoman state sold *berat*s to Muslims for a lesser fee (1,200 piastres). Muslim merchants were permitted to join the Muslim guild, the *Hayriye Tüccarı* (literally, "merchants of benefaction"). However, in the Ottoman status system, esteemed social positions arose from service in the Ottoman military, the civil bureaucracy, and the Islamic hierarchy, not from commerce. This in part accounts for the small number of Ottoman-Turkish merchants until the ideology of the Republic of Turkey promoted new careers.

The growth of European nationalism encouraged the Christian merchant class in the Ottoman Empire to become more vocal in its demands for more trading rights and in its criticism of the Ottoman state's limitations on merchants' powers. Increasingly, the merchants were supported by Christian groups outside the empire. Demands for independent rule from Arab countries within the empire in the second half of the nineteenth century also created problems of state control. Finally, internal dissatisfactions of the *millets* and the Ottoman Empire's continuing involvement in external wars threatened to tear the empire apart as the twentieth century approached.

The Countryside Around Smyrna

Dangerously close to nineteenth-century Smyrna were brigands of Greek and Turkish outlaws, who preyed on travelers, raided small villages, and attacked caravans carrying goods from central Anatolia and Persia. Ramsay describes in vivid detail his narrow escape from Circassian raiders on the Anatolian plateau as late as 1883 (1897:63 and ft.;186–89).

Despite the outlaws and ruffians, the British built a railroad in the late 1850s that linked Smyrna to the Anatolian hinterland. Extending up the Lycus and Meander valleys, the railroad was preceded by Christians who served as agents to extend the trading connections with the line (de Planhol 1958:528). A regular influx of Greek Orthodox Christian farmers followed the course of the tracks, developing small vineyards and plantations near the railways that radiated from Smyrna (Ramsay 1916:378–79).

Between Smyrna and the ancient port of Ephesus were remnants of the great Turkoman nomadic confederacy that had been a threat to the Ottoman Empire in the seventeenth century. The Turkoman had had a fierce and independent spirit and an ability to mobilize large numbers of cavalrymen. From the seventeenth century on, sultans made a concerted effort to break up the Turkoman confederacy and force these nomadic tribal groups to settle (de Planhol 1958:527). Tax collectors harried the Turkoman who, to escape taxation, began to migrate from the great central Anatolia plateau. Some came toward western Anatolia in smaller and smaller groups. Of these, some tribal fragments went to

Rhodes and Istanköy (also known as Kos) just off the coast of Halicarnassus, while others settled at points as widely scattered as Smyrna, Kusadası, and Ankara (pp. 528, 531). Turkoman nomads practiced transhumance—raising camels, sheep, and goats, and moving between a summer (*yayla*) and a winter camping ground (*kışla*). They lived in small groups with black tents surrounded by their herds of camels and goats.[11]

The railroad by the 1860s was encroaching on the ancient migration routes of the nomads and was especially threatening to the nomadic Yürük, who raised only sheep and goats. Many tribal fragments of Yürük and Turkoman migrated to the Cilician mountains, to the Taurus and the anti-Taurus mountains, where they could continue to escape government pressures to settle. Each group migrated at a different time, following its own migration routes. Meanwhile, some Turkoman near Smyrna had become employed by the railroad. They made charcoal, cut trees, sawed planks, and constructed sleeping cars. The Turkoman continued to be divided into tribal groups, were fond of hunting with hawks, which they carried on a gloved hand, and also developed a fine breed of greyhounds. The Turkoman had never been Islamicized, but continued in their pagan religion of *Yesidées*. Although government attempts to break up the large nomadic confederacies had been largely successful, smaller nomadic bands ranged all over Anatolia, Armenia, Northern Persia, and Turkistan. They had no traditions of cultivation; their only rivals at raising livestock and leading a pastoral existence were said to be the Kurds.

Like sultans before him, Abdülhamid II attempted to compel the nomads to settle down in permanent villages after the Russo-Turkish War of 1877–78; by then the most nomadic and thus the most resistant to settling were the Yürük (Ramsay 1916:389, 391). The Yürük (literally, "those who walk") were found in small scattered communities in the mountains and, to a lesser extent, on the great plains around Smyrna that stretched to the Eastern Taurus mountains (p. 388). By the mid-1880s, the countryside south of Smyrna was characterized as "cultivated [land], plantations of mulberry trees, orange trees, mud villages, scattered among whom is another population, the Turkomans, whom we saw in great numbers over the plain, living in black tents, surrounded by hundreds of camels" (Field 1885:62–63).

Between 1890 and 1895 an additional land development project was undertaken near Smyrna by Europeans, who induced the Ottoman government to "promise possession to squatters, who would plant vineyards and farm the land. The Ottoman Empire would guarantee permanent possession of the land to the worker as long as he was making full use of it. The result was a great extension of production in the Meander Valley, almost wholly by Greek-speaking, Orthodox Christians" (Ramsay 1916:380).

The multiethnic, diversified pastoral/farming economy of the western Anatolian countryside began to change as ethnic leaders fanned nationalistic yearnings at the end of the century. Increasingly, an incendiary situation developed between "Turk" and "Greek." After the complete dismemberment of the Ottoman Empire decreed by the victors of World War I and the invasion and burning of Smyrna by the Greek army in May 1919, Ataturk emerged as a leader to save the Turkish nation (Rustow 1957:71). The Greco-Turkish War lasted from 1919 to 1923, when the Greek army was driven off mainland Turkey, and most ethnic Greeks either assumed Turkish Islamic identities or fled for their lives to nearby Greek islands. The advent of World War I had forced the British, Dutch, and French to curtail their mercantile activities with Smyrna. When the sultan and caliph sided with Germany, the British invaded the Aegean coastline and were driven off in the fierce Battle of Gallipoli in 1915.

The division of the empire after World War I was the final blow to the Ottoman state. A new state, the modern Republic of Turkey, rose like a phoenix from the ashes of the burning, perishing Ottoman cities. The new identity and value system that developed was built on Turkish nationalism, populism, secularism, and statism. The imagined "community of Turks" would be embodied in Asia Minor.

Administration of Land Law in the New Republic

The new Republic, established by Ataturk in 1922, inherited earlier attempts at centralization of land administration, the most important being the following:

1. A centralized Land Registry Bureau (*defterhane*). Planned in 1847, it had been put into practice thirty years later in Constantinople (Karpat 1968:87). (See #5.)
2. A standardized system of printed and properly sealed land ownership documents. This replaced older existing deeds of the *sipahis*, *ayans*, or tax collectors.
3. The Ottoman Land Code of 1858, a "milestone of social history in the Middle East" (Karpat 1968:86). Intended to reassert the state's ownership of land, its actual effect was to enlarge the scope of privately held land.

4. The state's attempt to reclaim all lands acquired in unorthodox ways (such as communal pastures). Yet bribery and intimidation kept much pastureland in the hands of *derebeys*, who controlled entire valleys (Lewis 1966:442–45).
5. The 1876 *Law of Title Deeds*. In which the Office for Deeds was annexed to the Ministry of the *Defterhane* Administration of Constantinople and record-keeping was finally centralized.

Although title deeds were awarded and records kept under the Ottomans, and although the Ottoman Land Code of 1858 liberalized the right of succession to the benefit of land users' heirs, it did so within the context of the Islamic concept of absolute private property. The purpose was to induce landholders to improve the land, which now was worth doing because land could be retained in the family (Karpat 1968:87; Lewis 1966:443).

In the new Republic of Turkey, land title offices would be decentralized. Each *kaza* (county seat) would have a Land Records Bureau by 1950. Furthermore, legal categories of private land ownership were to be more fully developed to meet the dual demands of populism and of modern bureaucratic record-keeping.

In Ataturk's remarkable thirty-six hour speech of February 17, 1923,[12] to open the first economic congress of the new Republic at Izmir, he mentioned four groups whose welfare the state would now promote: merchants, farmers, artisans, and workers. This explicitly demonstrated that class-war ideologies were to be rejected.

During the 1920s, two more agrarian reforms were made. The first abolished the tithes, called *asar*, by the Law of February 17, 1925. Rooted in the medieval Islamic fiscal system, tithes had become seriously abused by tax collectors. Although the practice had provided important state revenues, it was a heavy burden on the peasantry.[13] By relieving the financial drain from rural villages, Ataturk assured village loyalty during the internal upheavals that followed.

The second major land reform related to ownership. When the Swiss civil code was put into effect in 1926, it unified and modernized the system of land tenure, thus legally terminating many remaining traces of the tax-farming system. A number of large landowners in the south and east of Turkey, however, continued to hold almost the same status as the earlier Ottoman *derebeys*. Although land redistribution laws were passed in 1927 and 1929, progress was slow. Between 1923 and 1934, only 711,000 hectares were reassigned. The most important distributions were in the eastern provinces where the government was anxious to break the power of the feudal and tribal chiefs that had led to the Kurdish rebellion of 1925.

In western Anatolian provinces and in Karaman, a new class of landowners with medium-sized estates developed when the lands formerly held by Greeks were given to Muslim immigrants (after the exchange of populations) and to veterans of the Turkish War of Independence. This latter group had close connections with the new government and often assumed the prestige and authority formerly held by the local landlords.

The forces most damaging to the privileges of former landowners were the branches of the People's Party that were opened in all rural areas. In Ataturk's Turkey the local party officials were the agents of the Kemalist revolution, giving advice to the peasantry on a wide variety of subjects. In doing this, they took over many of the powers formerly held by large landowners.

Land Reform Law of 1945

In his autumn speech of 1945, President Ismet Inonu agreed to allow the formation of an opposition party (Ahmad 1977:9). As the Republican People's Party became more populist, it introduced a land reform bill, meant to have far-reaching effects. After almost a year of parliamentary debate, it became law on 11 June 1946 (Lewis 1966:467). The land reform goals were to provide land for peasants with too little or no land to farm. To ensure the full and effective use of the arable lands of the countryside, land was granted to peasants along with twenty-year interest-free loans for agrarian development. The land for distribution was to come from unused state land, from pious endowments (which had been confiscated in the 1920s), from municipal and other publicly owned land, from reclaimed land, from land of unknown ownership, and from land expropriated from private individuals. All landed property in excess of 500 *dönüm* (123.5 acres) was to be nationalized. The distribution began in 1947 and involved only state lands and pious foundations. By 1950 only about 60,000 *dönüm* had been distributed. After further prolonged discussion in 1950, the nationalization limit was raised from 500 to 5,000 *dönüm* (Lewis 1966:468), a decision in favor of larger landowners and a clear bid for their support and loyalty at a time when Turkey moved to a multiparty system of contested elections.

Emerging Land Relations in Bodrum, 1950–1970

With the decentralization of land records, Bodrum received a Land Registry Office. It is the repository of all "legally" recorded land transactions taking place in the district. Until 1928 the Turkish language was written in the Arabic script, and so earlier land titles had been recorded in Arabic. The earliest registered title written in modern Turkish (Latinized script), used in a land case that I witnessed, dated to 1932 (Starr 1985a:Case No. 5).

An individual could gain a legal title (*tapu*) to land in four ways: through inheritance, purchase, court-decided legal title to usufruct land, or through validation of ownership by a cadestre survey team working in the area. The civil code stipulated that all lands of the patriarch were to be divided equally among all his children (regardless of gender or marital status), after the surviving widow received one-fourth. In practice, many factors intervened in carrying out these inheritance laws, for married daughters might relinquish inherited land to their brother(s) who remained in the village to farm the family estate. Also, a middle-aged widow often relinquished her share and chose to live with a married son or daughter. This allowed more land to be divided among her children.

The general term for court-decided inheritance cases was *veraset*, although variations on this term are listed in the court docket, such as *veraset et intikal vergısi*, i.e., inheritance and death dues. When inherited parcels were small and a number of individuals had rights to the land, or when problems concerning equivalence of diverse land occurred (orchards, woodlands, irrigated and nonirrigated fields, and house lots), the heirs could apply to the courts, and the judges would develop standards of equivalence for the division. The general term for a division of land among heirs is *taxim*. Sometimes there would be twelve to fifteen heirs with different degrees of rights to the land, such as a case in which the deceased patriarch left three children, one of whom had died and left three children. Each child's share was then one third of his deceased parent's share after the surviving spouse received one-fourth. Thus, degrees of kin relationship needed to be established by the court. In Bodrum in land division cases decided at court, the judge listed the names of all children, even babies in arms, in the court docket and later on the title deed, a practice followed earlier under Ottoman land title deeds (see Tute 1927:26). By applying to the courts in land division and inheritance cases, judicial authority and wisdom helped cut through a number of complex issues that often perplexed and hindered land division at the village level.

The second way of acquiring a legal title to a house and lot or to land was by purchase from someone who already possessed legal title. The new owner would register the land in his or her own name. In the 1960s no foreigners could own land or houses in Turkey unless they were married to Turkish persons or had Turkish partners. In both cases, the Turk would be co-owner.

The third means of establishing legal ownership was to open a court case to assert ownership by virtue of *usufruct* rights. A 1966 law stated that a person who had been farming land of less than 20 *dönüm*,[14] who could demonstrate that he or she had paid taxes on the land for eleven years or had farmed it or lived on it uninterruptedly for twenty years, during which time no one else had paid taxes on it, could open a court case for possession. Two witnesses who were in a position to have first-hand knowledge of the situation were required to testify before the court. If the suit was uncontested, the farmer would be given a title. In 1972 the law was amended to require tax records if the size of the land was more than 20 *dönüm*. If one owner claimed several pieces of land in one registration area (*tapulama bolgesi*) whose total size was more than 50 *dönüm*, again tax records were needed for proof.[15]

The fourth way to gain title was through a government cadestre team that was working in the district to clarify and grant land titles through usufruct rights. Starting in 1965, a nine-member cadestre team went from village to village in Bodrum, staying in each village until an entire map of legitimate titles to each parcel of land could be drawn. They used the same methods the Bodrum courts did, namely hearing testimony from principals and witnesses. The same standards of evidence were also used (for court methods, see Starr 1984). After two years' work, seven villages had been completed: Bites, Ortakent, Sazköy, Pınarlı Belen, Tepecik, Çomlekçi, and Kum. Bodrum judges were enthusiastic about the work of the cadestre team and one said: "When all the people in a village have a title to their land, we don't see anymore of these title problems in court, and all other land problems are minor ones. When titles to land are not clear, villagers are often using other people's fields or cutting or burning other people's woods."[16]

Under Islamic law a notary could issue a legally recognized land title. In the past, and even today, this form of legal title is recognized in Islamic and in civil law countries (see Eickelman 1985:26–27, 106; Nicholson 1987; Rosen 1980–81:220). Licensed by the state, these notaries gave certified titles, in Turkish called *Noter Senedi*. In the Bodrum district, poorer villagers still used these notes as a form of sale or purchase, but ownership of land purchased by such a note could be challenged in court. In a contest between a court-awarded land title (*tapu*) and a certified note, *noter senedi*, the former would win. A certified note, when contested, was not considered sufficient proof without further verification.

Another route to establishing ownership was to apply to the administrative director of Bodrum, the Kaymakam, who with his council (*heyet*) would investigate land claims and reach a decision. To enforce or to appeal his decision, a person needed to apply to the Bodrum courts. In the three-year period of 1965 through 1967, fifteen cases asking for criminal sanctions against individuals who did not comply with a Kaymakam decision were heard in the Middle Criminal Court in Bodrum (see Table 1, p. 62).

The Kaymakam's committee consisted of important representatives of the national government at the local level. These were the government doctor, the director of Land Records Office (*Mal müdüru*), the director of the Census Bureau (*Nüfus Memura*), the government-appointed veterinarian (an important person in rural areas, and particularly so in Bodrum because of his active participation in politics), and finally the Kaymakam's secretary (*kâtip*). In comparison to the courts, fewer cases were brought to the council because its methods were cumbersome and took time (as did the courts), but there was the additional problem that its decisions could easily be appealed to the Bodrum courts. The council also was responsible for looking into complaints against civil servants in the district, a task that took priority over land investigations.

Land Cases in Bodrum Courts

In 1967, in a talk with a Bodrum judge, I asked what the three most frequent types of cases he saw in the Bodrum civil court were. With no hesitation he responded, "Land." He continued:

Judge: The second most important case is divorce. We see about ten cases of land to one about divorce. The third biggest are inheritance cases.

Anthropologist: In regard to land cases, what are the biggest problems in civil court?

Judge: Titles and ownership of orchards.

Anthropologist: What are the problems with titles?

Judge: Boundaries. Slowly all villages are obtaining titles for land. We manage to title about four villages a year with the cadestre team.

Anthropologist: What types of land title cases create the most problems?

Judge: Forest cases.

Anthropologist: What kinds of forests are there?

Judge: Village woods, personal woods, and government forests.

Anthropologist: Which are the largest? the smallest?

Judge: Government, personal, then village. There is another kind of wooded property, that owned by Red Cross or Tourism for the good of the community. The Turkish government has surveyed all the forests by airplane. In areas where titles were given, there are no longer any problems. But where titles are lacking, there are still land fights. Sometimes the government is wrong; sometimes it is the people. When the people get angry, they might say, "If it isn't mine, I'll light a match to it."

Anthropologist: What are the most numerous land cases?

Judge: Giving title after twenty years of residency, aggression on someone's land, general titling, surveying, land division, and inheritance.[17]

Although the judge's perception is a good barometer of what creates the most work for him, in terms of actual numbers he provided the information in inverse order. Inheritance and land division provide the most cases, titling after twenty years the least (Table 1). To see what can be learned about land cases from court statistics, it is necessary to turn to the court docket.

Land Cases in the Court Docket

In Bodrum's civil courts in the three-year period of 1965, 1966, and 1967, land cases account for over half the cases heard. The total number of civil cases was 1,846, and the total number of land cases was 969, or 52.3 percent.

Table 1 provides an actual breakdown into types of land cases. The frequencies here are compared with all cases in both civil and criminal courts. The most frequent cases involve general "inheritance cases" with 295 cases, or 8.8 percent of all cases going through the courts in a three-year period. "Nullifying an old title and recording a new one" is second with 227 cases, or 6.6 percent of all cases in all the Bodrum courts. The third most frequent civil land case is to "reclaim a house or land" from someone using it, with 124 cases, making it 3.8 percent of the entire case load in the three-year period.

Requests for a "road to an orchard" occurs when orchards have been newly created from adjacent fields, or when an orchard is divided

TABLE 1

Land Cases in the Civil Courts of Bodrum, Turkey
1965–1967

Type of Case	No. Cases	Percentage of Cases in All Courts
Inheritance (*Veraset*)	295	8.8
Title: to nullify old and record new	227	6.6
To get own house or land back	124	3.8
Division of land	71	2.1
To object to forest boundaries	62	1.9
To record and correct number of *dönüm*	51	1.6
Certification of legal possession	30	.9
Increase and correct number of *dönüm*	29	.7
To evict from property	18	.5
To correct size of property	13	.4
To get a road to an orchard	12	.4
Violation of purchase option	10	.3
To get title through usufruct rights	7	.2
To void an inheritance	5	.2
To correct size and land location	4	.1
To take off a mortgage	4	.1
Minor: to buy, sell, or sue for inheritance	2	.1
To be allowed to use undivided field	1	.0
To establish a religious foundation	1	.0
To increase price of legal expropriation	1	.0
To take back rent-free real estate	1	.0
To void a written document of sale	1	.0
Total	969	28.7

among heirs. By law a person must be given a road to his or her fields, but because of the value of tangerine orchards, an owner might be reluctant to give up a portion of his orchard for a road for another person. The landlocked farmer, by going to court, can use the law to compel his opponent into compliance.

Regarding the 62 cases of forest boundaries, these civil cases should be considered in relation to the 155 criminal cases of violation of forest boundaries and the one case of cultivating a garden in the government-protected forest (Table 2).

The total of forest cases thus is 218 or over 6.3 percent of all the cases brought to the Bodrum criminal courts. The judges were holding the forest boundary cases in abeyance, while waiting for a third judge to be assigned to Bodrum to hear them. The temporary assignment of a third judge meant, as one Bodrum judge explained to me, that the government recognized the newly proclaimed "government woodland" had created problems in the region. The new state forest had been created from wooded areas that villagers dwelling nearby had always considered village-held, communal, or their own private lands. In sending an additional judge to hear these cases together, the court administration was recognizing an existing problem and attempting to provide a general solution that would establish boundaries, using the same criteria for settlement across a number of local complaints. Bodrum judges and higher court administrators preferred not to have these cases of disputed forest boundaries flow through the courts on a case-by-case basis, in part because the judges felt the courts were already busy, and in part because the court hierarchy hoped to resolve the problem once and for all times.

TABLE 2

Land Cases in Bodrum's Criminal Courts
1965 through 1967

Type of Case	No. of Cases	Percentage of all Cases in Bodrum Courts
To violate the forest laws	155	4.6%
Usurping village land	44	1.3%
Requests for criminal sanctions and evictions on cases decided by Kaymakam concerning someone using your land	15	.4%
To plant a field in the government-protected forest	1	.0%
Total	215	6.3%

Of equal interest are the cases at the low end of court frequency. For example, there is only one suit asking for the right to farm "individual land." In tobacco-growing areas in the eastern plateau area of Bodrum district, farmers told me that there were economic reasons to keep tobacco-growing land from being subdivided into smaller and smaller plots. Small plots occurred as a consequence of generation after generation of landholders dividing land among their children, according to the inheritance rules of equal land division among siblings under the civil code. Yet, in the three-year period only one household applied to the Bodrum courts to be allowed to "keep an undivided field together." This suggests that tobacco farmers may have continued to hold family farms as "joint family property," yet registered smaller and smaller plots in the Land Registry Office.

Another interesting aspect of the low end of the case flow is that only one case "to establish a religious foundation" appeared, although this occurred in the period of the relaxing of official state opposition to Islam and the beginning of the ground swell of public religious expression in some parts of Turkey. The fact that only one person brought a suit to create a religious foundation and no cases of criminal prosecutions for promoting illegal religious activities appeared suggests that in areas of economic development, like Bodrum, Islam is a less important focus of social life, a less significant way of gaining prestige, and a less certain way to mobilize public support.

Until the summer of 1968 Bodrum police would have been interested in supporting the law against religious propagandizing by Islamic groups, in part because notables in Bodrum were hoping to promote the sea town as a tourist center. But when the new chief of police, an ardent apostle of Islam, arrived in Bodrum in the summer of 1968, he ordered the closure of Bodrum's first *diskotek*, which had been opened in Bodrum by two enterprising youths from Ankara. Word around town was that the new chief was also getting injunctions against the state liquor store and the cafes that served wine, beer, and alcohol to urban Turkish visitors, young European tourists, and the local clientele. The *diskotek* remained closed only two days, however, for the town notables and the administrative director of Bodrum intervened on behalf of the entrepreneurs. Enterprising activity prevailed over religious sentiments.

Criminal Courts

Fewer cases about land are found in the criminal courts. The total number of criminal cases concerning land in the three-year period of 1965 through 1967 is 215 (15.9 percent of 1,355 total criminal cases).

Bodrum's land cases in criminal court are an important contrast to Aktan's (1966:324) research on crime and landownership. Aktan found that almost half of the reported four million annual court cases in Turkey relate directly, and many more related indirectly, to land. His interviews with men in jail led him to suggest that half the men in Turkish jails on murder charges had killed someone over disputed land. Although available data does not allow comment on the suggested relationship between land and murder (cases of premeditated murder were not heard in Bodrum), many more civil than criminal prosecutions concerning land were brought to the Bodrum court. This suggests (although further research would need be undertaken to verify) that when an area is undergoing increasing economic prosperity, many farmers choose legal redress over self-help in searching for a solution to land problems.

A counter to the "economic prosperity causes reduced violence" argument would claim that pacification of western Turkey was the key to less violent fights over land. Compared to eastern and central Anatolian districts of Turkey in the 1960s, the Bodrum district was firmly under governmental control. Admittedly, the visible presence of the gendarmerie and the Bodrum police was a factor in allaying violence, intimidation, and revenge killings, as were court prosecutions for carrying an unlicensed weapon. Yet the case flow data suggest, and personal interviews with rural men from many of Bodrum's local villages confirm, that even angry village men were willing to seek legal redress instead of violent methods of revenge.

Furthermore, an increasing economic prosperity of a district goes hand in hand with a willingness to turn to secular state courts for resolving disputes. Hobsbawm (1959) and Blok (1989) have demonstrated that propensity to violence and banditry is not just a value system. It goes with exclusion from economic resources, a low social status, and the inability to engage in other, more legitimate activities that provide social mobility.

Land cases heard in Bodrum's courts can also be used to address an additional research theme. In the late 1940s and early 1950s, rural social scientists asserted that many villagers made ad hoc arrangements about houses and fields at the death of the patriarch, and that such impromptu arrangements might continue across generations. These arrangements were said to be flexible adjustments, bound neither by the new official codes nor by local folk law (Stirling 1957:26–27; 1965:122, 273; Yalman 1979). Based on research in 1949–50, Stirling reported that villagers preferred to work out the redistribution of property informally after a head of household died rather than "to call in officials who will ruthlessly apply the legally correct rules and force all the permanent and final rearrangements of ownership to be made at once" (1957:26–27).

By the mid-1960s in the Bodrum district, land relationships had become so complex, and individuals who might legally have a claim to an inheritance had so multiplied, that many heirs were glad to apply to the courts for help in deciding land divisions. In Table 1, 295 cases of inheritance and 71 cases of land division appeared at court in a three-year period, which represents 10.9 percent of all civil and criminal cases heard in the same time frame.

Conclusion

For three centuries the Ottoman Empire had attempted to break up the powerful Turkoman confederacy on the Anatolian plateau by heavy taxation, by splitting tribes up to undermine tribal unity, and by forcing tribal segments to settle. By the nineteenth century remnants of the Turkoman were found as far west as the Aegean district near Smyrna, and some camps had migrated as far south as the Halicarnassian peninsula. Still nomadic, they shared migration routes to summer and winter pasturage with the sheep-herding, nomadic Yürük, each group migrating at a different time.[18]

Yet a new society was emerging in the western Anatolian countryside. Changes occurred, first through legal recognition, and later through the granting of political power to the dominant landholding groups. Land and land ownership remained a central problem for the Ottoman administrators at a time when they faced internal nationalistic upheavals and when Ottomans wished to compete with European powers in the field of trade and commerce (Karpat 1968:89–90).

Although the progression from multiple land use by nomads and farmers to intensive agriculture in the twentieth century required a revolution, some technological methods and personnel of the previous Land Ownership Bureau and some land use patterns continued from Ottoman times into the new secular Republic. The Ottomans and the new republicans both depended on cadestre surveys, on licensed agents such as *vekils* (legal persons who are not lawyers), and notaries to sometimes handle and record land transactions. Modern technology and statecraft has created better record-keeping and a less status-oriented taxation system, so that now all Turkish citizens are taxed more equally.

The movement of land from semi-feudal conditions of the Ottoman Empire into individual and state possession was incomplete at the time of my field research in the 1960s. Yet in one hundred years the western Anatolian region of Turkey had metaphorically crossed centuries of social and land use change and had become, in the twentieth century, a rich and productive area in the modern Turkish Republic. When allowances are made for size of the geographic area, western Anatolia is exceeded in productivity only by the province of Marmara.

Notes

1. The *timar,* or military fief, can be described briefly as a grant of land in return for which the *sipahi* (a cavalryman) was bound to render military service, in person and with as many men-at-arms as were required by the size and income of his grant. During the seventeenth and eighteenth centuries, more and more *timar*s were converted into crown lands and leased out to tax-farmers with purely financial and no military obligations. A peasant farmer had the right of *istiğlal* (usufruct) which could pass only to his sons. The peasant could not divide or sell the land, nor could he give it up or leave it. The *timariot*, or *sipahi*, appointed by the central authority, usually from among commanders who distinguished themselves in battle, represented the state and saw that the legal status of the land was maintained and that it was properly and continuously cultivated. Also, he functioned as tax collector, with a portion of the taxes serving as his own fee. In times of war, instead of being paid by a state treasury, the *timariot* paid the soldiers and contributed supplies according to his revenue.

2. Unless otherwise noted, the discussion in the remainder of this section is based on Lewis (1966:442–43).

3. *Derebey*s are feudal landlords.

4. One of these *çiftlik*s was at Teke in southwestern Anatolia, the other at Saruhan in western Anatolia.

5. See also Sunar (n.d.).

6. The discussion in this and the following paragraph is based on (Lewis 1966:442–44).

7. In European sources the Greek names of Smyrna and Halicarnassus continued into the twentieth century. In Ottoman sources Smyrna is called Izmir, and Halicarnassus is called Bodrum by the nineteenth century, but since I do not read Ottoman, I follow the European tradition until the advent of the Turkish Republic in 1922.

8. The discussion in the remainder of this paragraph is based on Frangakis-Syrett's lecture at the Columbia University Seminar, "The History and Culture of the Turks," delivered September 16, 1988; and on Kasaba (1988:92–98).

9. Except as otherwise noted, the discussion in this section is based on Lewis (1966:448–49).

10. See Cuniet's census of 1891 (Cuniet 1894:922–24, quoted by Galantı 1946:40–41).

11. Except as otherwise noted, the discussion in this and the following paragraph is based on Field (1885:62–63).

12. See Karal (1945).

13. The discussion in the remainder of this section is based on Lewis (1966:461–62).

14. A *dönüm* is a unit of land which has been standardized to refer to roughly one-quarter of an acre. Traditionally, before the National Land Survey Commission standardized its usage, a *dönüm* referred to the amount of land a team of oxen could plow with a needle plow in one day (Kolars 1963:xv).

15. Article 20 of the Law No. 1617 (July 26, 1972) amended Article 33 of the Law on Land Registration No. 766 (dated July 12, 1966). Personal communication from Professor Tuğrul Ansay, retired professor of law, Ankara University, Hukuk Fakultesi, December 14, 1980.

16. Interviews with Bodrum judges. Bodrum field notes, July 1967.

17. Interviews with Bodrum judges. Bodrum field notes, July 1967.

18. For a twentieth-century example of alternative use of the same pasturage, see Grønhaug (1974).

CHAPTER FOUR

BODRUM—ONE HUNDRED YEARS OF SOLITUDE

> In a small separate room, where the walls were gradually being covered by strange maps and fabulous drawings, he taught them to read and write and do sums, and he spoke to them about the wonders of the world. . . . [I]n that way . . . the boys ended up learning that in the southern extremes of Africa there were men so intelligent and peaceful that their only pastime was to sit and think, and that it was possible to cross the Aegean Sea on foot by jumping from island to island all the way to the port of Salonika.
>
> Gabriel Garcia Marquez (1970:24)

Although the title of Garcia Marquez's novel, *One Hundred Years of Solitude*, refers to the wilderness of the South American jungle, it applies an apt metaphor for Bodrum as well. Once a glorious city-state, the home of historians, philosophers, the first woman admiral, kings and queens, Bodrum had by the nineteenth century been reduced to a backwater port in the Ottoman Empire. For over one hundred years, Bodrum experienced social and physical isolation from the sources of Ottoman culture and society. It would spend the first four decades of the Turkish Republic as an authentic but small, unimportant sea town (much like all the other small towns in Turkey at that time), then in the 1970s become "discovered" and devoured by touristic development, losing, seemingly forever, the simplicity, innocence, and natural beauty it had once possessed in such abundance.

In 484 B.C., as the Persian city Zephyria, the sea town was the birthplace of the famous Greek citizen, Herodotus, known as the father of history and remembered for his remarkable description and analysis of the Peloponnesian Wars.[1] Some attribute Herodotus's historical vision to the fact that he lived at the corner of overlapping cultures—Greek and Persian. The city later became part of the Dorian Confederacy as Halicarnassus. About 375 B.C. Mausolus, who became king of Caria, moved his capital there from Mylasa. Mausolus married his own sister Artemisia, who reigned after his death and, when Rhodes declared war, led her navy to victory in 353 B.C., becoming the first woman admiral in history. She allied with Xerxes and fought at Salamis. The tomb Artemisia built for her husband/brother became one of the Seven Wonders of the World. In 334 B.C. the town fell to Alexander, who razed it. It then fell to Philip V of Macedonia (201 B.C.), and successively to Rome (129 B.C.), the Byzantines, the Selcuk Turks (end of the eleventh century A.D.), and became part of the Ottoman Empire during the reign of Begazit I.

One of Halicarnassus's most glorious periods was during the Middle Ages when Venetian trading ships sailed the Mediterranean, and the Christian Knights of St. John came to build the magnificent feudal castle on the site of the former Doric Acropolis. To do so, for ninety-eight years they dismantled the spectacular tomb of Mausolus, stone by stone. A local Bodrum historian, Professor Galantı, quotes Evliya Celebi who, when he visited Halicarnassus in 1671, found orchards, vineyards, and Seville oranges growing, cared for by government employees of the Ottoman Empire (Galantı 1946:211). Celebi also wrote that, beyond the castle toward the west, there were no houses.

In the eighteenth century an Ottoman admiral established a naval shipyard in Bodrum, and over the years all the pines on the surrounding hills were cut down to supply the yard with timber. It is from this time that Bodrum's tradition of boat-building dates (Mansur 1972:63). The contemporary yards are staffed by Turks, all of whom learned their trade from Ziya Usta, a refugee from Crete (p. 63). Before the Turkish War of Independence, they were owned and operated by Greeks.

Society in an Ottoman Sea Town

The town of Bodrum, in the nineteenth century, reflected the cosmopolitan, multireligious composition of the Ottoman Empire. At that time, France dominated the merchant trade with the Ottoman Aegean ports of Smyrna (Izmir) and Constantinople (Istanbul); Bodrum (its Turkish name) became a regional port for trade with nearby islands. Maps of the town, dating from C. T. Newton's 1857 archaeological expedition[2] to Halicarnassus for the British Museum, revealed plantations and farms held by both Greek Orthodox and Turkish Muslim family farmers. Newton found some remains of the Mausoleum—friezes, statues of Mausolus and Artemisia, and some great lions, all of which he took back to the British Museum (Newton 1862).

In the 1890s Bodrum town had over 3,000 Muslims and over 2,000 Greek Orthodox inhabitants. Eighty-six Jewish people and some foreigners (i.e., non-Ottoman subjects) also lived there. The Bodrum district contained approximately 14,000 people, about 11,000 of them Turkish-speaking while 2,000 were Greek-speaking (see Table 3).

Four ethnic groups populated the coastal area of Bodrum. One group was Christian orthodox Greek-speakers. They lived in Bodrum

TABLE 3

Population by Religion and Ethnicity for the Years 1894, 1912, 1927, 1946, 1965, and 1980 in Bodrum Town and Bodrum District

Bodrum Town

	1894[1]	1912[2]	1927[3]	1946[4]	1965[5]	1980[6]
Muslim Turk	3,605	—	—	—	—	—
Greek Orthodox	2,264	—	—	—	—	—
Jewish	86	—	—	—	—	—
Foreign	45	—	—	—	—	—
Total	6,000	—	—	5,524	5,137	10,000

Bodrum District

	1894	1912	1927	1946	1965	1980
Muslim Turk	11,613	8,817	15,871	9,871	20,738	—
Greek Orthodox	2,264	5,060	3	—	—	—
Jewish	86	—	10	—	—	—
Foreign	45	131	—	—	—	—
Total	14,008	14,008	15,694	9,871	20,738	38,000

Sources for Statistics:

1. Historical research conducted by Galantı, professor of history at University of Istanbul, who wrote two small pamphlets on Bodrum (Galantı 1946:40–41).
2. Soteriadis (1918:9).
3. Ümumi Nüfus Tahrırı 1929.
4. Bodrum local census, quoted from Galantı (1946:40–41).
5. Bodrum İlçesinin 1965.
6. Personal communication from Bodrum's tourist director, Mrs. Emine Cam, in letter, March 2, 1982.

town, small seaside villages, and sometimes isolated homesteads in the countryside. But, they liked seaside communities best where harbors were close to their villages, cafes, and agricultural lands. They grew olives, grapes, wheat, and vegetables. Some were good sailors and fishermen who maintained ties to Greek-speaking people on all the nearby islands. A household sometimes had farmland both on a nearby island and the Ottoman mainland. For religious and cultural reasons, Greeks and Turks did not intermarry.

Ethnic groups two, three and four spoke several different dialects of Turkish and were Muslim or pagan. The group with the highest status included Ottoman administrators and clergy who identified themselves as *Osmanlı*, had no pastoral traditions, and spoke Ottoman Turkish. (The *Imam* probably also knew Arabic.) The third ethnic group consisted of remnants of the once powerful Turkoman confederacy, which occupied an ecological niche on the higher, inland plain, lying about twenty-five miles east of the town of Bodrum.

The fourth ethnic group was the sheepherding pastoral Yürük (Ramsay 1897:31, 83). Like the Turkoman, the Yürük were Turkish-speaking and used summer pastures near the Bodrum sea and, unlike the Turkoman, they covered long distances on foot, migrating from summer pastures to places further inland. De Planhol (1958:526, 528, 531), a French geographer, suggests that various groups in Turkey known as the Yürük separated from the Turkoman confederacy much earlier than the seventeenth century, when the sultan forced the Turkoman "tribes" to disperse. Today the Yürük possess neither memory nor cultural traditions that link them to contemporary Turkoman groups.

Turkoman nomads were a familiar element in Anatolia as early as the twelfth century, and Ramsay (1897:282–83) places some Turkoman "tribes" near the Bosporus and Aegean Sea at that time.[3] Gradually, some tribal fragments migrated south, using as winter campsites eight of the villages on Bodrum's plain of Mumcular that they now inhabit permanently.[4] Turkoman women still make carpets on upright looms, spinning and dying the wool from sheep and camels. As late as the 1960s, the period of study, they carried their babies on their backs in slings, unswaddled, while the Turks living in the villages to Bodrum's west swaddled infants and carried two year olds on their hips with one arm supporting the child's body. A fragment of the Turkoman confederacy had been banished to the island of Kos in the seventeenth and eighteenth centuries (de Planhol 1958). This may account for the continuing interest of Bodrum village youth in marrying girls from Kos and other nearby islands (Starr 1984:95).

Old Turkish men who remembered the period before 1914 (i.e., before the intense ethnic hatred between Greeks and Turks) describe friendly relations between Greek and Turkish-speaking households. In addition to farming, Greeks were the carpenters, lime-makers, house-builders, and producers of most of the crafts of the area. The area now known as Gümüşlük was a summer campground (*yayla*) for Turkish-speaking transhumants who had no traditions of carpet-weaving. Earlier, roughly 1900 to 1919, the Greek population was also larger in summer than in winter, and the ruins of houses and cafes along Gümüşlük's 150-foot deep harbor in the 1960s attested to the vibrant social life that existed there not so long ago.

Social Control in Earlier Times

The population for the entire Bodrum district in 1912 was 8,817 Turkish people and 5,060 Greeks (Soteriadis 1918:9). In this period Turkish women from nearby islands were considered the most beautiful and were desired as wives by Turkish-speaking men. Older informants told me that, in earlier times, people had married across large distances on the Bodrum peninsula and the inland plateau. Such marriage practices created far-flung networks and were useful for transhumant groups. Marriage ties provided pastoral households with access to diverse pastures, lands, brides, and information. As settled agriculture developed and households made cash investments in land and houses, marriage preferences changed. Marrying within a village became a way for males to amass political loyalties and landholdings, and for females to remain near their natal families.

The earlier wide marriage-networks formed the underlying structure of social control in a situation in which the controlling power, the Ottoman Empire, maintained almost no political control over the households. Lewis has described how decay of rural administration in the Ottoman Empire occurred during the seventeenth and eighteenth centuries, and how the sultans lost control of the provinces to local *ayan*s and sheiks (1966:378–79). The provincial code of 1864 divided the Asian homeland into twenty-seven *vilayet*s, each governed by a *Vali* with extensive powers (p. 381). Bodrum district had a custom house with soldiers to collect tolls from ships passing by, but there was no gendarmes to keep the peace in those days.

Members of local households did not remember hearing older relatives talk about a garrison of Ottoman soldiers in the area. Nor did they remember belonging to larger tribal units or hearing stories about them from older relatives. It was marriage patterns and not "tribal" relations that provided widespread links and reciprocal relationships that could be called upon in an emergency. These patterns of marriage also kept women docile and under male control since any woman would be living among strangers and subject to the social control of a husband, a father-in-law, and agnatic females. Deprived of the emotional support of sisters, mother, and aunts, a young bride in a strange camp or village had to become submissive to survive.

Some households, of course, kept their daughters—when they were especially fond of them or, more likely, when there were no sons or brothers' sons to adopt. Thus, the institution of the *iç güvey* grew up—the son-in-law who marries in.

Trade and markets, rather than warfare and raiding, were the modes of social control practiced across Bodrum's language and religious groups. Vestiges of the rotation of local markets were still present in the 1960s: Bodrum's market days were Thursdays and Fridays, and on Mondays a small market still existed at Karatoprak. Festivals occurred in Bodrum town that also brought people together and marked the change of seasons. For example, "fighting camels," following the trade route of itinerant merchants, always appeared in early January in Bodrum.

In the first decade of the twentieth century, hostilities between Greek- and Turkish-speaking groups around Izmir increased. As ethnic anxieties spread to the Bodrum area, Greeks began selling their land and houses. During the second decade more Greeks left, and many who decided to stay took Turkish names and nominally adopted the Islamic religion. The years 1915 to 1923 were particularly hard in western Turkey. People old enough to remember those times did not want to discuss them, understandably so.

Bodrum: Turkish Administrative Center, 1923–1960

Events leading to the Greco-Turkish War (1919–23) and the establishment of the Turkish Republic irrevocably reshaped the town of Bodrum, condemning it to a comparatively isolated existence for three decades, much like the existence of other small district towns in Turkey. Population exchanges were undertaken by the League of Nations in 1922, when roughly 850,000 Greek-speaking people who had fled from Aegean and Anatolian Turkey became a problem to the Greek government.[5] Most of these families had fled precipitately, taking few possessions. As Greek soldiers advanced into Anatolia during the Greco-Turkish War of 1920–22, Greek-speaking people suffered. When news of the uprising of Turk against Greek spread to Bodrum, Bodrum Greeks sailed to nearby Kalimnos and Kos, where some owned land. They ultimately resettled in Greece. Whatever attempts they may have made to reclaim their land and houses at a later date is unknown.

Turkish-speaking groups from the Balkans and from Crete, Rhodes, Athens, and all parts of the empire were transported to Turkey by the League of Nations. The Turks who came or were sent to Bodrum chiefly settled into *Kumbaçhe mahallesi*, a former Greek neighborhood that had been called *Rum mahallesi* (Greek neighborhood).[6] The Turkish census of 1927 records a total of 476 Turks (232 men, 244 women) who, "born in Greece," came to the area in this period (*Ümumi Nüfus Tahrırı* 1929). The total Bodrum population for the district was 7,045 men and 8,649 women (see Table 4).

TABLE 4

Bodrum District, 1927 Census, Population by Religion[1]

	Islam	Catholic	Greek Orthodox	Armenian Christian	Jewish	No Rel.
Men	7,033	0	3	0	9	0
Women	8,648	0	0	0	1	0

Source for Statistics:
1. *Ümumi Nüfus Tahrırı* (1929:xcix).

Not all the Greek-speaking residents fled in the 1920s or took up Islam, however. Avram Galantı (1946:1), a Turkish historian, reported that in the 1940s a Christian population still lived in Bodrum. They sailed and fished, catching octopus that they dried; what was not consumed locally was sent off to Greece for sale. In 1967 Bodrum's Christian community no longer existed. It was then that an unused Christian church in *Kumbaçhe mahallesi* was deliberately destroyed.

The destruction of the church sheds light on the use of symbolic action in ethnic relationships between Greek and Turkish people. (The Jewish community had departed much earlier.) In the autumn of 1967, with talk of war between Greece and Turkey over Cyprus, rumors filtered back to Bodrum that the Greeks on the nearby island of Kos, who had been observing nightly blackouts, had attacked a Turkish mosque there. Although no one was hurt, feelings ran high in Bodrum town against the Greeks. Some townspeople began to pay more attention to the large empty Christian church and arranged to dynamite it. The dynamite was set up, the streets were cleared of traffic, the church and nearby areas were roped off and evacuated, but five minutes before the ignition of the dynamite, a court order obtained by some other prominent citizens prevented the explosion. Two days later a crane with a large wrecking ball was set up and demolition of the church began, instigated by the director of the Village Extension Program in Bodrum, a fanatical Turkish nationalist. Before another court order could halt the wreckage, much of the roof and dome had been destroyed. A second court order stopped the wrecking crew, but not before a newly created ruins stood at what once was a beautiful triangle in the heart of Bodrum town.

The dirt road linking Bodrum to Milas was finished in 1927, and that was when the secular grade school was also constructed. A camel track linking villages on Bodrum peninsula to the district town was slightly improved in the same year.

According to Galantı (1946:56–57), the technology of growing tangerines was learned by a Turkish man on the island of Rhodes, and the first modern tangerine orchard was planted at Akcaalan, near Karatoprak[7] in the 1930s. Before the technique of grafting tangerine branches was learned, tangerine seedlings were brought to Bodrum from Sicily and Rhodes. From the early 1930s on, tangerine seedlings were grown locally in Bodrum at Akcaalan, and tangerine orchards proliferated. Galantı estimated that over four hundred orchards were developed in the Bodrum district in the 1940s; Washington oranges were also grown.

In the 1940s Bodrum was Turkey's only sponge-diving center, and eighty-nine boats (see Table 5) employed 403 people (Galantı 1946:21).[8] For a brief period in the 1940s a sponge-diving company was organized

TABLE 5

Boats in Bodrum, 1940

Type of Boat	No.	No. employed
Motorized sponge boats, using nets	21	80
Sailing sponge boats, using nets	30	90
Old-style sponge divers in diving suits (i.e., *forma*)	11	165
Rowboats, with glass-bottomed bucket	27	68
Totals	89	403

Source for Statistics:
1. Galantı (1946:21)

by the Summer Bank to sell the products, but it soon closed because there was no profit. Nevertheless, interest in collecting sponges for a living continued (pp. 60–61), and in 1946 Bodrum shipped 20 tons of sponges out of the country to be sold (p. 21).

There were many fishermen in Bodrum, although only one boat had an ice-making machine, and it carried fish not sold locally to nearby Greek islands to sell. Heavy taxes by the Greeks soon put a stop to this practice, however (pp. 60–61).

In 1957 an embankment was built linking the Castle of St. Peter to the mainland. A sturdy sea wall made of boulders was created to block off half the western harbor, thus protecting the boat basin from the open sea. The majestic castle, once fortressed on its own island (on the spot of the ancient city of Zephyria), now peaked a peninsula, guarding Bodrum's twin harbors.

In 1966, there were four boat-building companies and fewer sponge-diving boats than documented by Professor Galantı in 1946. Greece was dominating the natural sponge market, and Bodrum boat captains claimed synthetic sponges were underselling theirs, an occurrence that soon would deprive them of a profit. Recognition of the need for a new industry in part accounts for the interest by captains and boatowners in Bodrum's nascent tourist industry. Camel fights were still a major event in January, the tobacco auction still took place in December and January. The town market was moved in the latter half of the year from its traditional place on the old soccer field to the paved cobblestone road in front of Bodrum's only bank, the Ziraat *Bankasi*. That same year saw the only street running from the castle to *Kumbaçhe mahallesi* paved.

Villages to the west of Bodrum, where all the tangerine groves were, were linked to Bodrum only by a partially graded dirt road, which in the rainy season was passable only by four-wheel-drive vehicles. In winter, for days at a time the road was impassable, as rain water cascaded off the hills moving pebbles and mud across it.

Bodrum, the Administrative Center and Its Institutions of Law

The modern town of Bodrum in 1966 (pop. 5,137) was an administrative center (*ılçe* or *kaza*) for the surrounding thirty villages that were located on the peninsula to Bodrum's west, and in the higher plains to the east.[9] The district was composed of 66,000 square kilometers, and contained three natural resources that are often settings for illegal activities: mountains, a state forest, and coastal beaches (difficult to patrol, two hours by motorboat from Greek territory). The population of the villages

MAP 3

Bodrum Town: Names and Locations of Bodrum's Neighborhoods in the 1960s

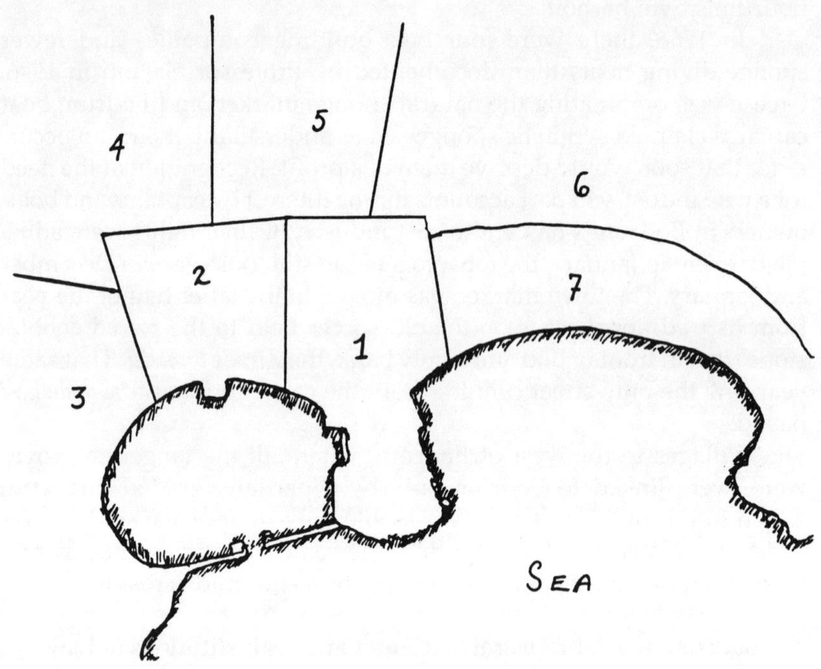

in the district was about 20,000 in the 1965 census.[10] Villages ranged in size from 293 to 2,019 people. They were essentially agricultural. Tangerines and vegetables were grown as cash crops on the peninsula to Bodrum's west. On the higher, more arid plateau to the east, tobacco, camels, cows, donkeys, and horses were the major sources of income. The economy of Bodrum town in 1967 was based on fishing, sponge-diving, agricultural production, and tourism. It was and is a southern port and the major Turkish ship-building center on the Mediterranean coast.

As the administrative town of the district, Bodrum contained numerous Turkish government bureaus. The Kaymakam, the district's administrative director, had an office that could investigate land disputes. He was responsible directly to the administrative director (*Vali*) of the province (*vilayet* or *ıl*), who had offices in the provincial capital, Muğla, a five-hour drive by Jeep from Bodrum. For administrative purposes, *vilayet*s are subdivided into *kaza*s (or *ılçe*s) and *nahiye*s (or *buçak*s). The latter is the smallest subunit of a district and is primarily a unit of control by gendarmes.

Bodrum had a number of institutions and offices of the central government as well as a municipal (*belediye*) administration. Those maintained by the central government included a post office (with telegraph and telephone), a customs bureau, a harbor authority, a maritime affairs office, a government agricultural cooperative, a forestry office, an immigration authority, a branch of the agricultural bank, a museum, a hospital (with a doctor and several nurses), schools (primary, middle, high), and a tourism bureau, plus directorates of finance, agriculture, religious affairs, village affairs, population, land registry, education, veterinary affairs, and health. Most of these offices were in separate buildings. The commandant of the gendarmes and the director of the (urban) police were both headquartered in Bodrum in different locations. The municipality was headed by a locally elected mayor (*belediye reisi* or *belediye başkanı*), who was responsible for maintaining standards of human and animal health, for business transactions (such as the use of scales in stores and markets), for fire protection, marriage licenses, and for the power and water supply. In the private sector, Bodrum had a number of shops, garages, inns, and small-scale craft industries. It also had two transportation offices, out of which buses and trucks were run to Izmir and elsewhere, as well as a number of individual operators who drove vehicles under contract.

In Bodrum town, law and order was the responsibility of the Bodrum police commissioner and his staff of five policemen. In the villages outside the town proper, law and order was maintained by gendarmes (military personnel on special duty), who are responsible to the gendarme commander in Bodrum. A village gendarme captain, however, may bypass the Bodrum gendarme commander to report a criminal case directly to the public prosecutor (*savcı*).

National dispute-handling agencies were the Kaymakam's office (for land cases and sometimes used for misconduct of civil servants) and the Bodrum law court. The court, with two judges and a public prosecutor, was divided into four courts of law: *Sulh Hukuk Mahkemesi* (lower civil court), whose jurisdiction was civil cases involving up to 1,000 liras (then about $100) worth of property; *Asliye Hukuk Mahkemesi* (higher civil court), whose jurisdiction was all other civil cases; *Sulh Ceza Mahkemesi* (lower criminal court), which heard minor criminal cases as defined by the Turkish criminal code; and *Asliye Ceza Mahkemesi* (middle criminal court), with jurisdiction over serious crimes up to and including involuntary manslaughter.

One judge presided over the lower civil and lower criminal courts, and the other was in charge of the higher civil and middle criminal courts. In actual practice, however, the judges often replaced each other at the bench. The public prosecutor took an interest in, and followed, all criminal cases, but he sat at the bench (to the right of the judge) only during the middle criminal court hearings.

Located on an unpaved side street in Bodrum, two blocks from the sea, the court was housed in an old two-story, whitewashed building, once inhabited by a Greek family. A whitewashed wall with a wooden door separated the courthouse yard from the road, which in winter became a muddy ditch. The court was not connected with other government offices, but was in a residential neighborhood, *Kumbaçhe Mahallesi*.

People waiting for their cases to be called sat or squatted outside the courtroom in a small square hallway, while inside the courtroom a formal atmosphere was maintained. Judges and the public prosecutor wore black robes over pants and shirts; lawyers wore ties and Western suits.

Individuals giving testimony were required to stand; women were expected not to cross their legs in court (even though they wore long dresses and/or baggy pants); and witnesses and observers were required to be silent. Only rarely was someone asked to give sworn testimony; I observed three instances, all of which involved old people, two of whom took the oath to tell the truth on a *Kur'an* and the other on a loaf of bread (a sacred object in Islam).

One of four male court stenographers sat at a table directly in front of the judge's bench during each court session. The judge questioned the plaintiff, defendant, and witnesses, and after each testimony he dictated the answers to the stenographer, who typed on a standard, manual Remington typewriter. Lawyers could not directly cross-examine principals or witnesses, but had to put their questions to the judge who, when the question was considered relevant, asked it. In a civil case, after the first hearing, a lawyer might appear instead of the defendant, who did not need to come, but in criminal matters the defendant was required to appear each time.

One stenographer acted as head clerk, court treasurer, the only notary in Bodrum, and also the official debt collector who oversaw seizure and sale of goods when a judgment was executed. Another worked mainly for the public prosecutor, who had his office in the courthouse. Another was associated with both civil courts, while the fourth worked with both criminal courts. In times of illness or vacations, either substituted for the other. Two other male employees were associated with the court. The younger, age 23, acted as sergeant at arms during court hearings. He instructed everyone to rise as the judge entered or departed, and he called out names of defendants, plaintiffs, and witnesses, admonishing people about talking or eating in court and women about leg-crossing. The other, a man about sixty, prepared and processed warrants, summonses, fines, and bills. Both were sent for coffee and ran other errands. Gendarmes delivered summonses and guarded prisoners. The only woman employed by the court acted as guardian of the Bodrum jail and prepared food for the prisoners; the job was not gender-linked, however, for before her employment a man had held this position. One of the benefits of this job was that its incumbent, in addition to salary, was given money to buy a new suit of clothes each year.

Bodrum itself had no lawyers (*avukat*) at the end of 1968. The nearest lawyers, of whom there were sixteen (two of them women), lived in Milas, a city 90 kilometers away by dirt road. Usually lawyers appeared only in serious criminal cases and in cases with wealthy defendants. A person wishing to hire a lawyer needed only to appear at court at the end of a morning's session and find one or two there. Bodrum's four *vekil*s (legal representatives), who lacked complete formal legal training, were allowed to represent clients only in civil land cases. These men also had vast knowledge of other aspects of law, and people asked them questions, paid them for legal advice, or employed them to write letters. *Vekil*s, like notaries, were legal officials in Ottoman times and are known throughout the Islamic world (see Inalcık 1964:44; Eickelman 1985:22, 83–84; Rosen 1980–81:220).

Court hearings were not continuous. The ideal was for a plaintiff and a defendant to state their claims and to name witnesses in the first hearing. The witnesses were heard about ten days to three weeks later and, hopefully, a judgment could be given in the third hearing. Since many different events and problems prolonged disposition, an average case (according to my statistical records of the three year docket) involved approximately six hearings and lasted three to six months. Certain types of crimes, such as those which threatened the security of the community (e.g., smuggling, possession of dynamite), fell into a special category that required them to be heard promptly to completion.

The Perils of Tourism

A brief forewarning of what full-scale tourism would mean for Bodrum occurred in March 1967, when an estimated three thousand Turkish tourists came for the three-day holiday of *Korban bayram*. Hotel and pension space was insufficient, restaurants ran out of food, and stores ran low on supplies. The traffic jam in Bodrum's narrow cobblestone streets was a city planner's nightmare. Most of the town notables thought it was a chance happening, marveling at the number of Turkish families that came to their town. They felt that the flocks of tourists would not appear again until two things happened: a good road was built to connect Bodrum to Milas and from there to Izmir, Ankara, and Istanbul; and an advertising campaign was undertaken after adequate hotel, pension, and restaurant space had been developed. But with the advent of a paved road in August 1968, even though not widened or rebuilt, people came in much greater numbers. The asphalted road marked the end of Bodrum's isolation and the beginning of Bodrum as a European and Turkish hot spot.[11]

By 1971 two more private hotels had been built, over a dozen smaller pensions begun, and the Tourist Association no longer provided small loans to families who wanted to convert part of their homes into pensions. In addition to the dozen or so boats for charter, there were now twenty-three boats sleeping from six to twelve people, and three new boatyards. The older boat-builders had learned to write contracts, keep records, pay social security to their workers, and pay their taxes.

Bodrum was attracting more professional people. A third doctor had moved to Bodrum, as had a certified dentist; two architects' and a lawyer's office had opened. Fatma Mansur, the author of the excellent ethnographic study of Bodrum town, so often referred to in this book, (1972), had even moved there permanently, as had over a dozen or so other Turkish intellectuals and artists. By 1971 Mansur reported noticing

> a perceptible stiffening of attitudes among the townspeople. A more exploitative, more impersonal, more competitive climate prevails in professional relationships. This attitude is even re-

flected in the dealings which take place between the members of the same family, let alone strangers. Small shopkeepers and craftsmen and the merchants no longer have much time to talk and laze in their shops. The distinctions between work and leisure is emerging, which is deplored by many although it is one of the best indicators of the fact that urban characteristics are gaining on rural ones in the town.

The turmoil and political unrest in Turkish cities in the 1970s seemingly did not affect Bodrum's growing tourist image, and the town continued to grow. By the 1980 census, Bodrum town had a winter population of 10,000, and the population of her surrounding villages had risen to 38,000 from its mid-1960s figure of about 20,000.[12]

The Fragility of Material Forms: Bodrum in 1987

The riveting view of Bodrum in 1966 attained after a six-hour drive from Izmir—Bodrum suddenly appearing unexpectedly around a turn after hours of traveling on dusty dirt roads, Bodrum dominated by a medieval castle snuggled in twin harbors—is gone. A beautiful scenic highway follows the coast; after having settled for several years it was tarred, and by 1985 Bodrum welcomed a road much more marvelous than anyone dared imagine two decades earlier—capable of bringing a hundred thousand tourists to Bodrum each month of the year. A newcomer approaches Bodrum now not over the old twisting, turning mountain road, but through Torba over flat land. This route protects the mountains, the pines, and the tobacco farmers from the tourists. Tobacco-growing villagers now have the choice of approaching Milas over the old Milas-Bodrum road that has been covered in asphalt or by the newly constructed scenic route, where they vie for space with Mercedes-Benz buses, opulent French automobiles, and English caravans.

In the summer of 1987 I made a brief visit to Bodrum, and in Ankara and in Çeşme I interviewed Turkish people who had made Bodrum their residence since 1982. They told me I could fly to Dalaman Airport, newly built near Bodrum, or spend time in Aktur Holiday village, a self-contained "Club Med" near Bodrum town.

Through these people I learned that Ahmet Ertegun, chairman of Atlantic Records, had in 1979 converted one of Bodrum's seaside houses into a villa. He is responsible for bringing, as one Turkish woman told me, the "beautiful people" to Bodrum. At his house Iris Love, the renowned classical archaeologist, who found the head of Aphrodite in Bodrum's coastal waters, and the first underwater archaeologist, George Bass, meet with the well-known celebrities who visit Bodrum. Princess

Margaret came in 1986, and Mick Jagger, the rock star, had visited previously. Artists and writers who had favored Bodrum a decade ago have moved on to quieter spots, because for three summer months an enormous all-night, open-air disco has laser light shows and blaring music until sunrise.[13] The avant garde have been replaced by the Turkish urban middle class who are buying summer or retirement homes. The water and electricity crises continue, as do traffic problems in town.

There are now 185 slips for yachts, already too few for the number of boats that appear there, and 200 *gülets*—motorized sailboats that take tourists out for a week to a month at a time. Gümbet, a deserted beach ten minutes by car from Bodrum where the gendarmes built a small shed selling soft drinks in 1968, now has many pensions and is known for its windsurfing. Three bookstores, one featuring English books and journals, are open in summer months. The winter town population on the 1985 census was 13,100 people, the summer population approximately 20,000, with many more tourists spread out in pensions and campgrounds on the peninsula.

The police station, a square cement building at the foot of the castle commanding a view of the main fisherman's cafe in 1967, has moved. The tourist office now occupies the space, and the building has been converted into an inviting whitewashed structure. Across the way the old fishermen's cafe, with its sturdy wooden chairs and tables, painted lively colors of blue, green, and red, has been turned into an ice cream shop. Now dainty, wrought-iron French ice cream chairs and tables, appealing to the international chic, replace the old fishermen's seats.

The simple whitewashed courthouse, with its modest sign *Adliye* (justice, law court), was abandoned and for sale in 1987. The court had moved to a new building, constructed to house the law courts, the police station, the gendarmerie, the Census Bureau, and the Land Records Office. Instead of *Adliye*, the Turkish government, using French models, now calls this centralized bureau the *Adliye Sarayı*, the "Palace of Justice."

Yalikavak, to Bodrum's west, now has seven beautiful minibuses that carry villagers all over the peninsula and run regularly to Izmir. Many summer cottages have been built there by Turks and foreigners, and it is always crowded in summer, although if one speaks Turkish, it is not too hard to find a place to sleep. The beautiful seaside village of Karatoprak had its name changed in the 1980s to Turgutreis, the name of a great Turkish admiral who was born there. Now sophisticated urban Turks rent time-sharing condominiums, built along Turgutreis's white beaches.

The tobacco market moved from Bodrum town to Milas in 1982, in part because the new highway makes Milas more accessible to the villages to Bodrum's north where tobacco is grown. But equally important, there is no longer space for the tobacco market—its trucks, its noise, its dirt, and disorder—in Bodrum's new image.

Camels, once an important beast of burden, were almost nowhere in use or in view in 1987. In 1966, my eighth day in Asia as we traveled south to Bodrum, we waited in a Jeep on a muddy bank for forty-five minutes at the Canakkale ferry, watching string after string of camels, piled high with bags of produce, being led off.[14] In 1987, I saw no camels between Istanbul, Canakkale, Izmir, and Bodrum. It was only as I approached a tobacco-growing village to Bodrum's north that I found a man with two camels. When asked about camel-keeping, he said it now was rare because their feed was so costly. They eat several buckets of grain a day, and it has to be purchased. Households preferred tractors to camels, but Bodrum's three banks had been too busy providing loans for construction in Bodrum to attend to peasant farmers' credit needs, he said. The tobacco-growing farmers had gotten together to form a strong credit union of their own, and it had helped many households buy tractors, large enough to pull wagons. Tractor-pulled wagons have replaced the four-wheel-drive jeeps (*dolmuş*) that used to transport villagers to town.

In 1987 I spent half a day in a tobacco-growing village I knew well twenty years earlier. Daily lives have improved there through the new prosperity, yet customs, rituals, marriages, and social relationships have evolved without disruptions and dislocations. The village still consists of dispersed family farms and has no central square or meeting area. They still bake bread in each household and do not buy bread from bakeries. Sons still bring new brides to live in stone or cinderblock houses built in their fathers' courtyards, and they still use family labor in the tobacco fields. When asked about brideprice (*başlık*), they told me they do not pay it now and never did. A boy and a girl still may elope together (still called *kız kaçermıs*), but no longer by forceful abduction, and the girl is no longer forcefully deflowered.

In 1969 electricity was brought to the village, and with it new customs. The bride's family now provides a refrigerator and a television set. As before, the boy's family provides the house and wedding gifts of gold jewelry to the bride. The girl's family still gets to choose the wedding date, an important prerogative, given the significance of girls and young women in tobacco planting and picking.

A family had invited us to sit on their veranda and talk, and as we ate delicious watermelon, I asked, "What would you wish for, if you were given one wish?" They answered that they already had a sacred place there that granted their wishes. "When our wish is granted, we sacrifice a calf and share its parts among the village." One of the things they had wished for was a village mosque, and in 1986 all the villagers had worked together to build themselves one.

Yet, we may wonder if this village's symbol of prosperity, a communally built mosque, expressed their "always felt lack" of a communal place of worship, or was it an attempt to become a part of a more nationwide expression of religious sentiments that in part was stimulated by politicians, hoping to capture the rural vote and by watching television?

Conclusion

Long ago, writing from the Persian island town of Zephyria (now a medieval castle and Tourist Information Office of Bodrum), Herodotus wrote of the foibles and triumphs of generals, female admirals, and betrayal in the great war between the Greeks and the Persians. He taught those of us willing to learn the lessons that can be gleaned from history.

Bodrum has played important roles in the cultural life of classical, medieval, and Ottoman societies, and remains a compelling community. I am glad to have known and loved Bodrum town and her townspeople in its early and authentic Turkish republican identity. When I think about her present incarnation, I try hard to avoid nostalgia, and to reconcile myself to her image as a chic summer gathering place, beloved by urban Turks, as the small fashionable sea town of Southampton is treasured by world-weary New Yorkers. As a vacation place for French, German, and English tourists, Bodrum continues to charm—an annual art exhibit is held every summer, amid trendy boutiques; sparkling whitewashed houses still line the hills and narrow streets.

Yet, I could not bring myself to impose new memories over those I still cherish from the village I knew so well, so I did not return to Mandalinci,[15] although someday I may. Nor did I look up my Bodrum friends, whom I also treasure, although someday I may do that, too.

Bodrum's metamorphosis into the cynosure of the Turkish tourist industry may only be the beginning for a process of change to the Aegean shore with the end result, in twenty to thirty years, closer to Cannes or Nice than the town of Bodrum everyone was so proud of in the mid-1960s. Even now the changes and touristic interest in Bodrum far exceed the hopes and dreams of Bodrum's notables, who with Ankara and Istanbul intellectuals, helped make it happen.

The cafes serving liquor and wine, the nightly dancing and merry-making under open skies, the emphasis on attracting sophisticated, secular Turkish and youthful European tourists are all forces of change undercutting the impact of Islam. Islamic fundamentalism openly opposes public contact between the sexes. It emphasizes sobriety, avoidance of contact with Westerners, no male/female dancing, the covering of the female body, and the control of female sensuality, except in the marriage bed. Tourism, the prosperity that followed for many in its wake, and the public license to explore new behaviors it carries, is a useful comrade to the secularizing elites who hope to move the Turkish state even closer to Europe and the Common Market, which many in the Turkish government hope to join in the 1990s.

Notes

1. Historical discussion is based on the printed pamphlet *Bodrum* (1966).

2. He removed most of the great statuary, which remains today in the British Museum in London.

3. For more details, see Field (1885:62–63), de Planhol (1958:526, 528, 531), and Ramsay (1897:100–101; 1917:31, 83).

4. Osman Nuri Bilgin, Director of the Bodrum Primary School in 1967 and a devotee of Bodrum's history, was the first person to bring to my attention the nomadic origins of some villages on the Muncular plain.

5. See Refugee Settlement Commissions' Quarterly Reports to the League of Nations 1924–1931 (c524, M.187). These are 27 reports of the work of the Greek Refugee settlement commission. See also Nansen (1922a, 1922b, 1923). See also Refugee Settlement, General Survey on the Work Accomplished up to the year of 1926 (Ser. L.O.N.P. 1926.II.32). Also Ladas (1932, chapters 32, 33).

6. For more details and a somewhat different interpretation of the origins of these Turks, see Mansur (1972:6–9). It may be that our informants differed, but it was clearly my impression then, and my field notes reflect it today, that what Bodrumites referred to as "Cretans" were all of the Turkish-speaking people who came to Turkey just before and during the population exchanges, not just those from the island of Crete.

7. Renamed Turgutreis by 1985, after a great Turkish admiral who was born there.

8. Fatma Mansur (1972:63) places the commencement of a flourishing sponge-diving industry a decade later than Galantı (1946) does.

9. The 1965 Bodrum census puts Bodrum town at 5,137 people, while the surrounding villages contain 20,738 people (Census of Turkey, *Genel Nüfus Sayımı* 1965:483).

10. Except as otherwise noted, the discussion in this section is based closely on the description in Starr and Pool (1974:537–40).

11. See Mansur (1972:83–88) for an excellent description of the political agitation for a new road; unless otherwise noted, the discussion in this section is based on Mansur (1972:253–57).

12. Personal Communication Mrs. Emine Cam, Director, *Bodrum Turizm ve Tanıtama Buro Müdürlüğlü* (Tourist and Information Office), March 2, 1988.

13. See Lamar and Allis (1987:66–67).

14. The Canakkale quay is now as sturdily constructed as that in Port Jefferson, Long Island, where I live.

15. A fictitious name for a Bodrum village I studied in 1966–67 (Starr 1978a, 1978b; 1984).

Chapter Five

Gender and Family Transformations

> The idea of a religious law—the concept that law, as well as other human relationships, must be ruled by religion—has become an essential part of the Islamic outlook.
>
> Joseph Schacht (1955:84)

In many ways the radical revolutionary groups dreaming of a new nation of Turks were conjurers. From a number of status and religious groups, some privileged, some oppressed, they imagined a new community of loyal citizens inhabiting a new symbolic world—that of secularism. Replacing Islamic symbols and the Islamic calendar, they would immerse males and females in a secular cognitive framework that would change people's very notions of themselves. Everything would be changed: their concept of time and calendar, their conception of self and other, the work world, family relationships, dress, names, language, script, alphabet, numerical system, neighborhoods, education, public behavior, and especially their "mentalities" at the hearth fires. Age-old male prerogatives in the rural countryside would be superseded by more egalitarian gender relationships.

Some institutional structures, already in skeleton form, merely needed to be used for new purposes. For example, required military service could be used to educate and inspire loyalties in young men as well as to discipline them. Public secular education could be made accessible for everyone, female as well as male, poor as well as rich, villager as well as city dweller. The small group of elitist dreamers surrounding Ataturk, inspired by the idea of restructuring a very old, war-weary society torn apart by ethnic hostilities, decided that the basic "thinking processes" of individuals would be, in one generation, transformed. Transformation would start with the very smallest unit, the domestic household. Starting with individual males and females, new selfhoods would flourish within ancient shrouded bodies; women would cast off their veils and seclusion, men would cast off their fez and baggy jodphurs and, joining in the classroom, all would learn to read and write the language of the peasant, the major language of the Anatolian plateau—Turkish. The language of the masses would be the language of administration and of the nation. New mentalities and new identities would be grounded in Turkish language, Turkish cultural identity, and national loyalty. For the next sixty years, Ataturk's reinvention of an old ethnic slur would be written on buildings in cities, on walls in rural villages, and into the very hills of Kurdistan: "How lucky I am to be a Turk!"

An instrument of social change was to enhance the status of all Turkish women through law. This chapter analyzes data from the Bodrum district law courts to suggest that this method was successful by 1950 in rural western Anatolian villages. Before urban ideas concerning equality for women had become widespread in the Bodrum region, rural women in villages had begun making choices to gain relief from oppressive family structures. Supporting evidence demonstrates that, during the next twenty years, women attempted to gain "psychological space" from their role as mother, wife, and agricultural worker.

The Islamic view of women defines them as daughters, mothers, and wives who need to be under the control of fathers, brothers, and husbands. Furthermore, traditional Islam does not regard religion and law as separate entities. Muslims define jurisprudence as "knowledge of the practical rules of religion" (von Grunebaum 1962:144). Historically, Islam was both a system of religious beliefs and practice, and also a "system of state, society, law, thought, and art—a civilization with religion as its unifying, and eventually dominating factor" (Lewis 1960:133). Its holy law, the *Şeriat*, was developed by jurists from the *Kur'an* and the traditions and sayings of the prophet.

Marriage, divorce, and family relationships have always been, to the Muslim mind, even more closely associated with religion than other legal matters, and therefore controlled by Islamic law (Schacht 1964:76). Thus, when the new secular Turkish civil code became effective on October 4, 1926, it created an anomaly—Turkish family law became secular for the first time in history, while Islam continued to be the religion of most Turkish citizens. The new civil code, based on the Swiss model, categorically endorsed monogamous marriage and rejected polygamy—"a marriage is null and void when at the date of the marriage one of the parties is already married" (Williams 1925:28). Under Islamic law and custom, marriage was a private matter between the families and the community; the state did not intervene until the twentieth century. Under the new Turkish Republic a marriage, to be legitimate, needed to be registered with the state. Under Islamic law and custom, women had no rights to divorce, although in the twentieth century the Ottoman family law of 1917 began to chip away at male prerogatives.[1] The new Turkish civil code gave women the same rights to divorce men enjoyed, and it stipulated that the grounds for divorce must be proven by witnesses in *court* (Williams 1925:33). For the first time, it allowed a Muslim woman to marry a non-Muslim man (Lewis 1966:267). It set the minimum age of marriage at seventeen for women and eighteen for men, although in exceptional cases both might apply to the courts for permission to marry at fifteen (Velidedeoğlu 1957:63). A woman also acquired various rights to property that previously had not been available to a daughter, as well as her husband's surname and citizenship when she married (Williams 1925:35, 37, 43).

The new secular civil law was meant to change the core structure of Turkish domestic life to bring it closer to models of nuclear family life known in western Europe. Anthropological and other studies in Turkey in the 1950s and 1960s, however, suggested that these goals were not achieved; Turkish Muslim women living in rural villages continued to be bound by Islamic and customary traditions and were subservient to males (Stirling 1965; Szyliowicz 1966; Yasa 1957). Other research has shown that much of the hardest agricultural work in Turkey is done by women (Kazgan 1981:145), and that in most rural areas of Turkey, the daily lives of women confine females to their own households, fields, and neighborhoods, thus limiting their knowledge of new lives for women and undermining any ideas they might have about more freedom within the household and within a marriage.[2]

Most Turkologists recognize that, in the twentieth century, urban elite Turkish women have had educational and career opportunities to develop their intellectual capacities and personal identities that nearly equal those of urban elite Turkish men (Abadan-Unat 1981a and 1981b; Fallers and Fallers 1976). Yet the idea that *rural* women are also making decisions that change their life situations receives little consideration in the existing literature. Abadan-Unat (1977) and Kiray (1976), for example, have argued that when male family members migrate to Europe, women left at home assume responsibilities for agricultural decision-making and children's education. Some even take over control of household finances , but relinquish these decision-making roles when the husband returns to the village or the wife joins him in his life abroad. Fatma Coşar (1978:131) reports that the position of rural Turkish women is better in western than in central or eastern Turkey, but she does not attribute this improvement in status to the women themselves. Rather, she argues that the climate is milder, the roads are better, landholdings are smaller (making women's work less demanding), Islamic practices are more sociable and view women less harshly.

My ethnographic experience with rural women and their households in western Anatolia (1966–68), however, left me unconvinced that these women are backward, submissive, and subordinate to male and Islamic controls. My research indicates that Ataturk's social revolution, initiated in the 1920s, had reached women in western Anatolian villages by 1950. I suggest that rural women's struggle for autonomy went unrecognized at this time by the press, social researchers, and the villagers themselves because the women had not formed a social movement to articulate values concerning their civil rights. In the rural countryside even as late as the mid-1960s, no ideology and no collective consciousness yet existed supporting better lives for women. Nonetheless, it appears that changes in female attitudes and behavior were underway. While traditional Islamic law did not permit women to initiate divorce, by 1950 at least some rural women exercised their rights under the secular law to escape from marital discord and to bring other conflicts with men to court. In addition, evidence indicates that the patriarchal extended household was breaking down between 1950 and 1970. Married women were interested in separating from the patrilocal, patriarchal household and establishing nuclear households with their husbands. They were also interested in limiting numbers of children. The diffusion of mechanized agriculture came later and therefore does not explain this reduction in family size.[3]

How did legal change come about? After Ataturk changed Turkish family law in 1926, elite women living in cities collectively mobilized to distribute information about the new rights. By 1950 this news had spread to rural areas of western Anatolia by word of mouth and through the multiparty system (introduced in the late 1940s) that brought hundreds of politicians to peasant villages to mobilize the vote. Each party had a women's wing, interested in women's issues. Additional information flowed downward from the national government, through the chain of command to the village headman, who was required to spread the word about the need for, and ways to acquire, the state-required, civil marriage licenses. He also was to inform villagers that divorce had been regulated, and was now controlled by the state. Finally, the involvement of Turkish soldiers in the Korean war of the 1950s created a strong push toward legitimizing unions. A woman in an irregular, nonstate–recognized union, did not receive her portion of her mate's pay check, or widow's pension.

Thus, new ideas concerning women's legal rights reached rural women in western Anatolia, although, of course, the discourse was not framed in terms of rights, merely that the district courts would act on cases concerning women's claims and grievances. Rural women began to use the courts for divorce as early as 1950, and later for protection in other kinds of conflicts. That the new secular legal system would begin to have effects on rural women's behavior suggests both the vigor of individual rural women in seeking better lives and the vitality of the legal system as a symbol of reform.

Ataturk's Revolution and the Introduction of New Values

Ataturk's revolution brought values of populism, nationalism, and estatism to the Turkish Republic. *Estatism* is the term used for centralized planning of the economy, which took the form of five-year plans. Briefly, governmental goals were to increase production and move Turkey to a sound economic base, since Turkey's economy had collapsed during the last years of the Ottoman Empire. Ataturk planned to raise Turkey to an economic status similar to that of industrialized states in western Europe (Kili 1969:106). This would be accomplished through increased agricultural production that would result from land reform programs and the introduction of industrialization. New generations of workers with a strong work ethic would be trained through free universal secular education, and also by male participation in universal military service.

Ataturk undertook a social revolution as well. Everything would be changed from Ottoman times—concepts of dress, time, the uses of public spaces, the calendar, the written language, its script, the numerical system. He introduced new ideas about family life and social relations within the family and in public settings. Major instruments of these policies would be carried out through secular education (for village girls as well as boys) and a now totally secular court system, based on western European models.

Ataturk moved quickly to achieve two announced goals in the early 1920s, destroying the sources of power of the Islamic hierarchy and bringing all Islamic structures firmly under state control. Since church and state had always been closely linked in Turkish-Ottoman society, placing Islam under state control did not violate previous ideas of their separation. Islamic leaders had demonstrated their treachery by supporting the traitorous Ottoman leaders at the Armistice of Mundros in 1918; if the hierarchy's power was not destroyed, they would form the main opposition to Ataturk's program of change and development. In Ataturk's view, Turkey's status would be raised by the degree that the country of farmers could develop a Westernized outlook.

By the early 1920s, Ataturk planned to eliminate the influence the Islamic clergy had on law and on education. Turkish parents were allowed to bring up their children as Muslims, although all children, regardless of gender, were required to attend secular schools until sixteen years of age. All Islamic schools were closed, and their land was claimed as state land under the new republic.

Yet by 1948 (ten years after Ataturk's death), the repression of Islamic structures and values was partly rescinded. For as Turkey moved to generally free elections with opposing candidates standing for election from at least two parties, politicians began to court what they perceived as Islamic values among rural populations and small shopkeepers and merchants who made up 85 to 90 percent of the population (Fallers 1974:107). This gain for electoral democratic processes was to have far-reaching consequences. As urban politicians reintroduced Islamic values into the rural countryside, Islamic elites were again to become consequential agents in nation-state politics, as events years later clearly revealed in the crisis in parliament in 1974. Indeed, the processes of oppositional politics are visible in almost every significant state structure and bureau in Turkey today.

Ataturk and Women

Ataturk's social programs included raising the position of Turkish women, the vast majority of whom were Muslim. His messages therefore had a strong consciousness-raising component. For example, Ataturk publicly praised the heroic deeds of rural Anatolian women in 1925 and announced his policy that women should enjoy the same educational opportunities and freedoms men already had (Abadan-Unat 1981b:11). Ataturk once remarked of rural women :

> In some places I have seen women who put a piece of cloth or a towel or something like it over their heads to hide their faces, and who turn their backs or huddle themselves on the ground when a man passes by. What is the meaning and sense of this behavior? Gentlemen, can the mothers and daughters of a civilized nation adopt this strange manner, this barbarous posture? It is a spectacle that makes the nation an object of ridicule. It must be remedied at once. (Kinross 1964:477–78)

Earlier in a speech at a cinema in 1923, Ataturk had said, "Win for us the battle of education and you will do yet more for your country than we have been able to do. It is to you that I appeal. . . . If henceforward the women do not share in the social life of the nation, we shall never attain to our full development. We shall remain irremediably backward, incapable of treading on equal terms with the civilizations of the West" (Kinross 1964:390).

In the late 1920s Ataturk made his position even clearer. A group of *hojas* (holy men) called upon Ataturk to protest the presence of women teachers at a conference of teachers in Ankara. During the conversation Ataturk learned that the women had been seated in a group, separated from the male teachers. Ataturk summoned the president of the Teacher's Association and in the presence of the *hojas* began scolding him: "What have you done in the teachers' meeting? How dare you do it? This is a shame!" Misunderstanding his objection, the holy men were quite pleased until Ataturk said, "You invited the female teachers to the meeting and then made them sit apart from men? Don't you trust yourselves? Have you no faith in the virtue of these women? Let me never again hear of the segregation of women" (Kinross 1964:419).

In 1930 Ataturk's government passed laws giving women the right to vote in municipal elections. In 1933, because Ataturk was sensitive to criticisms of his public policies that had been compared to those in fascist Germany, he gave women the right to vote in all elections, thus demonstrating to Europeans that his views were enlightened (Tekeki 1981:298). In 1935, with Ataturk's support, seventeen women were elected deputies to the Grand National Assembly. Once Turkey moved to the multiparty system, however, fewer women were placed on the ballot, and of these fewer were elected.

Women and the Courts

When basic values undergo change, courts can become the arena for deciding major controversies of the day. Courts also play a central role when status relationships are changing, when hierarchical positions among groups are threatened, or when there is a strong advocacy on the part of citizens pressing for their rights (Starr and Collier 1989a).

In western Anatolian Turkey among free, landholding farmers, the change from rural subsistence economies to production of agricultural products for the market changed older patterns of domestic labor; hence, household authority patterns were sometimes contested as previous cycles of household growth, expansion, and devolution began to break down. New groups from the agrarian countryside sometimes turned to the law for protection and/or to enhance their status. Included among these new groups using the law were married Muslim women.

In earlier times, few structures intervened between the household[4] and the state in the Bodrum region. The household was a unit of protection, as well as production and consumption. In rural areas like Bodrum, the least autonomous members of domestic households were young males and all females. Not only did the power of the household head exist unchecked by outside authorities, but the oldest male patriarch represented family members in all external affairs. He had authority to give orders to and demand obedience from his adult sons, while his wife supervised and controlled all the females in the multiple family household. All women were to be subservient to males. The ideological structure of the kinship system, and Islamic ideas and practices supported this power structure. Disobedient sisters and wives could be beaten, and under Islamic law wives could be divorced at will (*talâk*) by a husband saying, "I divorce you" three times.[5] Although the Ottoman Law of Family Rights of 1917 gave women certain rights in marriage, it was the new civil code of 1926 that fully overturned women's legal inequality. Yet officially granted rights would represent little social change for rural Muslim women until a changing consciousness led them to use secular law to improve their life situation.

Divorce Cases in the Civil Law Courts

This analysis is based on a hand-copied record of Bodrum's court docket.[6] It includes all the divorces recorded in 1950 (N=54), a particularly interesting time because Turkey moved to a multiparty political system between 1947 and 1950. As mentioned, this marked the first time politicians in large numbers visited rural areas and spoke at length with villagers, hoping to enlist their votes. The analysis also includes all divorces recorded on the docket in the three-year period of January 1, 1965, through December 31, 1967 (N=137) . Because no decision had been reached in four cases by the time I left the field in 1968, this data set consists of 133 finished cases.[7]

The docket is the courts record of cases. It contains the case number, type of case, whether a lawyer is involved, which of the four courts the case belongs to, the names of plaintiffs and defendants, the villages where they were living at the time of the lawsuit, the decision, and the length of time to the decision. It also includes whether the decision is appealed and the outcome on appeal. If a decision is overturned by the higher court in Ankara (the *Yargıtay*), the case is returned to the Bodrum court and reheard. If the Bodrum judge concurs in his earlier opinion, the case is returned to the Supreme Court within the *Yargıtay* whose decision is final. This second decision is also recorded in the docket.

After a divorce case is initiated, the court grants or denies the divorce, the case is dropped, the parties are ordered to live separately for one year, or the case is suspended. A suspended case occurs when the plaintiff fails to appear for a hearing or fails to notify the court in advance that he or she could not be present for a scheduled appearance. (This study ignores suspended decisions when the case was rescheduled. When not rescheduled, suspended cases are considered dropped cases, since the effect is the same.)

In divorce decisions the judge rules on custody of the children. Young infants are given to the mother. If there are two children, a boy and a girl over four years, the boy is usually given to the father and the girl to the mother, unless there are unusual circumstances. The judge also decides who pays which fines, the court witnesses, and which party pays the court expenses. The party with the greater degree of fault is chosen to pay the court fees. If there is no recognizable degree of fault, the judge requires the plaintiff to pay court expenses.

The Turkish civil code of 1926 recognized six grounds of divorce: (1) adultery, (2) plots against life, grave assaults, and insults, (3) crime or dishonorable life, (4) desertion, (5) mental infirmity, and (6) incompatibility (Ansay and Wallace 1966:122). Until 1963 the Bodrum courts were required by law to attempt mediation in all divorce suits; this pretrial reconciliation was *only* required in divorce cases. After 1963 new instructions to judges were sent from the Ankara high court to abandon this practice. Under Ottoman Islamic law, pretrial mediation in divorce has been introduced as a reform measure in 1915 to make Islamic law less harsh to women. It was expanded further under the Ottoman Family Law of 1917, which provided for three male family members to attempt to reconcile the couple before the case reached an Islamic judge—who probably would have granted the divorce to the husband. The decision made in Ankara to discontinue precourt mediation in the judges' chambers in divorce suits represented a step toward conceptualizing women as equal to men.

A decision to open a lawsuit for divorce brought two advantages, even if later the spouse decided to drop proceedings. Going to court acted as a warning to the other, and it established a public record of marital difficulty.[8] If the situation continued, the earlier court case gave additional validity to the assertion of incompatibility, which was the basis of divorce most favored by the Bodrum judges in the 1960s.

An examination of the cases of divorce initiated in the years 1950, 1965, 1966, and 1967[9] reveals that 54 cases were initiated in 1950; this number dropped to a steady 45, 45, and 47 a decade and a half later (see Table 6).

While the number of divorce cases initiated by women stayed constant over this period, the number initiated by men dropped substantially from 33 in 1950 to an average of 24 for 1965 through 1967. This difference suggests that men became relatively less powerful in initiating divorces in the later years. The drop in male-initiated divorce cases coincides with the abandonment of pretrial mediation in 1963, a change that may have discouraged divorce claims by males who wished to use the courts to threaten and punish wives, rather than because they were intent on divorce.

The outcomes for male and female-initiated divorce cases also reveal that women were becoming more successful in obtaining the divorces they sought. A comparison of the percentage of divorces granted to men and women who initiated divorce proceedings finds a substantial increase for women: from less than 33 percent in 1950 to an average of 68 percent in the 1965–67 period. (The comparable figures for men are 42 percent and 57 percent.) As a result, divorces granted to women rose in number from less than half of those granted to men in 1950 (6 versus 14), to the same number or more in 1965 through 1967 (15 versus 11; 16 versus 15; 14 versus 14).

Thus, the number of divorces resulting from cases initiated by women more than doubled between 1950 and 1965. For cases initiated by men, the number remained constant. These results indicate that women were making increased use of the courts to obtain divorces that had been unheard of before Ataturk's reforms, and that the courts themselves were growing more responsive to women's new role.

Changing Grounds for Divorce

Two cases from the Bodrum district courts illustrate changing attitudes toward women's rights in a marriage.

Case One. A letter from the plaintiff's lawyer to the court in a woman-initiated divorce stated, "He did not give his wife what every young girl wants—a separate house. She lived with his stepparents. She suffered. She waited. In 1965, after their baby was born, she became ill." A long list of other harms that befell her in the marriage followed, including the baby's death from her husband's neglect when she was hospitalized. It is not known how the judge weighed this evidence, but

TABLE 6

Outcomes for Divorce Cases Initiated by Men and Women

	Cases Initiated By Men					Cases Initiated By Women					Total Cases Initiated
	Granted	Not Granted	Dropped	Unfinished	Total	Granted	Not Granted	Dropped	Unfinished	Total	
1950 (N)	42.42% (14)	36.36% (12)	21.21% (7)	—	100.00% (33)	28.56% (6)	33.32% (7)	38.08% (8)	—	100.00% (21)	54
1965 (N)	47.85% (11)	17.40% (4)	34.80% (8)	—	100.00% (23)	68.10% (15)	18.16% (4)	13.62% (3)	—	100.00% (22)	45
1966 (N)	71.40% (15)	19.04% (4)	4.76% (1)	4.76% (1)	100.00% (21)	66.56% (16)	8.32% (2)	16.64% (4)	8.32% (2)	100.00% (24)	45
1967 (N)	51.80% (14)	14.80% (4)	29.60% (8)	3.70% (1)	100.00% (27)	70.00% (14)	10.00% (2)	20.00% (4)	—	100.00% (20)	47

the lawyer, in making a case for his client, clearly listed the woman's first grievance as the failure of the husband to establish a separate household. The divorce was granted.

Appellate courts, by the late 1970s and perhaps before, were recognizing as grounds for divorce the failure on the part of a husband to establish a separate home for his wife (Zwahlen 1981: Ansay 1983). Not only does this mean that national courts were recognizing married women's rights in opposition to the rights of the extended patriarchal household, but it also suggests that the modern Republic of Turkey has a vested interest in undercutting extended patriarchal households.

Case Two. A Bodrum woman asked for a divorce from a village man. They had been married eleven years and had three daughters. She stated that for the last two years the husband had been drinking and spending all his money on alcohol. He answered that he was not an alcoholic, that he had been drunk only once in three years, and that he was poor. He said he was an *iç güvey* (a groom who lived with his wife's family), and that she had made him leave her family's household. He said he did not wish to divorce. The wife brought witnesses. Two witnesses said that the couple had not gotten along for three or four years, that the husband had called the wife a prostitute, and that five or six months earlier he had left the household. A third witness said they didn't get along, and then added a surprising fact: The husband had left for Milas and later the wife asked this witness to go to Milas and bring the husband home again. The neighbor went. He found the husband, who refused to return, making a gesture expressing he no longer wanted his wife.

The judge decided they must live separately for one year, and that the husband must pay the court fees of 15 TL, which was the cost of bringing the witnesses to court (about $1.50). The judge wrote in his opinion that he could not grant a divorce because of the children.

Six months later the wife appealed this decision, writing: "Witnesses proved he called me terrible names and that we cannot get along together. He has not taken care of us for three or four years, and he left us five or six months ago. I asked him to come back, but he didn't, and this fact was proved by a witness testifying in court."

The appellate court overturned the Bodrum judge's decision, writing in part: "When a couple is told to live separately for one year under the law #138, there must be some possibility that after a year they will again be reconciled. In this case we cannot see any possibility. Children cannot be the reason to keep people from divorcing for a year." The appellate court wrote to the Bodrum judge, "You should have given her a divorce. Your decision was wrong, and we are overturning it."

The plaintiff then wrote to the Bodrum court to reopen the case, citing the appellate court decision. The Bodrum judge granted a divorce in the first rehearing of the case, even though the defendant continued to object to the divorce. The judge said in part, "The appellate court has objected to my former opinion, and I think they were correct." The defendant was granted the right to see his children each Sunday of the month. He was told to pay the court expenses of 97 TL ($9.50).

In this case we see that appellate court in Ankara may pay closer attention to the women's grievances in a marriage and be less interested in preserving the husband's rights to remain married than the local courts. An aspect of this case that may be relevant is the fact that the mother and children had always lived in her extended patriarchal household, which would continue to provide for them.

An analysis of Turkish divorce case decisions from the Ankara appellate court (Zwahlen 1981) found a substantive change in the concept of fault in divorce in the last decade. In a review of Zwahlen's book, Professor Tuğrul Ansay, formerly dean of the Ankara Law Faculty, wrote that before the 1970s, a plaintiff in a divorce proceeding had to be less at fault for the marital strife than the other party. After 1970, incompatibility of character or sexual incompatibility, and not fault of a spouse, was grounds for divorce (Ansay 1983:752–53).

In Bodrum courts as early as 1965, judges preferred a plaintiff to claim "inability to get along together" rather than to list the partner's faults. During hours of interviews with Bodrum judges, and discussions of particular divorce cases, fault in divorce in relation to who has the right to bring suit was not mentioned. A person became a plaintiff because of stronger motivation to divorce, or easier access to the Bodrum courts. The evidence indicates that some rural Muslim women in western Anatolia were willing to use their secular right to act on this motivation.

Other Female-Initiated Law Suits

In Bodrum town the Turkish court system was represented only by a lower and a middle criminal court. The highest criminal trial court was located in Muğla, the provincial capital.

When all criminal cases brought to Bodrum's middle criminal court were examined (Table 7), we found a significant increase in the number of cases brought by women against men in two time periods. In 1950 women brought only 20 percent of the cases (N=3) initiated against male defendants; by 1966 the figure rose to 34 percent, or 21 cases. Thus, there was a gain in women's use of higher criminal courts between 1950 and 1966 (see Table 7).

TABLE 7

Gender of Principal Complainant and Principal Defendant in Middle Criminal Court Cases

Cases Involving	1950	1957	1965	1966	1967
M against F	5	4	11	8	4
M against M	12	24	37	40	32
F against F	2	3	4	9	5
F against M	3	9	12	21	16
Total	22	40	64	78	57
F against M as % of all above	14	22	19	27	28

Source of Statistics:
Starr and Pool (1974:553)

Several reasons help explain why rural women in western Turkey first used courts to divorce men, and only later used the higher criminal courts to prosecute men for harms suffered. Once a decision was made to terminate an intolerable marriage, the woman might have been willing to go to court. But if a woman admitted being molested by a man in 1950, she would have brought greater shame upon her reputation than any satisfaction gained by seeing him punished. In the Bodrum countryside, even in the late 1960s, males thought that if they could get a woman alone in a house, a barn, the fields, or the woods, she would have sex with him. Rural males thus viewed women as temptresses and seducers and were slow to recognize male sexual aggression against women as violent and often unsolicited assaults, although the Bodrum legal system did.

A second reason for the increase in criminal prosecution by women plaintiffs probably was that under the older value system, the women's husband, brothers, and fathers were supposed to be her protectors. But, by the mid-1960s, women often brought these very kinsmen to court for beating them. In other words, males might still assume they had the right to chastise women as they saw fit, but women had learned that the law did not recognize this right of male kin.

The Changing Consciousness of Rural Turkish Women

Besides use of the courts to initiate divorce, other indicators reveal that subtle informal processes have also altered the consciousness of rural Turkish women. A decline in household size in Bodrum villages occurred between the two censuses of 1946 and 1965 (Table 8),[10] and women, supported by the national legal system, played a part in this decline in two different ways. First, women encouraged their husbands to move out of the extended patriarchal family household; the Bodrum courts and national appellate courts supported this desire. Younger married women might wish to leave patriarchal kinship units because these living arrangements tended to support male supremacy values (see Collier 1974). For example, several brothers living together might lend more support to the notion that disobedient sisters and wives should be beaten, a method of dealing with unruly females that informants said was an age-old custom.

The second way women were affecting household size was in their attempts to limit numbers of children. Ethnographic discussions with many rural Muslim women in western Anatolian villages revealed married women's interest in birth control. While my data do not allow me to identify which of these two factors was more powerful, either or both—limiting numbers of children and changes in household forms—could have produced the same result, namely a reduction in household size.

Censuses for the Bodrum district have been located for the years 1891, 1912, 1927, 1946, and 1965.[11] Census data for the years 1946 and 1965 revealed that for the villages that can be compared, the number of rural village households tripled, rising from 1,044 to 3,252 (Table 8). Yet population in all of Bodrum's villages, considered as a whole on both censuses, increased only by 60 percent (Table 9). Although an explanation for this increase could be that civil servant families and urban households whose norm was the nuclear family unit were moving into the area, these households would have chosen to live in Bodrum town, the only place with amenities like household electricity, indoor toilets, and running water. During this same period, however, the population of Bodrum town slightly decreased, from 5,524 in 1946 to 5,137 in 1965

TABLE 8

Population by Village and Household Size for 1946 and 1965 Census

	1946 Census		1965 Census			
	Population*	Households	Men	Women	Total	Households
Ağaçlı (Bitezköy)			625	647	1,272	322
Çiftlik	510	100	571	512	1,083	256
Kizilağaç			435	433	868	208
Konacık (Cirkan)			121	104	225	60
Mumcular	400	82	627	701	1,328	299
Bahçeyakası			215	206	421	82
Çömlekçi	173	32	319	338	657	144
Kum			214	177	391	73
Mazı	395	72	382	388	770	165
Pınarlıbelen			579	571	1,150	222
Saz			442	418	860	190
Tepecık	122	25	237	234	471	91
Yeniköy			408	421	829	181
Karatoprak	1,057	209	1,038	999	2,037	471
Akyarlar (Kefaluka)			150	148	298	71
Dereköy	219	41	221	224	445	128
İslamhaneleri			126	139	265	74
Karakaya	396	62	524	490	1,014	247
Peksimet			108	111	219	58
Yalıkavak	420	72	534	561	1,095	271
Dağbelen	308	60	141	150	291	73
Geriş	186	38	217	222	439	113
Gökcébel			336	353	689	170
Göl	71	14	207	240	447	105
Gündoğan (Farilya)	324	64	396	425	821	182
Gürece			144	133	277	74
Ortakent (Musgebi)	453	91	510	570	1,080	295
Türkbükü	261	52	210	194	404	113
Yahşi			145	151	296	77
Yaka	142	30	149	147	296	77
Totals	*	1,044	10,331	10,407	20,738	3,252 **

Note: 1927 census lists Bodrum district population at 15,694 total people, (7,033 men and 8,648 women).

* This is a portion of total population since the population for some villages is not reported.

** Counting only households that are comparable with 1946 census.

(Table 9). Thus, this doubling of households cannot be explained solely by an increase in the in-migration of people with different household forms.

TABLE 9

Population of Bodrum District, 1946 and 1965, by Villages, Towns, and Total

	Bodrum Town	Bodrum Villages	Total
1946	5,524	9,871	15,395
1965	5,137	20,738	25,875

Turkish demographers (e.g., Erder 1981:52) have suggested that the process of declining fertility in Turkey began in the 1960s. However, my analysis of national census data for Bodrum's villages indicates that the reduction of household size probably began earlier than the process of declining fertility. Although I am unable to distinguish whether the decline in household size resulted from changes in household forms, from women's efforts at birth control, or from both, my knowledge of one large village suggests that both were significant.

Information on village population and number of village households is provided on the 1946 and 1965 Censuses (Table 8). I have based my findings on sixteen of the thirty villages, because these sixteen villages were the only ones I could treat as comparable units for the two censuses. Village names changed between the two censuses, and other intervening factors[12] prevented me from determining village identity in the remaining cases[13] (see Tables 8 and 9).

Nevertheless, all the more populated villages from the 1965 census have been identified on the 1946 census, and these include villages from the two major contrasting cash-cropping areas in the mid-1960s. This is important because tobacco-producing villages differ markedly in ethnic origins of inhabitants, household organization, ritual life, history of settlement, yearly cycle of celebrations, and some other aspects of culture from those growing tangerines.[14] These census data clearly indicate a decline in size of households between the 1946 census and the 1965 census (Table 10); all but one of the sixteen villages show a decline in household size. The largest average household size in 1965 was 5.2; the smallest 3.55. These figures are somewhat lower than Duben's, but they support his general assertion that household size was "moderate in rural Turkey of the past, ranging between 5.3 and 6.5" (Duben 1985:88). A sign test on the differences in the number of people

TABLE 10

Average Number of People per Household
in the Years 1946 and 1965
by Certain Villages

Village	1946	1965	Change	Percentage Change
Karakaya	6.39	4.11	– 2.28	– 35.68
Yalıkavak	5.83	4.04	– 1.79	– 30.70
Çömlekçi	5.41	4.56	– 0.85	– 15.71
Dereköy	5.34	3.48	– 1.86	– 34.83
Dağbelen	5.13	3.99	– 1.35	– 26.32
Göl	5.07	4.26	– 0.81	– 15.98
Çiftlik	5.10	4.23	– 0.87	– 17.06
Gündoğan	5.06	4.51	– 0.55	– 10.87
Türkbükü	5.02	3.57	– 1.45	– 28.88
Karatoprak	5.06	4.32	– 0.74	– 14.62
Mumcular	4.88	4.44	– 0.44	– 9.02
Tepecik	4.88	5.18	+ 0.30	+ 6.15
Geriş	4.89	3.88	– 1.01	– 20.65
Ortakent	4.98	3.66	– 1.32	– 26.51
Yaka	4.73	3.84	– 0.89	– 18.82
Mazı	5.49	4.67	– 0.82	– 14.94

per family between 1946 and 1965, for the 16 villages, showed that the number of people per family has declined significantly ($n=16, p<.0005$). The average decline was 1.03 members per family.[15] For the Bodrum district these figures indicate that by 1965 village couples were generally living in nuclear families. In the one village in which household size increased between the two censuses, it was a quite moderate increase (from 4.9 to 5.2) (Table 10). In this case, the numbers are still well within the range of nuclear or uxorilocal marriage households,[16] so this increase does not suggest the reforming of multiple patriarchal households.

In 1967 I conducted a survey of households in three populated neighborhoods of one of Bodrum's larger tangerine-growing villages (total village households: N=347; village population: 1,002 people). Nuclear family households, uxorilocal, and virilocal[17] marriage households existed in each neighborhood. But the latter two forms included a widowed parent of *either* spouse, and the wife's mother was represented as often as the husband's father. At the time and in later analyses, I viewed these forms as a stage in the life cycle of households, and concluded there was no prevailing pattern of patriarchal extended families, although it represented an "ideal model" that villagers referred to (Starr 1968; 1978a:62–63).

Extended patriarchal households were more frequently found among the wealthy farmers. But again, such households might include a daughter and her spouse instead of a son and his, a finding that confirmed the *iç güvey* model (Starr 1978a:68, 85). When a married son continued to reside with his father, the father always belonged to a wealthier social rank in the village. Wealth meant a father was able to provide a young son's bridewealth (*başlık*), allowing a son to marry before compulsory military service at age eighteen. Often these fathers built a separate room onto their houses for the newly married couple, thus investing capital in return for the son's free labor. In this way a wealthy father put his son in debt to him and obligated the son to work on his fields (an inheritance that the son would some day share with all his other siblings). Sons who lived in the extended patriarchal household were also obligated to demonstrate loyalty and respect (sometimes excessively) to their fathers. When, through their labor, the young son and his wife had paid off the bridewealth debt six to eight years later, the couple often moved into their own house.

In poorer families the father could not afford the bridewealth; therefore, the son had to earn it himself. For a Turkish villager the costs of the bridewealth were considerable in the 1960s and villagers rarely had extra cash. In 1967 they ranged between 700 TL to 3,000 TL ($70 to $300) (Starr 1978a:72). Thus, youths from poorer families tended to marry seven to ten years later than wealthy boys (pp. 67, 73). More mature when they married, perhaps more worldly, sons from poorer families were less likely to be willing to follow the norms of submission to and respect for a father that living in multiple, patriarchal households entailed. Furthermore, these youths probably developed ties to other men in the village for whom they worked as sharecroppers or day laborers, or there was the possibility of marrying up the social ladder and becoming an *iç güvey.* Through social networks a man could find separate accommodations in the village. Thus kin, patrons, friends, and wife's relatives played an important part in helping poorer couples form a separate household. Also, when a man became a tenant farmer, he was provided with a house by the field owner.

A married woman wanted privacy and the opportunity to be mistress in her own house. With new ideas entering the village and secular grade school education available and compulsory for village girls, adult women's status was no longer based solely on the number of children (preferably male) that she bore.

Life in an extended patriarchal household could be difficult for a young wife. Most likely she had been brought to live among women she did not know well. If she were lucky, her marriage had occurred with a male from her own village, so that her mother, sisters, and friends were not too far away. She owed obedience to all the older women in the household, as well as to all the men and boys. In the beginning she was well treated as the new bride, but her status quickly deteriorated if she did not become pregnant. Her behavior was scrutinized and discussed by the other women. Even her nuptial bedding would be examined by household women for signs of virginity or its lack. Male household members also watched her demeanor and domestic skills. The newly wedded couple would have little privacy within the small house and would probably share sleeping quarters with members of the entire household after the nuptial night. Many compelling reasons, therefore, determined why the bride and groom would desire to form a separate household.

The Turkish "High Court on many occasions rejected the old tradition of the wife's living with the other relatives in the husband's extended family and recognized her right to demand a separate dwelling from her husband" (Ansay 1983:752). The reformist attitude of the appellate court, along with growing egalitarian norms in rural marriages, provided incentives that moved the rural western Anatolian household toward the nuclear family model.

Women's Interest in Limiting Family Size

Participant observation supports and complements the demographic materials presented above.[18] Together they present a strong argument that women were interested in limiting family size. The following information was obtained during the period I lived in or maintained contact with a rural, tangerine-growing village of 1,000 people (347 households) between 1966 and 1968 (Starr 1978a; 1984).

Neglect of unwanted babies was the most successful method of limiting numbers of children. No one ever spoke directly to me about infant neglect, and I never raised the subject. Occasionally, however, I'd hear oblique statements such as, "Isn't it too bad that she had a second or third girl," and subsequently I'd hear that the baby was ill. The following was blatant enough to be recorded in my field notes:

> A young mother of about 20 years of age already had two daughters under five, when she gave birth to a third daughter. Within days the female relatives told me the baby was sickly and she

didn't nurse properly. These middle-aged women (the grandmother and aunt of the newborn) never spoke joyously of the birth, only of a sickly baby. A month or so later these women began talking as if the baby would not live much longer. Within five months of birth, the baby died. No one was surprised. No one had suggested taking the baby to the government doctor in town for treatment.

A second method of limiting numbers of children is, of course, to avoid pregnancy. What I learned about village birth control techniques was acquired passively—by being present when the subject occurred. The village women were pragmatic and curious about urban and Western customs and, at one time or another, over ten village women asked me, "How did you, a married woman, manage to have only one child?" If I were friendly with the woman, I told her how I'd managed. Sometimes I'd mention that the government doctor in Bodrum had told me he would provide free birth control pills to any woman who came for an office visit and asked for them.[19]

The following exchange occurred during a nightly gathering of six to ten women who rotated visits among village houses. The men and boys of the households had gone off to a coffeehouse, a normal custom after the evening meal. As the women talked, a middle-aged woman, mother of four, indicated she wanted to tell me secrets about village sexual relations. She insisted the three unmarried girls had to leave the room. I was left sitting on the floor with four or five married women. She beckoned us closer. Lighted only by a candle, her face shining round and moonlike, she leaned toward me from her haunches, saying: "*Simdi, sene soleyim*" ("Now, let me tell you").

I waited breathlessly. No one moved. Slowly, she said: "*Dikkat, dikkat, dikkat lazım*!" ("Careful, careful, you need to be careful!")

Then, triumphantly, she sat back. No one moved. Everyone looked at me. I had been told. I was now initiated into the sexual knowledge of the village, the practices the virgin girls were not allowed to hear. The lengthy preamble led only to instruct me in the oldest form of birth control known besides celibacy—*coitus interruptus*.

Women's interest in limiting numbers of children did not translate into use of the government doctor in Bodrum town. He told me no village woman had yet asked about birth control in 1967. As far as I know, no active Turkish birth control program comparable to the one occurring in some areas of rural India during the late 1960s and early 1970s existed (Epstein and Jackson 1977). Yet rural Turkish women whom I met were acquiring piecemeal birth control information, and were open and receptive to birth control ideas gleaned from small, informal exchanges among women.

No visible social movement existed to protect women or to struggle for their rights in Bodrum district during the mid-1960s—no women's marches and no protests, and little visible leadership of rural women's causes.[20] In order to account for the change in women's behavior, therefore, an explanation might lie in the informal networks of social relations through which new ideas spread to women. Although some urban-to-rural outreach was provided by the women's units of the Republican People's Party, by and large Bodrum rural women did not identify with, nor were they mobilized through, party politics. The best source of information was by "word of mouth," which occurred through rural women's informal networks. These informal female networks stretched out beyond the household, neighborhood, and community. Women in uxorilocal marriages or in extended patriarchal households daily were under the control of household males and other household females. But at rituals and festivals, these women gained opportunities to exchange news and hear new ideas.[21] When nothing was happening in the outside world, there was no effect. But when changes started to occur, as in the case of district court judges enforcing the new Turkish civil code, then the women had new information to exchange.

Large festivals in the Bodrum district that brought women together were weddings, circumcisions, and mourning rituals. Despite cultural differences and differences in village histories, mode of production, and social organization, all of Bodrum's villages and towns observed these rituals. Seventy-five to fifteen hundred people might come from everywhere in the region of thirty villages, and sometimes from Aydin, Izmir, Istanbul, and even Ankara. Weddings among poorer villagers lasted three days, but most weddings lasted six. Circumcision rituals covered an entire day, bringing together women from nearby villages, while the mourning rituals after a death involved only women. These began in the early evening, usually forty-seven days after a Muslim death, and continued well into the night with recitations from the *Kur'an*. At weddings and circumcisions, men, women, and children were present, and the sexual segregation at these gatherings allowed direct exchange of information among women. When a drunken male once stumbled into a women's group at a wedding, a mature woman picked up a board and hit him over the head to drive him away (Starr 1978a:76). Mourning rituals (*mevlûd*) brought women together in smaller groups of twenty to forty. Coming and going from these rituals, women walked along paths and roads talking together. These outings had a festive air, and women exchanged news of marriages, births, deaths, crops, schools for their children, in fact, everything imaginable, including who was divorcing.

Even as a woman disapproved of another's divorce or someone's case against a husband for beating her, the knowledge was stored in memory against a future time when her own marriage might become unbearable.

By the late 1940s, politicians, turning to the countryside in great numbers to gain votes, facilitated the spread of new policies and ideas generally. By the mid-1960s about twenty households of the urban Turkish middle class lived in Bodrum town. Members of a circulating civil service elite, they brought new forms of behavior to the community. A companionable relationship between spouses was visible when husbands and wives strolled arm-in-arm in the streets along the waterfront in early spring evenings. It was visible when husbands and wives attended the cinema together. At their engagement parties and wedding receptions, married couples embraced in ballroom dancing to live bands imported from great distances for the occasion.

Although village girls and women did not aspire to this level of public congeniality and familiarity between the sexes, it was the expressed desire of every young married rural woman in the Bodrum area to have her own household and to live separately from the family of her husband. This, in itself, represented a movement away from male supremacy values, from the values inherent in Islam, and from the ideology that supported extended patriarchal households. Judicial decisions in the Bodrum district courts supported this desire, and so did the Turkish High Court that upheld a wife's right to divorce when a husband refused to provide a dwelling separate from his father's or brother's after marriage (Zwahlen 1981, Ansay 1983:752).

Other women's social movements started similarly—haphazardly through small, informal exchanges of information. A women's march protesting the reduction of free milk for school children in Chiswick, England, although unsuccessful, resulted in the women obtaining a community meeting place on grant from the village council, for the price of one peppercorn a year. During conversations in this hall, some women gradually revealed to each other that they had been severely beaten for years by husbands. The issue of battered wives was to follow a slow and chancy course for years before it emerged into a full-blown social movement for change in England (Dobash and Dobash 1979:1–2).

Conclusion

In late Ottoman times in the Anatolian countryside, the most oppressed groups were young males and women. My data suggest the movement from extended patriarchal households in western Anatolian villages was based on an increase in women's striving for autonomy, which was linked to structural and societal changes, including new legal rights. Under the secular Turkish civil code of 1926, women gained rights almost equal to men. Under the constitution of 1961, sons and daughters gained the right to migrate out of Turkey (Abadan-Unat 1986:326). These rights, granted by the nation-state to individual citizens, limited the male householder's prerogatives within the extended patriarchal family and played a part in moving rural Turkish marriages toward more egalitarian models.

Women were using district-level courts by 1950, and by 1966 they had increased their usage to include criminal prosecutions against males for harms suffered. The use of state courts demonstrates a changing consciousness among rural Muslim women concerning their self-worth and what constitutes appropriate treatment by males. The decline in household size between the 1946 and the 1965 censuses and the efforts to limit numbers of children provide further evidence that women's consciousness was changing.

The purposeful action by Ataturk and his secularizing elites in supplanting Islamic family law with secular European family law was meant to create a legal and regulatory environment that supported more egalitarian relationships within the household. Secularization, combined with a growing willingness by women to take action to improve their situation, made it possible for them to exercise rights they traditionally did not enjoy.

This research demonstrates that court use and the analysis of case flows through the courts are best understood by viewing the data within a broader context of societal change. For example, since secular elites believed the way to raise Turkey to the economic status of western European countries was to create family structures similar to European models, an aspect of their reform was to legally empower women. Women's use of the courts, along with judicial willingness to decide cases in their favor, tipped the balance in gender relationships toward more equality for rural Turkish women.

By "constructing" women as a status group and giving them legal autonomy, secular elites also undermined the control that the Islamic clergy would have over women. Islamic ideology defines women as inferior to men, needing male supervision and control. By raising women's status, Turkish reformers furthered their goals of economic reform, secularism, and republicanism in the new nation of Turkey.

Notes

1. The Ottoman Law of Family Rights allowed whatever school of Islamic law couples wished to use to be applied. This meant the most flexible rule of the

Hanefi school could be applied instead of the rule of one of the other three schools. It also allowed a woman to have written into her marriage contract a right to annulment should her husband take a second wife. And, it allowed women rights to divorce on grounds such as impotence, insanity or abandonment. If a woman wished to divorce her husband on grounds of extreme cruelty or incompatibility, the law provided that three male family members must first attempt reconciliation of the couple before divorce was possible (Starr 1984:102; Lewis 1966:335–36; Pearl 1979:109).

2. Ethnographic studies during and since the 1960s have stated that rural women's most important ties are based on kinship and neighborhood (Coşar 1978:126–29; Kandiyoti 1976; Olson 1982:62, 64; Starr 1978a and b; Kağıtçıbaşı 1982:5, 8).

3. No tractors were in use in the entire Bodrum district when I left in autumn 1968; by the early 1970s, when Mansur finished her study of Bodrum town, only four tractors had been purchased (1972:34).

4. I use the term *household* to mean those people who live together in a domestic unit, membership in which is usually based on kinship through marriage and descent. A household is simultaneously a dwelling unit, a unit of economic cooperation (at least in distribution and consumption), and the unit within which most reproduction and early childhood socialization takes place (Netting, Wilk, and Arnould 1984:xvi). Most people spend considerable time as members of a household. An *extended patriarchal household* is a household in which most power, authority, and responsibility for household decisions resides with the males in the domestic unit. This usually means that the oldest male in directly ascending line is household head, a position he retains until senility or death. Such a household is an integrated unit for "cooperative work, shared meals, ownership of livestock, financial exchanges, and types of reciprocity in distribution and consumption of food and child rearing practices" (p. xxiv). The mere physical nearness of conjugal families is not an adequate index of integration into a household organization.

A *nuclear household* consists of two or more people related by marriage or descent. Thus, a married couple or a mother and child is a nuclear household, as is a father and child or two siblings who reside together and meet some of the criteria of households described above. An *upwardly extended household* is a nuclear household with a relative or relatives from the older generation living with them. Elsewhere (Starr 1978a:84–87; 1984), I discussed household forms as relating to sources of household income, diversification of the household productive system, and sex of the oldest and youngest child.

5. Pearl (1979:89).

6. During ethnographic observations in the Bodrum court for over a year (1967–68) I witnessed many hearings of divorce cases. This led me to seek permission to copy the entire dossier of a number of divorce cases (N=57). This series runs from January 1, 1966, to September 1, 1967 (1.9 years), and provides in-depth knowledge of what happened in divorce litigation, in addition to those

cases I actually witnessed in court. For this book, I have returned to my hand-copied records of the court dockets from the years 1950, 1966, 1967, and 1968.

7. For greater accuracy, I returned to the original hand-copied data set, and not the computerized data set used in Starr & Pool (1974), which accounts for a slight discrepancy in number of divorce cases (133 cases not 132, and four, not six, unfinished cases).

8. Wife-beating cases at the Bodrum courts were prosecuted as assault and battery cases, which is why I cannot get an accurate count of them from the court docket. In the three cases of wife-beating I saw prosecuted, the two Bodrum judges attempted to reconcile the couple by persuading the female plaintiff to drop the case against her husband before a judge would have to reach a decision and penalize the husband with a jail sentence.

9. While these figures represent all divorce cases recorded in the docket during these years, the trends reported are based on relatively small numbers of cases.

10. There is no evidence that the census definition of *household* changed between 1946 and 1965.

11. Census sources are as follows: for 1891 (Cuniet 1894, as quoted in Galantı 1946); for 1912 (Soteriadis 1918); for 1927 (*Ümumi Nüfus Tahrırı* 1929); for 1946 (Galantı 1946); and for 1965 (*Bodrum Ilçe Nüfus Sayımı* 1965). Galantı (1946) and local Census Records from the Bodrum District Office were available to me in Bodrum during field research. I used these rather than the official Turkish government censuses because of the discrepancies between the local census statistics, the names of villages, and the official published record, published as the national 1950 census. For consistency I again used local census records for the 1965 census rather than the official Turkish census of 1965. In general by 1965 the discrepancies between numbers and names of villages had decreased between "the official" and "the local" Turkish records, but the former slightly overcounted males. Galantı's census (1946) and the Bodrum census records for 1965 are on file with the author and are available on request.

12. There were twenty-eight named units in 1947 and thirty in 1965. Changes in subdistrict (*nahiye*) jurisdictions changed some villages from one subdistrict to another between the censuses of 1946 and 1965. Some village names also changed during this period. Some smaller neighborhoods were joined to villages, and thus disappeared. Although I do have information for some of these situations, I could not identify all.

13. In an unsuccessful pursuit of the name changes between the 1946 and the 1965 censuses, I consulted older and newer maps, as well as the 1960 and 1984 *Gazetteer of Turkey* (1960, 1984), for changes in the names of Bodrum's thirty villages.

14. All the larger villages (population over 800) were engaged in cash-cropping and selling cattle at market. Villages to the west of Bodrum tended to

grow tangerines, other citrus, and early spring vegetables for markets. Villages to Bodrum's east produced tobacco, carob beans, a little wheat, and considerably more animals for sale.

15. I wish to thank Professor Nancy Mendell, Richard Senno, and David Stock who, at various times, helped with these statistics.

16. A *uxorilocal* marriage household is one in which one or more married daughters live with their husbands at the home of *her* father and mother.

17. A *virilocal* marriage household is one in which a married man and his wife live at the home of *his* father, brother, or uncle.

18. This argument was stimulated by Carl Degler's brilliant use of census materials to demonstrate that, beginning at least a century earlier, the necessary groundwork for the American movement for female emancipation occurred as women began to limit numbers of children. He thus demonstrated that it is no coincidence that the women's emancipation movement occurred at the same time the modern American family emerged (1980:vii).

19. A government doctor worked in the state-supported hospital in Bodrum town. When I arrived, the doctor was a male physician in his middle years; at the end of summer 1967 he was replaced by a younger female physician.

20. I went to all the public events I heard of in the year and a half I participated in activities in Bodrum. The only public event in which women were addressed was at the ceremonial opening of the new school in Mandalinci village. The following is a description of this event, taken from my field notebook:

> As all the women and children (sitting in a segregated group) were leaving after two hours of speeches by males, the village headman called the women back to hear the almost forgotten speech by the president of the Women's Group in Bodrum, a young woman teacher from the Bodrum high school. She spoke of Ataturk's goals of equal education for women and the nation-building needs that required women to be equal partners of men. She talked against the women's custom of wearing long shawls and covering the lower parts of their faces in public. Birth control, possibilities of divorce, and the use of the legal system for protection against violence were not mentioned. Nor did any women I knew discuss her speech afterwards. This leads me to conclude that there was little or no active consciousness-raising activity by more educated women in relation to the peasantry in Bodrum's thirty villages.

21. This Turkish situation contrasts strongly with S. Mizzi's Ph.D. thesis on working-class women in Malta. In that community, females did not continue friendships with other females after marriage. Their female associates were their mother and their natal sisters. This had consequences for the intensification of centripetal family structures, especially since houses and house lots were owned matrilineally (Mizzi 1981).

III

The Development of Secular Law

Chapter Six

Managing Disputes at the Village Level: Cultural and Legal Forms

In the 1830s an Englishman, Captain Elliott, avoided a severe storm by anchoring in the deep water harbor of Mandalinci, where he remained for several days. He reported that the hills held ruins of a classical Greek town and about the port were fragments of an "unknown city. . . . Not a human habitation exists within a mile and a half of the ruins" (1838:161–64).

One hundred and thirty years later the classical ruins were still in Mandalinci, and the waterfront village still stood in ruins. Uninhabitable one and two-story buildings, mostly without roofs and floors, standing open to the sky, marked the passing of a nineteenth-century Greek sea town.

It was in Mandalinci, a representative[1] Bodrum village (fictitiously named for this study's purposes), that my intensive inquiry into rural Turkish cultural and legal forms of dispute resolution[2] took place in the mid-1960s. A sixty-six year old village man told me then that his house had belonged to his grandfather when his had been the first Turkish farm in the central valley for "maybe" three hundred years. I surmised from Turkish informants' life histories that in the late nineteenth century, the seashore was inhabited by Greeks, while sheepherding, Turkish pastoralists sometimes visited the plain and coast, gradually establishing rights to pasturage in both places.

The first permanent Turkish houses were built on the mountain (which by the 1960s had become a neighborhood of Mandalinci but, unconnected by roads, was only accessible by a half-hour trek from village center). The dwellings in the mountain neighborhood were in the ancient house style, constructed differently from those identified with the Greek seafaring culture at the waterfront. A mosque in the

MAP 4

Mandalinci Village: A Dispersed Settlement

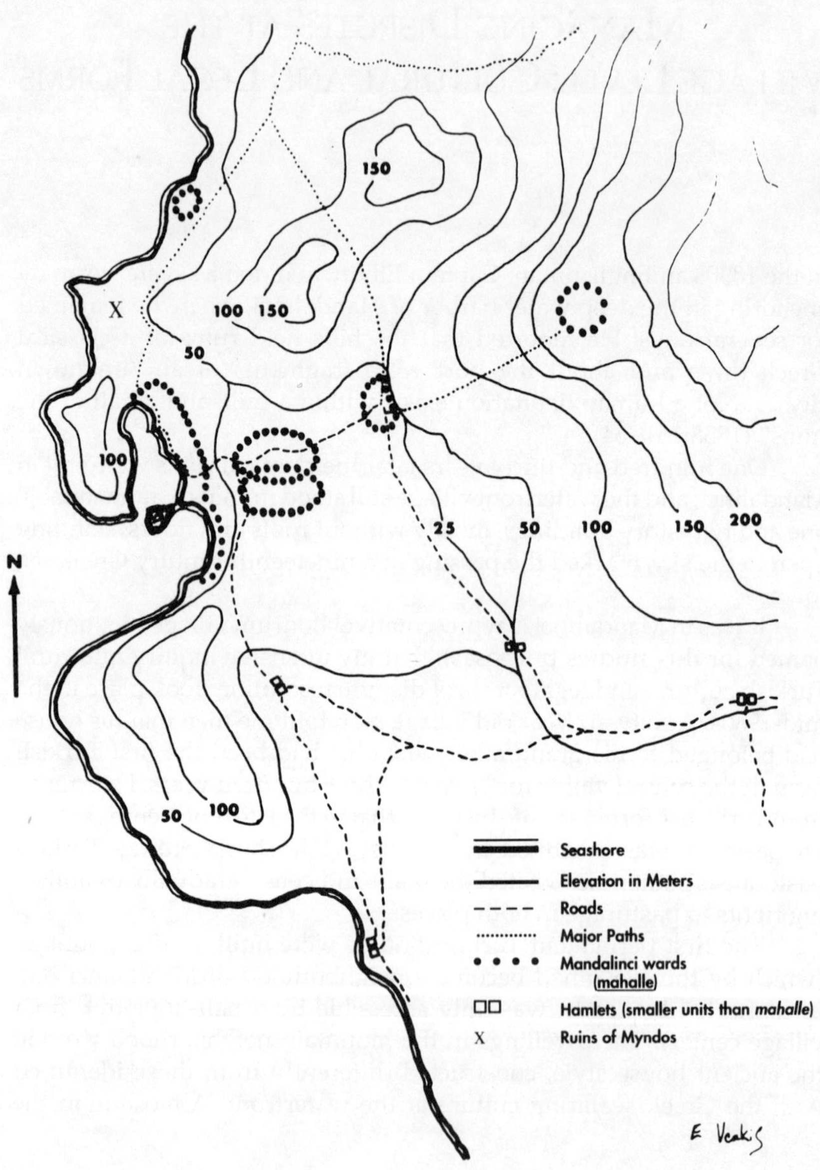

mountain habitat, built by a grateful sea captain who weathered a storm in Mandalinci's 150-foot deep harbor, is inscribed with the date 1907.

The Greeks left the area in the first two decades of the twentieth century and, at the beginning of the Turkish Republic in 1923, some Turkish officers were awarded Greek farms along the shoreline. Several Turks from the Balkans were also given village land, and some of the pastoralists gradually moved in and took up settled agricultural life.

In discussions about this period with older informants in the village and in Bodrum town, no one mentioned that Islamic judges or Islamic clergy had played a significant role in their lives. Nor did they mention tribal gatherings, or large ceremonial activities by either the Islamic or Catholic clergy. (There had been a small Catholic church on a hill above the harbor, now used as a barn.) Soldiers had not been garrisoned in the area, although one seventy year old man said that when he was small, there was a gendarme station and a customs house in the village, and that from a small lookout station on the top of the largest hill, a soldier always watched the sea. Every boat coming from north or south was required to stop in the harbor and see customs officials. The waterfront houses were all inhabited by Greeks, and at least two casinos along the waterfront were crowded with Greek men dancing and gambling at night.

A seventy-three year old man told me, "In those days everybody carried any weapon he wanted. We had long knives and double pistols with short handles and wore turbans." In his particular narration of village history, printed below, he describes an incident of contact with the Ottoman state:

> About a hundred years ago a Greek man, named Demetrius, came to Mandalinci. He was a tailor and had five or six daughters. He lived in the valley and sometimes made shirts for people. About this time there were no more than ten houses, inhabited by Turks, in the flat land or seaside. When the Turkish people offered to pay him, he said, "Ah, don't give me money. Give me some land so that I can be your neighbor." In this way he acquired ten plots of land. Later two other Greek men came. One became the owner of the western part of Mandalinci, the other owned all of the eastern land from here to the next village. When a Turkish warship went to Kalimnos with the Ottoman Sultan Aziz in the nineteenth century, all the Greek people ran away up into the mountains. One of those Greek men called them back down. He killed forty sheep for the Turkish soldiers on that warship. In Istanbul the sultan Aziz gave him a golden tobacco box and I have seen it. He also

> received a long saber and a medal for his generosity to Turkish soldiers. After he died, however, the government took back the medal and the saber.
>
> Later more Greeks came. At the end there were about twenty Greek families living here all year. The others came just for the time of reaping, and then returned to Kalimnos (field notes, *Mandalinci History*, 9 May 1967).

Ottoman warships occupied these waters during the reign of Sultan Abdülaziz, who reigned from 1861 until 1876. Thus, the account of the warship and feast may be accurate. The narrative reinforces the impression that, in those times, Greek-speaking households outnumbered Turkish ones. The ruins of two-story, cut-stone houses along the waterfront (Turks used fieldstone, fragments from ruins, and built one-story houses in the village until 1968) suggest a larger, sea-oriented population. (By the 1960s, with the exception of Bodrum town, Turks in this district were practicing mixed farming and animal keeping. They had neither stone-cutting skills nor seafaring traditions.) As the Turkic nomadic transhumants settled, they built their houses inland in the mountains or in sheltered areas on the plain. In the past, many Greek and Turkish households that used the area came for only part of the year, suggesting that the old man exaggerated the number of Turkish households in the flat plain around 1900.

In a fluid situation in which neither "tribe" nor state maintained strong control, the major mechanism of social control was kinship. Informants stated, and older marriage patterns confirmed, that in earlier times Turkish-speaking people married across large distances on the Bodrum peninsula and on Bodrum's inland plateau. Such marriage practices created far-flung networks and were especially useful for transhumant groups, because marriage with kin groups living elsewhere gave pastoral households access to diverse pastures, lands, brides, and information. With the development of settled agriculture, households made cash investments in land, and marriage preferences changed. Marrying within a village became a way for men to amass political loyalties and landholdings.

These wide marriage networks formed the underlying structure of social control in an outlying region where the controlling state, the Ottoman Empire, maintained little political control besides tax collection. Marrying women to groups farther away provided links, ties, and reciprocal relations which could be called upon in an emergency.

Other forms of social control would be needed in this multiethnic region to mitigate against interethnic violence and killing. In the absence of a strong presence of state power,[3] markets and trading relations provided peaceful social controls and strong incentives toward continued peace, which stretched across religious and ethnic boundaries.

Islam and Popular Legal Culture

In order to understand how Islam influences popular legal culture, I have turned to comparative anthropological research. For example, here is how the lawyer/anthropologist George Bisharat describes popular legal consciousness among West Bank Palestinians:

> Disputes are affairs of great interest in Palestinian communities. In fact, it is typical that many people, even anonymous bystanders, intercede in streetside quarrels and attempt to mediate between the disputants, who themselves seem to welcome a public hearing. Thus what may begin as a private confrontation often rapidly assumes the dimensions of a community event. Gratitude is showered on the mediator who can produce a resolution on the spot and a boost is given to his status in the community. Conflicts that are not immediately resolved become the topics of discussion and speculation. Those with knowledge of the relevant principles of *shari'a* or *'urf* (customary law) hold forth, it being an occasion for public display of religiosity and general wisdom. (1989:32)

What is particularly striking is the intervention of mediators who are knowledgeable about principles of the *Şeriat* and *'urf* (customary law), and that this is a path to higher status. As will be apparent later, informal mediators are also used in Mandalinci, but their references to Islam, customary law, and even contemporary Turkish law is noticeably lacking. No one, for instance, in a quarrel even quoted a legal maxim from the *Kur'an* or the *Mecelle* (i.e., the codification under the Ottomans of the *Şeriat* book of *Fıkıh*).

Interviews with the Mandalinci village *Imam* in 1967 further supports the assertion of the lack of Islam in popular consciousness of ways to resolve troubles. He said villagers discussed neither their private nor public troubles, quarrels, and arguments with him. They sought his advice only in spiritual matters, and that only rarely. His primary function was to lead the Friday prayer service in the mosque attended only by men, and to perform the simple marriage ceremony which took place in private in the groom's house after the six-day wedding ceremony. A few old women studied the *Kur'an* with him. Two village men had made the trip to Mecca much earlier and were called *Haci*. Although the village was Muslim, interest in Islamic religion and daily Islamic practices was noticeably absent, except during Ramadan.

In fact, in the 1960s conversations with hundreds of Bodrum's villagers and town dwellers, and research in the courts, all suggested that the Bodrum region had accepted the legitimacy of national secular dispute-resolving institutions—the Bodrum district courts and the district director of the county.[4]

Notaries and *Vekils*

Legal functionaries, used in Ottoman times, are still used in the new republic. Notaries had been used (then and now) to certify many kinds of legal documents and to provide these services to villagers and townspeople in the Turkish Republic. A *vekil*, a legal official in Ottoman times, could be used to ask for a lower tax status, to correct a tax status, and to represent someone at court. A *vekil* (then and now) is someone possessing knowledge of civil law who has not obtained a law degree or joined the Turkish bar association. Notaries and *vekil*s are found throughout the Islamic world today (see Eickelman 1985:22, 83–84; Rosen 1980–81:220).

The third legal functionary from Ottoman times was "the witness." In all Bodrum's villages this was an informal office that grew up through practice and can be identified as pre-Turkish civil code. In oral law traditions, the act of witnessing land and other transactions is important and even existed among the naked, head-hunting *Ifugao* (see Barton 1919:39, 59). Witnessing was important in early and classical Roman law of property transfers (see Starr 1989a), and even today in Islamic law courts, one or more males are necessary to bear witness to the "facts" in a case. If no males are knowledgeable, then two female witnesses are considered equivalent to every male witness (Rosen 1989a; Messick 1983a, 1983b).

In Bodrum's villages a village resident, always an adult male, became the person to witness and remember all oral land transactions. Often this witness knew how land and houses had been assigned and reassigned across four generations of agnatic kin.

In two different Bodrum villages I heard these witnesses testify in open-air court hearings. (In Turkish civil law, when land is disputed or a crime has been committed, the judge, court recorder, and surveyor must travel to the site of dispute or crime to view and diagram it, and hear testimony there.) A land transaction witness testified, in a village to Bodrum's west, to an earlier land division. With several other old men he presented "expert testimony" to the court that the sea had not receded in thirty-five years, which meant the plaintiff owned the seaside land now claimed for the village by the village headman (Starr 1985a: Case Five).

In Mandalinci village the land transaction expert, testifying on-site, said that two disputed houses and one lot had never been divided. As he spoke, he stood with his hand resting on his nine year old son's shoulder. No doubt the son would one day take his father's place as the village's expert in land transactions; as a child he was witnessing transactions and hearing his father recall earlier settlements and divisions.

The two houses in this case belonged to an elderly sister and brother, but the lot had passed to them without being divided; in fact it had never been divided. Recently, the brother had "sold" some of his land to another without consulting his sister, and then the sister had "sold" her house and lot to a member of her younger kin without consulting her brother. (Although the testimony specified "sold," it was equivocal whether money actually changed hands; perhaps the villagers thought "selling" rather than "giving" would bear more weight in court.)

In this way the land transaction expert's testimony became the key to unlocking the issues in dispute and resolving the case (see Starr 1978a:215), illustrating how the oral tradition of conflict resolution can still influence modern legal practices.

The Village Headman and Council's Role in Conflict Resolution

The village council consisted of seven elected members, one being designated as headman, or *muhtar.* The village schoolteacher and the village *Imam* were council members by law. The other members and the *muhtar* are elected by secret ballot by all adult men and women of the village and hold office for a four year period. In Mandalinci, there was no regular day for council meetings, but the council could be called together whenever a problem was brought to its attention. Although the law allowed a woman to be elected to a village council position, and although women have served as mayors of rural towns, the *muhtar* and others told me with great conviction that no village woman would ever be elected to the council in Mandalinci.

During my stay in the Bodrum district, the Mandalinci council did not meet at all. When decisions had to be made or work needed to be done that would benefit the village, the *muhtar* went to speak individually with men sitting at the coffeehouses or in their homes.

In regard to the responsibilities of the village council, in every instance Mandalinci villagers told me that it was the duty of council members and the *muhtar* to see that village affairs were handled smoothly. When asked if someone would take a quarrel or dispute to the council to be heard, they answered that he or she might. When asked for an example of a dispute that had been heard by the council, they either were evasive or responded that they did not know of any. Although reticent to talk about council meetings and disputes he might have heard in private attempts to question him, the *muhtar* did respond once when I again broached this topic because he was sitting with a visiting schoolteacher and some influential villagers. I asked what kinds of cases his council might hear.

"Trespassing, for instance, when sheep or camels go into someone else's fields; arguments over boundaries to fields, or other kinds of land problems; when neighbors or husbands and wives fight," he answered. He added that the council can fine an individual up to 500 TL ($50), but that it does not have the right to sentence a person to prison. If an offense of such seriousness occurs, the case must be taken to the Bodrum law court.

"Tell me about a village council case," I said. The *muhtar* answered, "Suppose I tell people they must come to work on the road. They don't come. For the first day I fine them ten liras; if they don't come on the second day, I fine them an additional twenty liras." When I asked, "When did you last fine someone" he answered that during the five years he had held office as *muhtar* (he had just been reelected), he had never fined anyone. Nor did he know of instances when past *muhtars* in Mandalinci had fined any villagers. In another context he told me that the most serious case a council can hear is stealing.

If the *muhtar* or his council hears of a village quarrel, they cannot intervene and insist that involved parties bring their dispute to council. The council can only hear cases when a principal asks their help. I asked the *muhtar* what a wife did when her husband mistreated her, and he replied, "She will go to her father. Her father won't do anything. After a while her husband will come for her, and her father might talk to them both at that time." When I asked him what the last case was that he or his council heard, he changed the subject.

In sum, in discussing methods of conflict resolution, no villager ever stated that the way they handled conflict was in accord with Islamic precedents, that they sought out advice from respected Islamic elders (i.e., those who had made the trip to Mecca), or that they prayed to Allah for help. Nor did villagers seek help from the republic's secular forums—the village headman and his council—which were created to resolve conflict in the village. The villagers, therefore, had to resort to other means of resolving conflict, short of going to court.

Village Methods of Conflict Resolution

So many anthropological ideas of rural conflict resolution have come from classical studies in tribal Africa (Colson 1953; Bohannan 1957; Gluckman 1955; Gulliver 1963, 1969; Epstein 1954; Turner 1957; and Van Velsen 1964) or from American Indian councils (Llewellyn and Hoebel 1941) that we tend to think in terms of village councils, judges, or religious leaders; of courts, town meetings, or moots—all visible and more or less corporate bodies where issues, grievances, arguments, and community-wide problems are handled, debated, and sometimes resolved.

Yet Gulliver (1963, 1969, 1971) has convincingly demonstrated, in research among the Arusha and Ndendeuli of Tanzania, that in face-to-face communities disputes may be settled despite the lack of developed legal institutions, such as judges, law courts, or adjudicators. In most societies, if two people from the same community get into a dispute, "hostility or the constant threat of it must give way to discussion, negotiation, an attempt to reach some kind of *rapprochement*, and a settlement of the matter in dispute" (Gulliver 1969:25). By paying close attention to detail—to the statuses of, and roles played by, the principles and their supporters, to the *timing* of the shifts in the argument, to the emergence of different roles in the negotiation process—a researcher can study dispute-managing processes occurring outside of a court or a clearly defined legal field.[5]

In Mandalinci there were no special settings, times, or contexts for handling disputes. Villagers did not form action-sets to negotiate in small groups or larger moots. There were no public assemblies for dispute management, no village council meetings, no persons who consistently played mediating roles, and no lineage feuding. Agnatic lineages consisted of from three to ten male members and were recognized kin units in the village. However, kin members were not recruited to support a principal in a conflict or crisis. When trouble occurred between individuals, and even between hot-tempered boys and men, no one thought of fetching a hunting gun or of getting their brothers together to help decide a course of action or to threaten the adversary.

My study of out-of-court conflict management in Mandalinci thus focused on the settings, contexts, and social situations people used for pressing and arguing about claims. This led me to scrutinize dyadic and triadic interactions as the raw data for dispute-behavior, and through this attention to detail, patterns on the village level of conflict resolution became clear.

Dispute Negotiations in Unstructured Situations

To search out the data of Mandalinci disputes before they reach a mass meeting, a professional mediator, a court of law, the local gendarme, or urban police, is to look for pattern and order embedded in "unstructured situations"—that is, behavior that occurs between people carrying out ordinary activities of everyday life.[6] Unstructured situations are given no special, ritualized significance of their own; they are not council meetings, board meetings, faculty meetings, or village moots. An analysis of patterned behavior associated with dispute in unstructured situations conceptualizes conflict as being enmeshed in the social life of a community: When a particular point in time is singled out to be examined, persons in conflict can be identified along with their supporters, their goals, and their interests. But goals and interests change through time; people in conflict today may find interests in common tomorrow.

By studying conflict as it occurs and is handled outside of law courts, we learn what attempts are made to resolve issues in the village context, what constitutes a valid claim, and which types of disputes between what social agents, in particular social relations, are amenable to a negotiated village settlement.

The cases of dispute in this chapter were collected in 1966 and 1967.

Dyadic Negotiations

Turgot, a thirty-one year old married man from Mandalinci, motored by boat to a seaside village, about an hour's run from Mandalinci. When he returned, he had a string bag full of cauliflower. A week later Turgot took me, my field assistant, and some others to that same village because I wanted to visit an old woman who made reed baskets. As we were leaving the old woman's house, a villager took my assistant aside and told him that there was some trouble between Turgot, the captain of our boat, and one of the village men. The villager advised that we leave quickly.

The next day in a Mandalinci coffeehouse I heard Turgot telling another captain the following story:

> "When I was in that village, that man, Ethen, stopped me, saying, 'Who is the captain of that boat?' "
> " 'I am,' I said."
> " 'Then you took some cauliflower from my garden about a week ago. How many did you take?' "

" 'Six cauliflower.' "
" 'That will be six liras then. A lira for each cauliflower.' "
" 'No, now I remember. I only took four.' "
" 'Then give me four liras [40 cents].' "

Five or six men, including Yusuf, Turgot's brother, were present when Turgot recounted this incident. The man to whom he told the story is a nephew of Ethen's. While discussing the encounter with Ethen, Turgot, who previously had been sitting quietly in his chair with his feet up, suddenly began squatting on his chair and moving rhythmically up and down in an agitated manner.

"If he asked me to pay fifty liras, I would have had to since some children saw me take the vegetables," Turgot added.

The Analysis: The encounter between Turgot and Ethen and its retelling the next day illustrate patterns villagers use in handling interpersonal conflict and in disseminating information about a person's character. The retelling of the event in the coffeehouse the next day in front of a nephew of Ethen's, another captain, suggests the interpretation that Turgot, Ethen, and other villagers attributed to these interactions.

The most significant event was Ethen seeking Turgot out on the road when he was alone to demand repayment for the cauliflower. Confrontation by someone when alone has overtones of threat. This fact becomes apparent when all cases of dispute from Mandalinci have been analyzed, interaction by interaction. Violence only occurred in direct confrontation of one aggrieved by another in a private setting. If claims were pressed in the presence of others, other people interfered when physical violence seemed imminent (see Starr 1978a:131–34, for a more detailed case discussion).

It is significant that Ethen demanded restitution of the stolen cauliflower and asked for repayment in terms of the cost of the cauliflower in market season. Ethen let Turgot haggle about the number he took, which suggests that Ethen was more interested in showing he would not tolerate theft of vegetables than in obtaining exact restitution.

The appearance of another captain, Ethen's nephew, in the Mandalinci coffeehouse the next day suggests that the time span for event and counterevent is short (in this case the next day); and that if Turgot's relatives, friends, and associates did not know he was the kind of person who steals vegetables for the household he shared with his wife's father and mother, Ethen's nephew would come to the village to tell them. No villager gains honor by stealing vegetables, and it is common knowledge that only a poor man, a man without fields of his own, would stoop to such behavior. Turgot recounted all events himself, but he clearly did so under the pressure of Ethen's nephew. Telling the events himself reduced to some degree his sense of shame at being caught as a thief and at giving in so readily when confronted by the field owner.

This was a dispute handled in an unstructured situation—claims were pressed and outcomes found by the aggrieved and his opponent. The final result of the dispute process in this instance was to make public Turgot's theft and thus reveal his character to his closest male associates.

In the second dyadic example, Yasar, a man aged between sixty-five and seventy-five years, the owner of one tangerine orchard and some sheep, came to Kurt Lessing's home in Mandalinci. Lessing, a middle-aged German journalist, had rebuilt an old stable as a home for himself in the village and had been living there for nearly a year. The old man appeared at his house. He seemed excited as he told Lessing that Pluto, Lessing's large hound dog, had just killed one of his sheep.

"What! My dog kill a sheep? Impossible," said Lessing.

"It happened," said Yasar. "My brother saw it happen, and if he had not chased your dog away with stones, your dog would have killed a second one."

Lessing asked to be taken to see the sheep and saw teeth marks on its neck. Yasar asked 100 TL for the sheep, which Lessing gave. Lessing had another villager skin and cut up the meat, which Lessing ate.

The Analysis: Lessing told me that the sheep cost more than if he had bought it alive and had it killed, but under the circumstances he was willing to pay more than its normal value, for the man could have demanded that his dog be killed.

We can assume that the Mandalinci villager pressed a claim in a way he deemed appropriate to seeking restitution from a foreigner who resided in his village. As in the first example, again the setting was private—Lessing's home. Because Lessing complied, the grievance was settled and no further disputing-interaction occurred. But as soon as the settlement became known in the village, another man appeared who pressed claims that the dog had killed his chickens (Starr 1978a:135–37).

In the third example, I asked Oktay, a self-made village entrepreneur, about a dispute between himself and Ahmet, another villager. When Ahmet was a youth, Oktay had taken him on as one of his workers. Ahmet came from very poor parents, so his association with Oktay, then a rising entrepreneur, was profitable to both and they became close associates. Ahmet worked as waiter and cook in Oktay's coffeehouse, did much of the supervision of the men who loaded Oktay's trucks, handled some of Oktay's accounts, and usually did Oktay's bookkeeping when villagers transported their produce on trucks hired by Oktay.

Oktay related the following:

"It was the season of quince. I was in Bodrum. I sent Ahmet a message to buy more quince from villagers. 'Buy whatever you can. I am planning to rent two trucks.' When I returned to the village, two men were boxing quince. Ahmet was lying on the grass. I asked why he hadn't bought more quince. Ahmet answered, 'If you get angry with me, I am not going to work for you anymore.' 'However you like,' I said, and Ahmet left his job with me."

"Before that I had overheard Ahmet say to another person, 'If they are going to order me about, I am going to take up my jacket and go home.' "

"I paid him for each job, sometimes 100 liras, sometimes 25, sometimes 300 liras. It depended on the amount of work. Ahmet's mother and father are sorry about what he has done. He was just like somebody from my family, like a son. Ahmet's father always came, and I would give him a pack of cigarettes or some tobacco. His father said to me, 'He is a crazy boy.' "

I went to Ahmet's house to ask why Ahmet, after eight years, no longer worked for Oktay. Ahmet was not at home, but his wife, a friend of mine, invited me in, gave me some food, and provided her version of the events.

"Oktay owed Ahmet 700 liras for work, but wouldn't pay him. After Ahmet quit his job, Oktay sent word to him, 'Come let us add up our bill.' But Ahmet wouldn't go. Now, Ahmet works in the coffeehouse next door to Oktay's."

The Analysis: Here the aggrieved, an employee of a powerful village patron, claimed his dispute concerned lack of pay and being ordered about, while Oktay claimed the younger man had been insubordinate and lazy. Oktay could have gone to Ahmet, apologized, and given him back pay. But the price might have been too high. Indeed, both might have thought this an appropriate time to terminate their patron-client relationship. After all, Ahmet was no longer a youth, and he resented being ordered around like one. Oktay's son was old enough to work in the coffeehouse and now could take on the responsibility of supervising those who worked for Oktay. The outcome was that Ahmet and Oktay avoided each other.

Triadic Negotiations

At least four types of third parties, or representatives, appear in the Mandalinci data: (1) *household heads* who are invited into the dispute to represent a household member, (2) *patrons* who represent a client or supporter, (3) *village gendarmes* (soldiers on special assignment to keep peace in the Turkish countryside) who are brought into a dispute by a principal or his supporter, and (4) *outsiders* to the village, such as government officials, bureaucrats, gendarme commanders—all of whom appear by chance in the village at a critical point in a dispute and are asked to intervene by a principal or his supporter.

The features that distinguish Mandalinci intermediaries from non-village third parties are these: (1) Mandalinci intermediaries are not impartial, but act on behalf of one of the disputants, and (2) they have no authority to enforce a resolution outside of the pressure they can bring by virtue of their rank, status, power, and personality. An intermediary or representative lends his or her weight to one side or the other (but one side only), although he usually is not as partial and shortsighted about a situation as the principal he represents. His presence then injects a certain amount of "good sense" into the process and sometimes hard negotiations as well. Non-village third parties possess different attributes: They are brought into the dispute because of their structural position in Turkish society rather than their particular relationship to a disputant.

When a dispute is reported to village gendarmes, it is handled in one of several ways: A gendarme might decide that evidence warrants reporting a "crime," that further investigation is necessary, or that the grievance ought not be reported. When reported, the public prosecutor in Bodrum conducted an investigation to see if prosecution was warranted. If an outsider to the village was asked to intervene, his power position in Turkish society made his judgment authoritative and enabled him to mediate disputes (a mediated settlement seeks the best possible outcome for both parties).

In this triadic example, a twenty-two year old youth, Yusuf, agreed to go sponge-diving with a captain from another village. Divers usually work for an entire season, which runs from April to mid-September. They are given a part of the seasonal earnings in advance, and the rest later. Yusuf did not discuss his diving arrangements with his father, Rauf.

After Yusuf had been diving off the boat for a while, Rauf's brother came to Rauf and said, "Yusuf is afraid of diving. Some days ago blood came from his nose; he doesn't want to go back with that boat when it goes to sea, but he is afraid to do anything about it. You have to do something."

Rauf found his son that afternoon and questioned him closely. Yusuf admitted that his nose had bled and that he didn't feel safe diving with that captain. Rauf asked his son if he owed that captain money.

"About 50 liras [$5]," said Yusuf.

The next day Rauf took his donkey and went to the village where the captain lived, a journey of about five hours. Finding him, he said, "How can you take my boy without my permission? I can put your two feet in one shoe" (a proverb expressing how much trouble he could make for him, if he wished).

Rauf then asked how much money Yusuf owed. The captain added up the advance he had given Yusuf and deducted the cost of Yusuf's food. He subtracted the sponges Yusuf had found and decided the debt was about 50 liras. Rauf paid him this amount, took Yusuf's blankets and mattresses, and returned home.

The Analysis: Yusuf did not approach his father directly to ask his intervention, but instead gave an account to his father's brother, who passed on the information. After obtaining the facts from Yusuf, Yusuf's father acted as a third party and went to see the captain. The father suggested he could cause much trouble for the captain, because the contract was made without his permission while his son was still living in his household and thus under his authority. The captain agreed to terminate the contract, and there was no disagreement concerning the debt between Yusuf and the captain. The father's intervention in this dispute, therefore, resolved it to the satisfaction of all.

I never found out if Yusuf was afraid of diving, or if there was trouble between the captain and Yusuf. A careful captain inspires confidence in his crew, and the blood from Yusuf's nose suggests that he was being asked to dive long periods without proper decompression.

As in the previous dyadic example, when a Turkish village man has a grievance against his employer, he may choose to terminate the relationship instead of pressing claims against a person who has more power.

In a second triadic example, a sixteen year old boy, Ismail, was going to Milas. Fatma, a village wife, heard of his trip and asked him to bring her a beautiful dress from a store there. She said she would pay him when he returned. He bought a metallic dress fabric, which at least four people saw. "Who is that dress for?" they asked. "Your mother?"

Ismail just laughed. "Can my mother wear that shiny thing?" (To villagers, the most beautiful material is metallic; such dresses are worn to weddings.)

Ismail gave the dress to Fatma and asked for his 70 lira ($7), but she said, "I'll pay you later." Whenever he asked her, she always said the same thing. Finally, he began to get annoyed. He went to her, saying, "I am going after sponges, can you give me my money now?" She thought a moment, then said, "Come to my house at night. I will put a big copper pot outside. You can take it and sell it. If you get more than 70 liras for it, give me what is left over."

Late that night, as Ismail was carrying the pot away from her house, a friend of his, another youth, saw him. Ismail said to him, "Come, let's hide this somewhere. Later we will sell it and divide the money." The youth helped him, but then went to Fatma's husband, Adnan, and told him how Ismail had taken his pot and where it was hidden.

Adnan went to the Mandalinci gendarme station with the story. In the evening, Adnan and a gendarme waited together near the pot. When Ismail came along to pick it up, the gendarme and Adnan surprised him. They took Adnan to the *nahiye* (subdistrict) gendarme station in the next village to question him and to make out a police report. This led to criminal proceedings against him for theft in the Bodrum court. (For a flow chart of how village disputes reach the courts, see Figure 1.)

Fatma was called to court as a witness. The judge asked her, "Do you owe any money to Ismail?"

"No," she said, "I have no debt to him."

The judge then asked Ismail if he had brought witnesses. "No," he replied, "but material such as her dress is made of cannot be found in the village. Such material is not even sold in Bodrum."

At another hearing, Ismail brought four people who had seen the material before he gave it to her. Each said, "We saw this material when he had it before he gave it to her, and in fact she is wearing that very dress in court today!"

When the judge turned to Fatma and asked her to take an oath that Ismail had not paid for this dress, she began to cry. The judge said, "Don't spill tears on your new dress."

Fatma asked that her pot be returned.

The judge said, "Pay the money you owe and you can have your pot back." After the court decision, Adnan paid Ismail 70 lira and took his wife's pot back to her.

FIGURE 1

Chain of Jurisdiction Pertaining to Civil and Criminal Cases

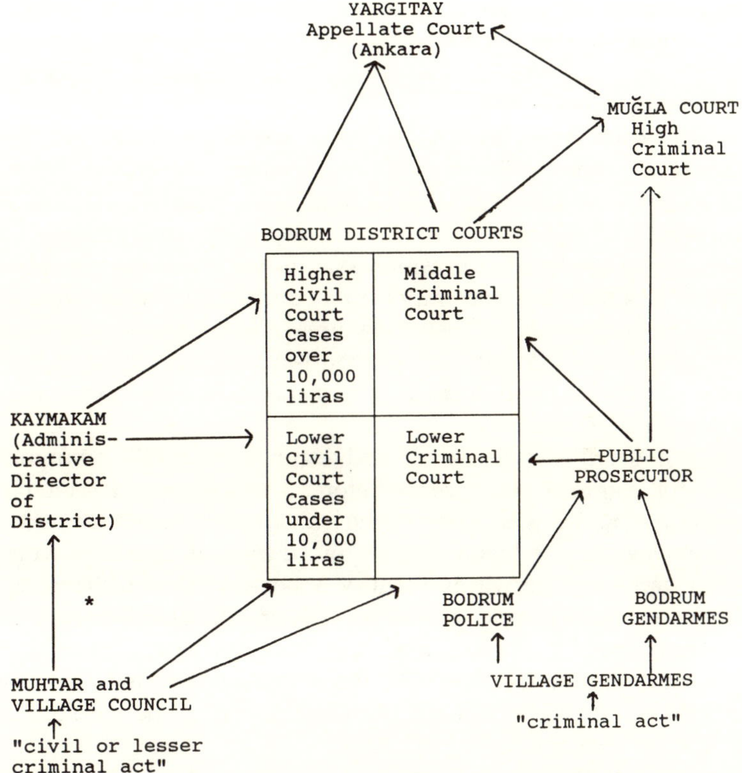

A case can be terminated at any level. Cases ordinarily do not go from lower civil or lower criminal court to the next higher courts, although occasionally an administrative error places a case in the wrong court. If so, the judge has it transferred.

* In other areas, the office of *nahiye müdürü* (subdistrict administrator) may play a role in communications between *muhtar* and *kaymakam*.

The Analysis: This case illustrates what happens when a youth is outmaneuvered in two-party negotiations. Ismail ought not to have accepted Fatma's arrangements concerning the pot for, intentional or not, the situation made him appear a thief. Again we find the disadvantage a minor has in successfully managing two-party negotiations with an adult. In retrospect, we see that Ismail made a series of imprudent choices: He accepted complicity with Fatma by agreeing to take the pot at night, and when discovered in the compromising position, he attempted to buy the youth's silence.

When Adnan learned of the theft, he went to the gendarme, knowing the outcome he wanted: a charge of theft uncomplicated by his wife's misconduct.

My early interviews with Fatma had revealed her undisguised interest in clothes and money. Court hearings established that Fatma did indeed have a new dress, which had been bought by Ismail. When Fatma refused to testify under oath whether she owed money for the dress, the judge decided in Ismail's favor and acquitted him. Here the authority of the judge was important in unraveling the facts in dispute.

The final example, illustrating three different types of negotiations, shows how a person may opt for a court-arbitrated decision as a way of terminating what has become a bothersome liaison. Four of the involved parties we have met earlier.

A married woman, Fatma, had begun an affair with an unmarried youth of eighteen some years before. The lovers met secretly, and although other villagers knew of the liaison, the husband seemed not to notice. One day the lover, Ahmet, forced himself on Fatma when she didn't want sex. Afterwards, Fatma sent her son to her husband, saying, "Come quickly, Ahmet is injuring me." Ahmet fled to his patron, Oktay, who hid Ahmet in a shed in his tangerine orchard. The same day a gendarme commander came to the village. Oktay felt that spiteful enemies of Ahmet would tell the commander of the incident, so he invited the commander to his house for a meal. During this hospitable occasion Oktay told the commander the problem, that Fatma was known as a loose woman, and that she and Ahmet had been lovers for over five years. The commander asked to interview Ahmet. He asked him if he were carrying any of her possessions. "Yes, some letters, a picture, and a small head scarf," said Ahmet. The commander then called her husband, showed these things to him and said, "How can you give this man to the court?"

Several years later Fatma's mother-in-law caught the lovers together. She made Fatma go with her to the village gendarme to report Ahmet, but after Ahmet explained the situation, the gendarme did not begin a case against him.

Years passed, Ahmet married and terminated his affair with Fatma. She was angry, but for a time did nothing. One day Ahmet and his wife, now noticeably pregnant, passed Fatma's house. Fatma began throwing stones at them, shouting, "How dare you walk past here?" Ahmet left immediately for the subdistrict gendarme station, located in a different village. There he reported the incident, saying, "I want to take her to court." The gendarme wrote an official document and attached her letters and head scarf to it. A court case was opened against Fatma by Ahmet for "insult and assault" and, within a day and a half, Fatma opened a countersuit against Ahmet and his wife for "insult." Fatma was found guilty and sentenced to one month in prison and 180 TL fine ($18). Ahmet and his wife were also found guilty and sentenced to one month in prison and 250 TL ($25) fine, but because it was their first offense, they were given suspended sentences. Fatma sent the judgment to appellate court, where it was upheld. She did not serve her prison sentence or pay a fine, however, because of the general amnesty granted after the national election in 1966.

The Analysis: Ahmet and Fatma were lovers for seven years. For much of that time others—Fatma's mother, mother-in-law, and children—knew of the liaison, so it can be assumed that Fatma's husband, Adnan, also knew, but chose to do nothing to reveal his knowledge until Fatma sent word that Ahmet was injuring her. Fatma's message made the liaison public, forcing her husband to take action. When Adnan met Ahmet on the road and glanced away, he was making an implicit statement of nonaggression toward Ahmet. Of course, he did not know all the facts yet.

Ahmet showed he knew that a serious event had happened, because he went to Oktay (who may not yet have become Ahmet's patron, but already was an influential villager) and asked for a hiding place. By hiding him, Oktay extended his protection, so that when the gendarme commander turned up in the village, Oktay found a way to involve the gendarme commander as third party in the dispute.

The commander demonstrated his talents at mediation when he asked for trophies that a lover might carry. These tokens of affection revealed the sexual liaison. It was clear to everyone that the husband's case would not stand up in court against a lover's tokens.

After Ahmet married, he attempted to terminate his liaison. Ahmet went to the subdistrict gendarme station instead of the village gendarme because of the previous record there of trouble between Fatma and himself. Since he meant to prosecute Fatma in court in order to inhibit her aggression, he needed to start procedures in a forum that would be ignorant of past difficulties. His change in marital status not only changed his relationship to Fatma, but meant that he needed to take a strong stand against her. Taking her to court signaled that he intended no further interaction with her. In this dispute, escalation to court was used to terminate social contact between the parties. Regardless of how the judge decided the case, thereafter their relationship would be characterized by avoidance.

Thus far I have presented some ethnographic data in the form of dispute cases and case interpretations to illustrate the pattern in two- and three-party negotiations. Now further analysis is possible.

Rank and Status Effects on Dispute Negotiations

Mandalinci villagers recognize divisions in the life cycle—for females; child, girl , woman, and old woman; for males; child, boy, youth, young man, and old man. Youths and girls tend to remain in their father's house and thus under his authority, except when males are away for wage labor or military service. A male and female gain adult status when they marry. Girls who marry at fifteen gain the status of woman, while males from poor families who remain unmarried even at twenty-eight or thirty are still considered youths. It is the goal of every male to marry and become head of his own household, and of every woman to marry and have children.

Status positions in rural Turkish society, arranged in ascending order of power according to village perceptions, are as follows:

Insiders to Village Social fabric:
- Household head
- Patron (i.e., large field owner)
- Entrepreneur

Outsiders to the Village Social fabric:
- Gendarme
- Minor Turkish officials and bureaucrats
- Important Turkish officials (i.e., judges, gendarme commanders)

These status positions are relevant to the disputing technique that an aggrieved person chooses (see Table 11). That choice relates to his or her status vis-à-vis his opponent's, and to the decision of whom to choose as mediator when third parties are brought into the process.

Table 11 summarizes disputes, episode by episode, occurring in Mandalinci in which claims were pressed in two- or three-party negotiations. Although these data are suggestive rather than conclusive, they illustrate patterns in village disputing processes.

Only three outcomes were unsatisfactory from the aggrieved's point of view. A man claimed another's dog had killed his chickens, but

TABLE 11

Out-of-Court Disputing Strategies
by Grievance, Status Relationships of Disputants, and Category of Disputes

Case No. Starr (1978a)	Aggrieved	Opponent	Grievance	Status Relationship	Disputing Technique	Outcome	Who Is Intermediary
Mandalinci Villager versus Mandalinci Villager							
13.	adult female	adult female	breaking contract	E–E	direct confrontation: public	S	
14.	adult male	his wife	adultery	H–L	direct confrontation: private	S	
17.*	two youths	adult male	sex with their woman	L–H	direct confrontation: private, beating	S	
17.	adult male	two youths	beating	H–L	public insult; later refusal to aid ill relative	S	
9.	youth	adult male	debt	L–H	terminates relationship	S?	
21.	youth	adult male	debt	L–H	direct confrontation: public	U	
21.	youth	adult male	debt	L–H	intermediary	S	household head: aggrieved youth's mother
22.	adult male	youth	adultery	H–L	public scene: later intermediary	S	household head: opposition's father
23.	adult woman	girl	taking job	H–L	intermediary	S	girl's mother, aggrieved's sister
28.*	youth	adult female	debt	L–H	direct confrontation	U	
28.*	adult male	youth	theft	H–L	gendarme, then court	S	
32.	youth	youth	unknown	E–E	direct confrontation: private fight	death	
29.*	adult female	youth	rape	lovers	tells husband	??	

continued on next page

TABLE 11 (Continued)

Out-of-Court Disputing Strategies
by Grievance, Status Relationships of Disputants, and Category of Disputes

Case No. Starr (1978a)	Aggrieved	Opponent	Grievance	Status Relationship	Disputing Technique	Outcome	Who Is Intermediary
29.	adult man	youth	rape of wife	H–L	intermediary who gets gendarme to mediate	??	opposition gets patron to act as supporter; the patron gets gendarme commander to mediate
Mandalinci Villager and Villagers Living in 25-Mile Radius							
4.	adult male	Mandalinci adult male	theft of vegetables from field	H–L	direct confrontation: private	S	
20.	youth	adult man, different village	risky boat Captain	L–H	intermediary	S	household head: aggrieved's father
Mandalinci Villager and Foreigners Resident in Village							
5.	adult male	foreign adult male	dog kills sheep	E–E	direct confrontation: private	S	
6.	adult male	foreign adult male	dog kills chickens	E–E	direct confrontation: private	U	

Key

H–L = Higher status aggrieved
L–H = Lower status aggrieved
E–E = Equivalent statuses (but both are low status in terms of village-wide ranking system)
S = Outcome satisfactory to aggrieved
U = Outcome unsatisfactory to aggrieved
* = When case has two phases (or remedies are attempted at different legal levels) it may be charted twice.

presented no evidence. The other two involved minors negotiating with adults: In one, the female household heads successfully pressed the claim later; in another, gendarme and criminal proceedings intervened before the facts clearly emerged (Starr 1978a: 134–37).

The negotiating pattern can be stated as follows: When disputants were of roughly equivalent rank, the aggrieved used two-party negotiation in a public or private setting. A private setting was chosen when the aggrieved hoped to keep his or her grievance and/or the negotiations secret, or to imply a willingness to resort to physical violence in order to force resolution. A public setting was used when the disputant wanted to appeal to widely shared community norms or to avoid physical violence, since others would intervene to separate disputants if violence seemed imminent. When the aggrieved had a higher rank than the adult opponent, he or she used direct confrontation in private, unless the satisfaction of the grievance under older village law-ways called for violent retaliation (as a response to the following offenses against household honor—molesting a married woman, adultery, rape). When the aggrieved was an adult and the opponent a minor, or if the grievance called for violence, the aggrieved invoked an intermediary. When the aggrieved was of a lower rank than the opponent, he or she might have used two-party negotiation, but with the expectation that it would be unsuccessful. If the aggrieved wanted restitution, an intermediary was needed. If all that could be hoped for was revenge, an aggrieved male might have beat up a male opponent, thus shaming him, since virility and manliness are considered essential components of male honor. Or he could have terminated the relationship, thus withdrawing friendship and support.

The purpose of using an intermediary could not have been the same for both a higher- and lower-ranking disputant. A higher-ranking person invoked an intermediary because it was undignified to dispute with a lower-ranking person. There was always the possibility for him to dispute directly, however, and then his higher rank became a factor.

There is only one example of a mediated dispute (Starr 1978a; 210),[7] and that involved an outsider coming to the village by chance. Here the gendarme commander had such high status and authority that he was a suitable person to impress on the husband how foolish he would appear in court.

The question of *enforcing* a solution is problematic in many societies, and ought to be considered as a separate issue from *seeking* solutions to grievances, especially since a disputant may change his mind about what constituted an acceptable solution. The cases presented here do, however, provide certain insight into enforcement, since it is apparent in Table 11 that a considerable number of aggrieved persons use public settings to press claims or make accusations. (The final resolution to the first case presented in this chapter was to force a public acknowledgment of theft).

In addition, a study of dispute and settlement needs to include ample documentation of how normal problems and grievances are routinely handled in everyday life, and how simple disputes are negotiated, if only to discover the cognitive dimensions of the community involved. More complex disputes may have more, and more *different*, stages and settings and, of course, cases of trouble in Llewellyn and Hoebel (1941:24–29) show how conflicting norms may be manipulated by a variety of principals and their supporters. In Mandalinci village the cases ranged from a broken contract, debt, insult, theft, adultery, and assault, to molesting a woman. Although lawyers might find trivial a dog's killing of a sheep or theft of chickens, from a villager's point of view all these incidents represented were challenges to male honor, and breaches that threatened social relations and public order.

Evidence presented in Table 11 suggests that intermediaries entered disputes where there was a status or rank inequality. Only one female entered disputes as an intermediary, and only household heads or patrons were within-village intermediaries.

The pattern of dispute negotiation in unstructured situations in Mandalinci can be summarized as follows:

1. Minors ought not act, or be acted against, in disputes (although they sometimes do and are),
2. Representatives tend to be used where there is a threat of impending violence,
3. Public confrontation is only appropriate between equals,
4. Individuals of higher status lose face in public confrontations,
5. Confrontation is the true forum of the powerless,
6. Islamic conflict resolution and Islamic notions of the good and the just solutions are nowhere in evidence,
7. Turkish secular law, Turkish legal maxims, Turkish civil or criminal codes, or Turkish concepts learned in court are never stated in presenting or arguing claims,
8. Patrons and household heads are the major informal mediators,
9. Gendarmes both mediated and created conflict, and
10. The village headman and the village council were not used to allay conflict, nor did they provide "policing" functions.

Disputes at Court

Court decisions were sanctioned by state law, and frequently involved the application of law and legal sanctions. Judicial styles of hearing and resolving cases involved mediation, adjudication (the latter being the prevailing form), and persuading litigants to drop cases.[8] Bringing disputes to court required a different mind set, for there was a pervasive legal culture at Bodrum courts that differed from the values and culture in the villages. In court a different set of social realities existed from those in the village, which continued to be embedded in age-old gender biases supported by Islam. In court, litigants were social equals. Adult women were as important as men and were guaranteed the same freedoms that men enjoyed. When a Turkish villager went to court, he shifted from the reality of village life, where social standing, reputation, social worth, gender, kin group, and one's past behavior all were evaluated, to a new arena in which much of his identity and possibly his past behavior could be concealed. There were new standards by which human worth was measured, new ways of conceptualizing appropriate behavior, and new directives for action. This not only involved making use of different legal documents, but also manipulating the reality of the social context. For example, judges did not accept testimony concerning witchcraft and other associated mystical beliefs, even though at times a villager tried to testify that "blowing on an egg" or leaving a "loaf of bread" at someone's door was relevant.

To take a case out of the village is a calculated risk for a villager. Yet villagers who continue a dispute at court will become knowledgeable about court procedures, what decisions to expect, and how to use the court to their advantage. (For chain of legal jurisdiction, see Fig. 1 and appendix II.) As Galanter (1974) has shown, litigants who are "repeat players" in court have a strategic advantage over first-time users because they have acquired knowledge of how to open and pursue a lawsuit, how judges reason and make decisions, what services lawyers give in exchange for their high fees, and what aspects of law can be used to help a litigant win. If an individual is an opportunist, going to court for the first time is a new learning process, a new arena in which to compete with his rivals and adversaries, and a new exercise of his political and diplomatic skills. Furthermore, following his own case through its many hearings and watching the procedures of court personnel and judges in the courthouse give a rural villager opportunity to see, hear, and learn the bureaucratic and ideological basis of the Turkish state. For some it is an intimidating and overwhelming experience, and they do not want to venture into the courtroom again. For others it opens up new vistas.

For instance, a leader of a Mandalinci village faction eventually pursued a dispute over an orchard against his brother through the appellate court in Ankara, where he attempted to use connections to gain information concerning the outcome of his case. (A fuller version of this case appears in Starr 1978a:223–46). The first principal in the dispute was Murat, a seventy year old man born and raised in Yugoslavia, who came to Turkey during the population exchanges and was given land in Mandalinci valley. It is his land that the aforementioned brothers at different times began converting to a tangerine orchard, and that became the focus of the dispute. The second principal we have met before: the Mandalinci entrepreneur Oktay. The tangerine orchard was essential to his power in the village, because it was his principal source of wealth. His rival in village politics owned two orchards. The third principal is Oktay's younger brother, Nebi, thirty-nine years of age, who was a day laborer in Bodrum town, but would move back to the village if he could establish his ownership of the orchard. The brothers are not related to Murat.

The dispute, which began about 1960, ranged over four years and included a number of lawsuits, which were as follows:

> Two major suits to gain land title were opened against Oktay. Murat's 1966 suit was decided in Oktay's favor because Murat only had a certified note signifying ownership, while Oktay had a title registered at the Land Registry Office; and Nebi's 1966 suit against both Oktay and Murat, which was decided in Oktay's favor at the Bodrum District Court and was sent to appellate Court by Nebi. A decision came two years later which upheld Oktay's ownership.
>
> Three major suits concerned debt. The first was Nebi's suit against Murat in 1964, at which time Murat gave all his possessions to Oktay so there would be nothing to collect from him, regardless of the court decision. Murat's suit against Nebi was filed in 1965, and his third suit came in 1967—against both Oktay *and* Murat—to recoup his losses of 36,000 TL (about $3,600). (The actual amount of the debt is questionable, although it would not be less than 15,773 TL, the amount of Nebi's earlier suit against Murat.)

A sixth lawsuit occurred because of a street fight after a court hearing in Bodrum in 1967 between Oktay, Nebi, and their wives, and was heard in criminal court. It was broken up only by the intervention of the Bodrum police, who (because the couples would not reconcile at the police station) opened a case for street-fighting against them in criminal court. These charges were dropped only after seven court hearings, and only then due to clever judicial strategy. In hearings the judge had been pushing for the litigants to say that they were reconciled. When they finally did so in the seventh hearing, on threat of everyone being sentenced to jail, the judge quickly dismissed the case.

The three principals and court records are in agreement over the following points:

1. The land prior to 1959 belonged exclusively to Murat.
2. In 1960 Murat sold (or gave two *dönüm* of his field to Nebi by certified note (*noter senedi*). Nebi may have established a tangerine orchard on these two *dönüm* prior to the certified note that established his ownership.
3. Oktay gave his younger son to Murat for legal adoption in 1964 as a way to give Murat an heir; this adoption was Oktay's way to gain control of the orchard.
4. At different periods Nebi and Oktay made exclusive arrangements with Murat: Nebi and Oktay each would provide the capital and managerial skills necessary to improve the orchard and produce tangerines; Murat would provide the field and sign notes on loans at the credit union.
5. In order to avoid paying debts to Nebi, Murat gave or sold land title for the orchard, excluding Nebi's two *dönüm*, to Oktay in 1965. (Oktay told me that Nebi's two *dönüm* were included in his agreement with Murat, but Oktay's lawyer's letter to the court does not mention Nebi's two *dönüm* in the title dispute, so we can assume that Nebi's rights to the two *dönüm* can be substantiated, and the lawyer could not find a legal ground to challenge it.)
6. Nebi's suit against Murat, his former partner, for 15,773.67 TL can be substantiated by receipts.

In dispute are:

1. The nature of Nebi's and Oktay's rights (ownership or usufruct) to the orchard.
2. Whether cash changed hands between Nebi and Murat, and between Oktay and Murat, for ownership rights, and if so, exactly how much.

3. How much Oktay and Nebi spent when managing the orchard and how much profit each made.

An additional pertinent aspect of this land dispute is that Murat's letter to the court and Nebi's receipts establish that Nebi paid out at least 15,775 TL while managing the orchard. The Claims Bureau established that Murat had no assets. Thus, Murat must have *given*, not sold, the orchard to Oktay. Otherwise, Murat would have had cash or new property. There was no mention of other debts to pay in addition to those to Nebi. Even if Nebi won his suit over debt against Murat, he would be unsatisfied, because Murat could not repay him, but winning the judgment was important to a further debt suit opened against Murat *and* Oktay. Then Nebi could claim that Oktay assumed ownership of the orchard when there were liens against the property, namely, Nebi's expenditures. Fickle Murat may have been willing to substantiate this, because his letter in Nebi's title suit against himself and Oktay indicated that Murat was now siding with Nebi against Oktay (all points in Murat's letter substantiate points in Nebi's letter).

The resolution that emerged: Oktay would keep title of the orchard, because his title (*tapu*) was established by the Appellate Court decision. Oktay lost the debt suit. The Bodrum judge required Oktay to pay some money to Nebi, because Murat owed Nebi money and probably gave the orchard to Oktay to avoid paying him.

A situation this complicated could not be resolved through current village methods of conflict management. The discontinuities between disputing processes in Turkish villages and disputing in court represent a situation of legal pluralism (i.e., two legal cultures existing within the same geographic area [see Collier 1973:42]). For example, "folk" notions of resolution of conflict are different from national legal culture as it is practiced in Bodrum's court. In court, a person with a dispute needs to comprehend the meanings of the legal vocabulary, and to recognize that different norms of evidence, proof, and remedies exist in courtroom practices. The gulf between ideas of what constitutes an adequate settlement in the village and in the court is so wide it conforms to our definition of legal pluralism.

Conclusion

Given the current growth of Islamic fundamentalism in Turkey, rural villagers in Bodrum in the mid-1960s were comparatively irreligious. In Mandalinci, rituals of death and mourning were Islamic, as was worship at the village mosque on Friday. Circumcisions were celebrated;

Ramadan food and drinking taboos were observed; and two men were called *Haci*—much earlier in their lives they had made the trip to Mecca. However, no one but the village *Imam* said his prayers five times a day; in fact, the call to prayer was not observed.

Islamic maxims and quotations of prescriptions of conduct from *Suras* of the *Kur'an* were not cited in village conflict resolution, as among some Islamic communities (see Bisharat 1989:40–41). But neither were prescriptions of secular law or references to the Turkish civil or criminal codes. In Mandalinci and other Bodrum villages, no one searched out Islamic sages to discuss an appropriate Islamic resolution to the dispute. Finally, no one considered it odd to take serious problems to the village-based gendarmes or to the district courts in Bodrum in an attempt to resolve the matter at hand or to seek revenge.

In resolving disputes outside of court, villagers used social networks, intermediaries, mediators, or self-help. Although pithy Islamic sayings or quotations from the *Kur'an* were not offered, age-old Middle Eastern patterns of clientism, patronage, and social networks did play a major role in allaying conflict. The marked secular nature of conflict resolution in Mandalinci and other of Bodrum's villages, considered in light of the increasing value of land and produce as marketable commodities, and the increasing economic development of the Bodrum region may explain in great part the willingness of villagers to accept secular, nation-state law.

The pragmatism of the villagers meant they were willing to use district courts when serious problems occurred. The lack of Islamic sentiments in Bodrum's villages and town during the period of study account for the visibility of secular courts and law enforcement agencies. At that time and in that place, no open, or clandestine, movement existed with the expressed goal of returning local people to Islamic justice and Islamic solutions to conflict.

Notes

1. The village was representative of all tangerine-growing villages in the area. Its population of approximately 1,000 fell between the smallest village, at 219 people, and the largest, at 2,000 people. Because the village was at considerable distance from the district courts (over dirt roads and a mountain), I surmised that village methods of managing conflict probably existed. Local transportation to the district courts (for the villagers) involved traveling over bumping, dirt roads in a four-wheel-drive jeep on a trip of about four hours, and costing a day's wages. For further discussion of "representativeness," see Starr (1981:598–603). For more information on conflict resolution in this village,

see Starr (1978a, 1978b; 1980; 1984). For a summary of the case method in the study of law, see Epstein (1967) and Nader and Todd (1978). For a discussion of how "interests" affect disputes, see Starr and Yngvesson (1975).

2. A dispute is defined as occurring in a social relationship between two or more persons in which one or more parties decides to stress the conflict in the relationship (Abel 1974:226, 227, 246). A disputant may press claims, seek revenge, or decide to bide his time and wait. I use the term *law* to refer to codified law, legislative law, administrative law, and law decided by judges in court decisions. The term *legal* is used in a broader sense, as in a *legal field*. A legal field is defined by the researcher as a focus of study. It may or may not be recognized as such by an informant. At the minimum, in this book a legal field is any situation in which a claim is pressed. See Moore (1973) for a discussion of how norms are generated in semi-autonomous fields.

3. See (Shaw 1971) and Lewis (1965:378–79) for descriptions of the decline of the Ottoman Empire's administrative control of the provinces in the seventeenth and eighteenth centuries.

4. All *Imam* were trained in government schools and appointed through government channels. They were not instructed in conflict-resolving methods, in part because the government did not wish to create alternative Islamic forums which would compete with existing secular models of conflict resolution: at the village level the headmen and council; at the district level the courts and the district director and his committee.

5. For definition of a legal field, see ft. 2, this chapter. See also Moore (1973) for a theoretical development of the concept.

6. A number of researchers have studied and provided the theoretical framework for analyzing social situations. The most important for this analysis are Garbett (1973), Garfinkel (1967), Gluckman (1961), Goffman (1961), Boissevain (1968), Schutz (1967), Turner (1957), and Van Velsen (1967).

7. This case was analyzed earlier in this chapter.

8. Following Fuller (1963:24–25, ft. 20) *adjudication* is defined as a style of decision-making in which the affected party must present "proofs and reasoned arguments" according to written law of the province or nation-state in courts of law.

CHAPTER SEVEN

JUDICIAL DECISION-MAKING IN DISTRICT COURTS

In the 1960s and 1970s, close to 70 percent of the Turkish population lived in small villages and rural towns. This meant that over half of the citizens who took disputes to courts went to rural district courts in county seats, like Bodrum. The problem created between villagers' notions of custom and national law was early recognized by national reformers, for Article I of the *Turkish Civil Code* (*Türk Kanunu Medenîsi* 1926) states:

> The law must be applied in all cases which come within the letter or spirit of any of its provisions. Where no provisions are applicable, the judge should decide according to existing customary law and in default thereof, according to the rules which he would lay down if he had himself to act as legislator. In this he must be guided by approved legal doctrine and case law.

Thus, the Turkish Civil code clarifies the relationship between village customary practices and state law. First, when statutes pertain to a situation, they should govern. Second, when statutes or legislation do not cover the issues, judges should use customary practices, which can be discovered by consulting knowledgeable villagers. And third, if custom is vague or nonexistent, the judge should decide the case himself according to case law (compare Guriz 1987:34). Legal training and apprenticeship with experienced judges teach fledging judges how to reach decisions in indeterminate areas. (Güriz 1987:3–4). And, in addition to their legal training, judges have developed methods that allow them to move a case through sequential stages towards a disposition. This chapter focuses on that process.

Turkish judges organize, shape, and build up a series of facts, information, and evidence by inferential processes. Their method inheres in the Turkish legal process and is not readily apparent to an outsider. However, because the method has a structure of its own, an observer who records hearings can, over time, build up an empirical collection of observed cases for later analysis. What I observed for over a year and a half was an integrated state legal system at the district level, functioning compassionately and effectively within a well-developed and articulated set of legal principles and guidelines.[1]

John Gumperz has posed and solved the riddle of inferential processes in sociolinguistic analysis. He suggests that "seen from the perspective of individual disciples, analyzing inferential processes presents what must seem like insurmountable problems." Yet pointing to "certain dialogic properties" that conversational exchanges have, he notes "these differ from other sentences and written texts." This allows us to "avoid, or at least bypass, some difficulties involved in the study of isolated messages" (1982a:5).

In recent decades progress has been made in the study of legal processes and of language use in law, as sociolegal researchers bring empirical methods of study to the observation and analysis of courtroom processes.[2] At the same time, empirical progress has been made in studying many courts in diverse countries. No longer do researchers assume that judges in common law and civil law systems use the same methods of hearing cases and of assessing evidence. No longer do researchers assume that precedent plays the same role, or that witnesses' testimony (as truthful or lying) is evaluated by the same standards in courts within the same country, region, or jurisdiction.

Empirically oriented researchers assume that judges exercise a degree of autonomy and discretion within their courtrooms and that they utilize a variety of legal norms and customary practices for deciding who is out of order and who can speak, on which topics, and at which times. My research supports those scholars who claim that the process of judicial decision-making needs to be studied empirically, that it cannot be inferred from the court docket or from the rules governing testimony and evidence.

The renewed interest in courtroom studies parallels the interest in contextualized meanings in the humanities, in literary criticism, in philosophy, in law, and in cultural anthropology. Some scholars concentrate on unloading hidden structures and implicit assumptions underlying written texts. Others focus on deconstructing grafted ideas thrust into the center of supposedly new theory.[3] Paralleling this interdisciplinary focus on textual analysis is an interdisciplinary interest in meaning and structure in conversational exchanges. Sociologists, sociolinguists, philosophers, and anthropologists have made striking advances in conceptualizing patterns of meanings, which can be unveiled through discourse analysis or conversational analysis[4] to reveal hidden dimensions of coercion and ways of speaking that suggest one hearer doubts the truth of the other's statements.

Most of these studies were conducted in common law countries; therefore, how truth and lying are determined by judicial inquiry in a civil law country adds to our cultural understanding. The Bodrum courts have been governed by the civil law tradition since 1926, when Ataturk adopted the Swiss civil code and the Italian penal code to govern civil and criminal law respectively (see chapter 1).

The first theme addressed in this chapter is how judges determine whether a witness is truthful or deceitful.[5] The cultural norms by which a social group or a society determines this, and the intuitive or relatively conscious methods by which narrative accounts are classified as honest or lying, is too large a topic to be undertaken in this exploratory analysis. Several areas, however, are available for study; linguistic exchanges between a judge and litigants or witnesses; the methods Turkish judges use to determine the validity or falsity of statements; the supporting testimony or documents judges call for, which can then be used to support or deny assertions made by a principal or witnesses, etc. My point of view is that of an informed anthropological observer of the court. I am less interested in what "standards of evidence" or "rules of law" are taught in Turkish law schools than in how Turkish judges perform in practice.

The second theme, an analysis of judicial decision-making, emerges from the examination of how judges move a case from the fact-finding stage to the decision stage. This involves a process of evaluating evidence and determining whether a witness is lying or truthful. Decided cases may not resolve the problem or grievances that brought the litigants to court, and a "decided case" does not necessarily mean the "end of grievances" (see Abel 1974; Nader and Todd 1978; Starr 1978a:269). But in addition to the litigants' *multiple* points of view (they may never agree on the facts in dispute or the optimal outcome), there are other ways to study courts. When courts are studied as organizations, when judicial decision-making techniques are scrutinized, or when a court case load is the analytic universe, then techniques judges use "to reach a closure on the matters at hand" become relevant.

Common Law and Civil Law Systems Compared, with Special Reference to Turkey

The adversary system of justice is the structural model of law court practices found in the common law countries of the United States, Great Britain, their colonies, and newly independent colonies. The civil law system is found in European countries: Belgium, the Netherlands, France, Germany, Italy, Spain, Portugal, Greece and Turkey (which considers itself a European country). It is also found in many of the ex-colonies of Europe, including much of Latin America. The European civil law tradition has a long history, stretching back to *jus commune*, associated in many minds with the Holy Roman Empire. That association is incorrect, however, for the emergence of modern nation-states in Europe destroyed much of this legal unity. The law of the *jus commune* was formally "received" in parts of Germany, but in parts of Europe where Roman law was not formally received, the process of building a national law took place under conditions and the assumption that *the legislative act* was subject to no other authority, either temporal or spiritual. Furthermore, legislative acts were not subject to any limitations from within the state, such as local or customary law (Merryman 1985:20).

The common law tradition developed from the Magna Carta, the great charter of English liberties delivered by King John at Runnymede on June 19, 1215. The common law is thought to be more evolutionary in character than civil law, without direct breaks in its form and substance (p. 21).

When Ataturk set aside over six centuries of Islamic family law in Turkey, he and his legal advisors looked to Europe for new legal models, adopting the law they knew, the Swiss civil code, to govern family law. The criminal code had been reformed in the latter half of the nineteenth century, also based on "received" European models. Ataturk introduced a new penal code to define criminal acts in republican Turkey, based on the Italian penal code. The Italian criminal code had recently been "received" in Italy from Germany. Earlier in the twentieth century, new Turkish administrative law had been introduced, based on French models. Under this code the modern Turkish Republic had been divided into sixty-seven provinces, administrative towns, and villages, with law enforcement in the countryside under the control of gendarmerie.

Under common law, the prosecution and defense are said to be involved in a legal battle in which each side vigorously presents evidence supporting its position.[6] A plaintiff or defendant in a criminal case may allow the judge to decide the case or may request a jury trial. When a jury has been assembled, the jurors sit passively listening; they can neither ask questions nor conduct investigations on their own. Testimony is taken in shorthand on special, silent typewriters by a court recorder, and later transcribed into a verbatim transcript of the trial. When the jury is deciding the case, they may call for parts of the written record in order to review testimony, but they are not given the entire recorded case to review. In adversarial procedures, the judge's role is to listen and decide on points of law. A judge does not actively question witnesses, plaintiffs, and defendants, but a judge does instruct the jury as to the legal grounds on which to make findings of fact.

In common law processes, lawyers actively coach witnesses beforehand, and in trials they lend support to those witnesses they have called to give evidence for their side and aggressively cross-examine witnesses for the opposition. In criminal cases, the district attorney has been active in conjunction with the police in developing the evidence in the case and deciding the legal grounds for prosecution. In courtroom practices, he or she plays the major role in presenting the case and in examining and cross-examining witnesses and the defendant. In criminal cases, the crime victim is not considered a plaintiff, but a "complaining" witness. The state is the plaintiff against the alleged offender.

Turkish law does not recognize trial by jury, and in other civil law countries, juries are rarely used (Merryman 1985:131). Under civil law processes, lawyers assume more passive roles, and the judge (or judges) is more active in developing the case and in assessing evidence. It is the judge, not a lawyer, who questions all witnesses. Cross-examination by lawyers is not allowed. In the Bodrum courts, when a lawyer wants to question a witness, he or she has to suggest the question to the judge. The judge then decides whether to ask that question or not, and sometimes substitutes his or her own words or inverts the order of the questions.

In theory, witnesses under civil law are not for the prosecution or for the defense, but appear on behalf of the court. Because a judge examines them (not a lawyer favorably disposed toward one party or the other), coaching is less helpful, for it is harder to predict the direction judicial questioning will take. Witnesses who live in a different region or expert witnesses may send written testimony. An expert witness (such as a committee of doctors deciding if a wound will leave a scar), sometimes will give testimony before a judge in a court where the witness resides. As with all types of testimony taken in a different locale, the transcript is signed and mailed to the trial court, hearing the case.

Usually witnesses are not given an oath of honesty, as is the custom in the adversary model. I saw only three witnesses sworn, all of whom were very old. The judge used the *Kur'an* in two instances. The *Sergeant d'Arms* was sent to find a *Kur'an* while the court waited. Then an old person was asked to place his right hand on the sacred text and repeat a simple oath of honesty that the judge made up that he promised to tell the truth. The *Kur'an* was used in two cases. In the third, a loaf of bread, a sacred symbol in Islam, was the ritual object. (Witnesses in

Islamic courts do not take oaths of honesty. This use of sacred Islamic symbols and the oath itself perplexed me, and after that day's session, I spoke with the judge who said, "These people are old. They still believe in the efficacy of symbols, and in each instance, the witness's truthful testimony would be a decisive factor in disposing of the case." Thus, the judge creatively exercised his prerogatives, granted under Article I of the *Turkish Civil Code*.

In a Turkish trial a judge asks a series of questions and, when satisfied with the answers, summarizes the testimony and dictates it to the court recorder. Sometimes, during dictation, a judge checks with a witness to verify the accuracy of the summary. After the judge finishes dictating the witness's testimony, the witness is required to sign it. If he or she does not know how to write, a thumbprint is placed on the document. Thus, an "official" record of a court hearing was compiled. In the Bodrum courts, regular (non-silent) Remington typewriters were used, adding staccato pounding to courtroom noise.

A high point of a common law criminal trial occurs when the defendant is cross-examined by the prosecution. Other high points are the impassioned closing statements by lawyers, and the announcement of a verdict by a jury or judge. In a Turkish trial, the defendant has given his account several times, first with the public prosecutor, then in the first hearing. What the defendant or his or her lawyer says before decision and sentencing does not come as a surprise. Closing statements in Turkey by a defense lawyer and by the public prosecutor are not impassioned speeches. A lawyer and the prosecutor address one or more judges. All share the same legal training, and legally sophisticated judges are less moved by passion and rhetoric. With only two law faculties in Turkey at the time of my research (1967–68), one at the University of Istanbul, the other at Ankara,[7] almost all judges and public prosecutors knew each other and formed social networks. (Today six law faculties exist in Turkey. They are located at Istanbul University, Ankara University, and four created by the new Education Law of 1983, the University of Marmara, the University of the Aegean in Izmir, at Konya, and at Dilçe University in Diyarbakır.)

When juries are assembled in common law countries, the trial is heard on consecutive days, because assembling a jury is expensive. While reaching a verdict, a jury is sometimes sequestered and kept from exposure to pressure from friends, neighbors, and biases expressed by media coverage. Juries are not used in Turkey, and so cases are heard discontinuously, except for cases that threatened public safety (e.g. possessing dynamite, firing a gun in an inhabited area, street fighting etc.).

In rural Turkey, the principals in a case need be present in court or represented by an attorney on the day of the decision and sentencing. The decision cannot be mailed to them.

Courtroom researchers have described the model of the civil law trial as a gradual "unfolding" of the evidence toward decision (Thibaut and Walker 1975), or as building the case in a "step-like" fashion (Caesar-Wolf 1984:220). In contrast to these "unfolding" or "building-block" models, the common law model is full of high points and suspense: the movement toward the cross-examination of the defendant, the impassioned defense lawyer's final statements, the prosecutor's last remarks, and the wait for the jury's verdict. Common law jury trials are focused, oral, and full of dramatic moments. Civil law trials in Turkey are marked by discontinuous hearings, less oral testimony (with more written documents submitted), and these trials are less dramatic.

The crucial comparison between the two systems is, however, whether one system discovers the truth better than the other. Because the judge in the civil law system performs both the role of fact-finding and of judging, Mirjan Damaska (1975:1098) argues that too little protection is given to the rights of the defendant. He suggests that the structure of the common law tradition, in theory and often in practice, allows the defendant to be aggressively defended, and that this acts to counterbalance jury and/or judicial bias.[8] But John Merryman, a long-time observer of both systems, disagrees with Damaska's criticisms of civil law processes and suggests that the debate about which system is fairer to the accused is "clouded by ignorance of the law and practice in civil law nations and by preconceptions that are difficult to dispel" (1985:132). An anonymous comparative law scholar who has made extensive study of both systems once remarked (as quoted in Merryman): "If he were innocent, he would prefer to be tried by a Civil Law court, but if he were guilty, he would prefer to be tried by a Common Law court." Merryman, in fact, explicitly states that "criminal proceedings in the Civil Law world are more likely to distinguish accurately between the guilty and the innocent. . . ." (1985:132).

Beatrice Caesar-Wolf studied civil law litigation after a traffic accident in a West German court. By analyzing verbatim transcripts, she demonstrated that the judicial technique of controlling the sequence of question/answer responses is crucial to understanding how decisions are generated. A German judge reached a decision in a step-like manner "by gradually narrowing down the range of alternative readings of the case, until a final 'indivisible' reading emerged" (1984:220). In regard to truth-telling and lying, she noted that judges needed to establish consistency and achieved this by building a coherent narrative in the written record of courtroom proceedings.

Turkish Judges

In producing a final decision for each case in "situations of uncertainty," the judge is constrained by the knowledge that his opinion may be subject to the scrutiny of the appellate court, for the loser can have the case sent there on appeal. In civil cases, the plaintiff or defendant can have the case forwarded to the *Yargıtay* appellate court in Ankara. In criminal cases, the plaintiff, defendant, or public prosecutor might send the decided case to the same appellate court (the *Yargıtay*) for review. Once a year members of the legal hierarchy come to Bodrum (they spent ten days there in 1967), examining the case records and looking over decisions. Knowledge that his decisions are subject to scrutiny and review act as one type of constraint on a judge.

In the 1960s, as well as now, a second constraint on Turkish judges was their membership in the Turkish elite. Only 5 percent of the Turkish population received a college education then, and merely being a judge accorded high status, comparable to that of a federal or Supreme Court justice in the United States. High status and salary made judges less likely to succumb to bribery.

A third constraint is that, unlike judges in the United States who are either elected or appointed, in Turkey all judges are career civil servants. Posted first to rural areas, if they do well they are moved in three or four years time to courts in metropolitan centers. As a member of the urban elite, a judge's goal is to be posted to the most cosmopolitan Turkish cities; Istanbul, Ankara, or Izmir. Too many cases sent on appeal, too many cases overturned by the appellate court, and the record against the judge will not allow him to obtain a secure urban post for his later years. Thus, a Turkish judge is always aware of constraints on his discretionary powers.

Article I of the *Turkish Civil Code* (*Türk Mendenî Kanunu*) instructs Turkish judges about deciding cases. First, the "law must be applied in all cases which come within the letter or spirit of any of its provisions" (*Türk Mendenî Kanunu Şerhi* 1967:9). Second, when the law is unclear, the judge should decide according to existing local practices. And if both things fail, third, he should decide as if he himself had to act as legislator, but he needs to be "guided by approved legal doctrine and case law" (p. 3). Unlike the law passed by the Turkish assembly, a ruling that a Turkish judge has laid down as a lawmaker is binding solely for the concerned case.

Analysis of numerous judicial decisions suggest three findings concerning Turkish trial judge practices. First, Turkish judges look for legal norms by which to decide a case. Second, when no overriding legal norm is present and both parties are at fault, Turkish district court judges attempt to reconcile the parties, thus allowing the parties to accept a decision of "case dropped." Third, a judge looks for weak legal arguments rather than strong ones. When one party has presented a clearly weaker argument, the case may be dismissed or decided in the favor of the other. Thus, cultural ideas about the construction of legal arguments and about purposeful action enter into the judicial decision-making process.

The cases examined below demonstrate that situations of conflict generate at least two accounts of the events. In deciding these cases, a Turkish judge validated one version and disregarded or discredited the other. Like judges everywhere, Turkish judges know that multiple interpretations of social action occur. Badly presented evidence, falsified evidence, information obtained through threat or duress, all tend to weaken a case.

The Courtroom Setting

In Bodrum, the court held sessions Monday through Thursday, and on Friday a judge, court recorder, and surveyor went to visit the site of crimes, disputed houses, and disputed land. This was called the *keşif* (literally, "the viewing"). Court began in the mornings about 9:00, and lawyers who wanted to discuss a case would see a judge in his chambers after court was over (12:00 or 12:30 p.m.). When too many cases piled up and mornings did not allow enough time, afternoon sessions would be scheduled.[9]

In all trial courts language is an important means of obtaining evidence. In the four rural Turkish courts I studied, "courtroom talk" was the means by which "facts" were presented, clarified, and later accepted or rejected. Conversational exchanges between the judge and each litigant in turn, and later between the judge and each witness, provided the major conduit through which the judge learned about the case. As in courtrooms everywhere, there were explicit written rules governing what would qualify as evidence and how evidence should be elicited and, as elsewhere, there were unwritten, customary procedures that governed the everyday workings of the court and its personnel, which made each court unique (Nader 1965a:16).

Unwritten customs included the court page telling all persons in the courtroom to rise when the judge or public prosecutor entered, witnesses standing directly in front of the judge's bench to give testimony, the plaintiff placed on the judge's right and giving the first testimony, the defendant placed to the judge's left and testifying second, small tables and chairs near the plaintiff and the defendant for their attorneys to sit on, and the prevention of people in the courtroom from crossing their legs when seated by the court page.

How Cases Reach a Courtroom

A case is defined as an item, with a reference number and a case-type title, and is listed in the court docket.[10] It also contains names of the parties, what action has been taken, case disposition,[11] fines, jail sentences, and whether or not the case has been sent on appeal. Two or more cases, centering on different issues, may occur between the same parties in the same time period or sequentially.

A civil case commences with a letter from the plaintiff to the court. A court appearance is scheduled by the judge and written on the court calendar which he maintains. A criminal case begins with a police or a gendarme report to the public prosecutor. The public prosecutor is required to interview all parties to the dispute to decide if there are legal grounds for a case, and what charges are to be brought against the defendant. The public prosecutor interviews a defendant in private, but a record of this conversation has to be dictated by him into the record. If he thinks a case should be brought to trial, he schedules a court appearance and sends official word to the defendant.

Both civil and criminal cases have at least three hearings. In the first hearing, the plaintiff (or in criminal cases the complaining witness) states his position, and the other party tells his. Each is asked by the judge if they wish the court to call witnesses. Names of witnesses are then recorded in the dossier. The witnesses are witnesses for the state, not for the plaintiff or for the defense, although the party on whose behalf they are testifying is required to pay the costs of their transportation. The first hearing establishes the nature of the grievances and who the witnesses are. If all witnesses come to the second hearing and testify, the decision is announced in the third court hearing. But when a witness, a report, or a paper from another bureau has failed to arrive on time, the case is postponed, usually for three weeks. Discontinuous hearings of a case in turn affect the court calendar. As many as twenty cases can be scheduled for a morning's session, and frequently witnesses will fail to appear. Thus the judge might call and reschedule between eight to twenty cases. The Bodrum town court almost never had afternoon sessions. Only cases that were considered a threat to public safety in Bodrum town were heard continuously. Even simple cases, such as one involving an uncomplicated issue where the facts were not in dispute, might take up to six months to reach a decision.

Analysis of Data

For purposes of this analysis decided cases, collected in the Turkish courtroom, have been sorted into three categories. *Type A* cases are those decided on legal grounds. For example, a law has been broken, a legal title (*tapu*) of ownership exists, or a policeman has witnessed a car accident. Statements by officials and/or the existence of legal documents allow a judge to analyze the case in terms of legal norms or according to clearly set, legal guidelines to produce a "legal decision" that others in the law court hierarchy and the legal profession would recognize.

Type B cases are those in which no legal norm is clearly applicable, or Turkish judges assume that the application of legal norms will create harsher consequences than the grievance or crime that brought the parties to court. Such cases include situations in which neighbors have argued, husbands have beaten wives, adult children have been disrespectful to aging parents, or an ex-lover has become angry or threatening. In these conflicts, the Bodrum judges do not produce a legal outcome, for that would mean a neighbor, husband, daughter, son, or ex-lover would be sentenced to jail, creating more resentment in the relationship rather than healing it. I call these *social relationship cases*, as opposed to the legal dispositions of Type A cases.[12]

Type C cases are routine, nondisputational cases in which court approval is required by law (e.g., examining the accounts of an orphan, certifying guardianship, or allowing the recorded sex or age of a person to be changed on a birth certificate). Cross-cultural research on courts has established that "official" courts everywhere engage in routine work which may take up between 15 to 25 percent of their courtroom time (see Abel 1979b; Engel 1978; Friedman and Percival 1976).

Judicial Decision-Making

To demonstrate how judges reach decisions, it is necessary to know how a case is built up and what gets into the dossier. The two cases that follow show how a judge controlled the topic of discussion, elicited information, checked understandings, compared competing versions of events, and checked accuracy and truthfulness of witnesses and litigants. The first case illustrates a legal disposition, the second a social relationship decision.

The first case began with a letter from the director of the grade school (*ılk okula*) in Bodrum to the public prosecutor's office (in the mid-

1960s this office was two adjoining rooms in the Bodrum courthouse). The letter, dated December 30, 1966, stated: "Mehmet O. is not sending his daughter to school. I want you to prosecute him with the Education Law 222, paragraphs 56–58."

On January 2, 1967, the prosecutor sent a letter to the Bodrum police, instructing them to bring Mehmet O. to his office for a pretrial hearing, which is a necessary precursor to a criminal trial. The public prosecutor was required to determine if there were legal grounds for prosecution and enough evidence to proceed to court.

On January 4, 1967, the police sent a letter to the Bodrum Census Office that asked the daughter's age. (Children are required to attend school until the age of sixteen.) Police brought the father to the prosecutor's office for pre-trial questioning on this date. At no time in the case did the defendant use a lawyer. What the defendant said to the prosecutor was written down by one of the court recorders and became a permanent part of the case dossier: "My daughter's name is Emine. She is studying in the *Ataturk ılk okula* in the fourth grade. I have wanted her to attend school, but she doesn't want to go. So she does not go. I have to go to work. I cannot be watching her all day. The Bureau of Education wrote me about her. I don't have anything more to add to this statement."

The public prosecutor sent a memo to the judge asking him to open criminal proceedings against the defendant. The defendant was charged with violation of the compulsory school attendance law. The memo noted that "he has twice paid a fine to the school (this money goes to a government office), but he continues to do the same thing."

The first court hearing was also held on January 4, 1967. In this hearing, the following dialogue took place:

Defendant: "I have eight children. I am very poor. I have to work every day just to get money for bread. She doesn't want to go to school. A few times I took her to school, but she left and returned home again. I asked her, 'Why don't you want to go?' She said, 'For seven years I have gone to school, but I do not learn anything. I want to work.' Yes, it's true the school has fined me a few times because of her non-attendance."

Judge: "We need to hear the girl's testimony. The case is postponed until she can be brought to court."

The judge scheduled a special afternoon session to which the defendant brought his daughter. Thus, the second court hearing occurred:

Judge: "How old are you? What is your name?"
Girl: "Emine O. I'm fourteen years old."
Judge: "Will you be a witness or not?"
Girl: "Yes, I'll be a witness. I have gone to the Bodrum Ataturk fourth grade class for three years. We have six brothers and sisters in my family. In the tobacco season, my father goes to Mumcular to work in the tobacco fields, and we go there together. That is the reason I am still in the same class. [Tobacco planting in the Bodrum region begins in March.] Now I will not go to school. My father took me two times to the school door, but I ran away. He didn't keep me from school."

The judge decided to hear the school director as witness and postponed the case until he could be summoned to court. The third hearing was January 18, 1967, with the school director as a witness stating:

"His daughter ought to be in the fourth grade class in our school. Because she didn't come to school, I asked her father to see me. He came and said, 'I am very poor. I can't buy her dresses or books.' I told him, 'Send your daughter to me. We will buy those things for her.' And we did buy her a dress and the books she needed. But her father didn't send her again, and I am obligated to follow the law. He didn't bring her to school by her hand, and he didn't do anything to help her finish her studies."

The judge asked the defendant what he had to say to this testimony. He answered that the testimony should not count. In this same hearing, the judge reached a decision, which in part read:

"He told us, 'I took her to school myself,' and she also said the same thing. He said, 'I am not at fault.' But the school director's testimony and the papers in the dossier proved to us that this man is not speaking the truth. With Law 222 and with the Laws 56 and 58 we will give this man ten days in prison. With the Law 647, paragraph 4, we can change this imprisonment to money. For each day five liras will be paid; ten days in prison thus equals 50 TL. Every week he must pay ten Turkish liras. If he doesn't pay every week, we will take him immediately off to jail. Instead of going to jail, he can pay money; for each day in jail he must pay 10 TL."

A male field hand earns 10 TL a day, a woman 7 TL. 10 TL was about a dollar in 1967; it purchased two loaves of bakery bread.

On March 3, 1967, the prosecutor wrote to the Bodrum police; "this man hasn't paid his weekly fine. Send him to me immediately." The police sent him the same day, and he was fined an extra 50 TL.

The Analysis: The testimony established that the girl was not attending school. A note from the Records Office stated that she was a minor and, therefore, school attendance was obligatory. The judge found the father guilty of breaking the law that required school attendance for minors, and in an attempt to treat the defendant and his daughter in a humane way, the judge heard their testimony. The daughter asserted that she has refused to go to school and that her father could not compel her to attend. Her reason was that she was doing so badly. According to her, she would rather work.

To evaluate the girl's testimony, the judge had two sets of "evidence" available: his knowledge of local norms and customs, such as the power structure in local Turkish households and the inequality in age and gender relationships; and the school director's testimony (remember that the latter initiated the criminal proceedings). The testimony of the school director made clear that the school had taken an interest in this girl, even providing her with a dress and schoolbooks. He also explained that the father had twice been fined by the school for not ensuring that his daughter complied with the school attendance law. Now the director was seeking legal remedies in accordance with national law.

The judge, familiar with local values, knew that education was considered by rural villagers to be more important for males than females. He knew, too, that poor families counted on children's wages to supplement household earnings.

What the judge may not have known were local attitudes toward tobacco agriculture. In the villages where tobacco is grown as a major cash crop, women and children are the most desirable workers—not only because they are a more docile and less expensive workforce, but also because the fingers of children and adolescent girls are the most nimble. Nimble fingers are useful in quickly planting and transplanting seedlings. Later in the season, children and adolescent girls are again important laborers in the daily picking of the tender, young leaves, and stringing them for airing and drying.

The judge gave more weight to the school director's testimony than to the father's or daughter's because they were interested parties. The judge shared with the school director an interest in promoting the

Ataturkian vision of the new Turkish nation—that everyone, including females, ought to be educated. He realized that a poor man would view his daughter's wages as an added source of income and would be more interested in money than human potential.

A written record supported the school director's contention that the father was at fault for not sending his daughter to school. Furthermore, the judge could discount the daughter's testimony that she had free choice in this matter. In the Bodrum region everyone knows the importance of paternal authority in a household. A father could compel a daughter to go to school or to lie on his behalf. More generally, in the Bodrum region everyone expects kin to elaborate the truth, or not to tell what they know about kinfolk, or to actually lie on behalf of kin who are in dispute with more distant kin, with strangers, or with Turkish authorities.[13]

The judge and local people also knew that officials could be bribed or corrupted, but the defendant did not build his defense by asserting that the school director had a grudge against him. His case was based on suggesting that he could not control his daughter's actions and on her testimony that she chose not to go to school. The school director undermined this version when he stated, "We gave her a dress and books," a statement never denied by the father. In fact, all the father did when asked to respond to this testimony was to say he did not want those words in the record. This is the weakest response any defendant can make. It appears regularly in the dossiers of legally unsophisticated defendants, just before the judge gives a decision.

A function of the law court in Bodrum was to establish the hierarchical order of values. By finding the father guilty of breaking the law of compulsory education, the judge was enforcing the Turkish Republic's value of female education against the value of the subordination of females. This is one of a number of cases in which the court opposed male arbitrariness to establish and preserve rights of females and minors.

The preceding case illustrates the application of legal norms to the facts. In the Type B case which follows, the violation of a legal norm is considered less important than the social relationship aspects of the case.[14] When both parties appear at fault, then the judge may work toward a decision in which both parties drop their charges against each other. In cases of this type, the judge attempts to create structure and introduce values into relationships where social norms have dissolved, are ambiguous, weakly developed, or never occurred.

On August 6, 1967, two neighbors were arrested for fighting. One day later a case was opened in lower criminal court by the Bodrum police. Both parties were named plaintiffs and defendants, and everybody was charged with "Wounding, Trying to Hit, and Insult." The litigant Hatice was a stout woman, and her eleven year old daughter was a witness. The other parties were a husband and wife, who had brought their two small children, three and five years old, to court. They told the court that they had moved from Milas to Bodrum five years before. (After the case was decided, the wife told me that she had been a school child in Bodrum and had been forced by her husband to elope with him when she was thirteen years old [see Starr 1984:99]).

Hatice was the first to testify in the first hearing:

> "The children from both families were playing on the seashore. That man was near there. The little children were pouring water on each other. He asked why they were doing that. He threatened to hit them. My little four year old girl came to me and said, 'That man is going to hit me.' Later, he came into my yogurt store and called me bad names. I had a yogurt scoop in my hand. I didn't want to hit him. I made a gesture and said, 'Get.' It was just an accident. Then his blood came. Later his wife came and threw a stone at me. I picked up the stone and threw it back at her. Later people came and kept us apart."

Erol, the next to testify, was the man who was struck by the yogurt scoop. He had a blood-caked wound on his left forearm in the first court appearance: "I went swimming. The children were playing there. They got wet. I said to them, 'I'm going to hit you.' Later I went home, and she was sitting there in her yogurt store. She attacked me. She wanted to hit my head, but I put up my arm, and she hit my arm instead." His wife then provided additional testimony: "My child came to me and said, 'Father's hand is bleeding.' I went there and she threw a stone at me."

During the earlier testimony, Erol's wife continually interrupted everybody's story. She was shushed several times by the judge, who finally shouted at her to be quiet. Then he turned to her husband and told him to keep her quiet. Three or four times her husband threatened her. The sergeant at arms of the court also admonished her about silence, but she still continued to try to speak. Twice when the judge yelled at her, she started to cry. The point of including this description is that she was unaware of the norms of behavior in the courtroom.

The first witness for the court was a sixteen year old boy: "I was on my way to fetch water. I saw Erol on the street. His hand was bleeding. Later, his wife appeared and saw it too, and then she threw a stone into the yogurt shop. But I don't know if she hurt that woman or not. Hatice then threw the stone from the inside to the outside, aiming at the wife."

Turning to the three litigants, the judge asked if they were ready to make up. The three were furiously angry, and it was impossible. So the judge decided to postpone the case for two weeks. He dictated details of the case into the record and included the need to write to the police station to see if any of the parties had prior convictions. In the second hearing on August 15, the case was postponed pending arrival of the letter from the police station.

The third hearing took place two weeks later, on August 29. Hatice had sent a letter to the court, saying that she was sick in Milas and could not attend the hearing. The young married couple was in court, and the hearing commenced:

Judge [to Erol]: "We have received a letter from the police station. It says you have six convictions."

Erol: "They were only for traffic violations."

Judge: Do you think a traffic conviction is not a conviction for a crime? Be quiet."

Then came the fourth hearing, on September 12:

Judge [to Hatice]: "Why didn't you come last time?"

Hatice: "Because of my children."

Judge: "We waited for you. Do you have another witness? What do you want to say?"

Hatice: "I want to continue the case."

Judge [reaching out and gesturing toward Hatice]: "What does that mean? Don't you get along yet?" [Turning toward the other couple]: "The public prosecutor has written that you are all plaintiffs and defendants. He says that Erol, because of his actions, will have to spend four months in jail for insult, and two more for threatening, and two more for something else." [Turning back to Hatice]: "You will have to spend six months in prison for wounding, and your daughter will have to spend two months in prison for her behavior." [Turning to the other principals]: "You are all guilty. That's what the public prosecutor said. What do you say to that? [This last was spoken very rapidly.]

Hatice's eleven-year old daughter: "Well, what can we do? If that's what the law says, we will have to go to prison."

Judge: "Well, my sister, decide what you are going to do. Ask other people and come back to court on October 10."

In the fifth hearing on October 10, the judge decided to postpone the case to hear Hatice's daughter's testimony again and to find someone to present expert testimony on the instrument that caused the wounding. The sixth hearing took place October 24, but the case was postponed to allow time for the two witnesses to come.

In the seventh hearing on December 5, all principals and the two witnesses appeared. Hatice's eleven year old daughter was the first to testify:

Girl: "I was playing on the seashore. Those two children made me wet. I told them to stop, but they didn't. Then their father came, and he threatened me."
Judge: "How did he threaten you?"
Girl: "He threatened to run me over with his car." (She is very tearful.)
Judge: "Then what did you do?"
Girl: "I went to tell my mother. He came, too. My mother was putting yogurt into pots. She said, 'Get.' And by mistake she hit him. She didn't mean to. It was a mistake."

The director of the Bodrum Draft then was called to give expert testimony on the weapon. He appeared in court, dressed in his soldier's uniform. Removing his soldier's cap to testify, he said, as he looked at the tagged yogurt scoop of one foot in length: "This is a yogurt scoop, made from tin. This is not what the law means by a weapon." He demonstrated the flexibility of the spoon: "It cannot kill someone. It is not very sharp."

The children accused of throwing the water were led to the witness position in the courtroom. The girl was five; the boy three. The judge asked the girl: "What is your name?" After she slowly gave her first name, he continued: "Please explain what happened." The girl was too shy to answer, she was guided back to her seat by her father.

The judge then implored the litigants: "Don't you want to make peace; don't you all get along now? You are all guilty." Then specifically to Hatice he added: "Will you drop the case?" Hatice sat stolidly, unmoved. Slowly she said without animation, "I will if they will."

The younger woman had already left the courtroom with her youngsters in order to quiet them. Her husband remained. The man, hardly moving, says: "Okay, we will drop it also."

The judge quickly said: "This case is dropped, but make peace among yourselves. Don't be fighting again. I don't want to see you in court again. Now go. Be quiet neighbors." Judge's decision: Innocent of threat, other charges dropped.

The Analysis: This is an example of parents coming in conflict because their children fight. It was treated by the judge as a social relationship case (Type B) because all adults had been charged as defendants and plaintiffs by the Public Prosecutor. The judicial solution was to attempt to get all parties to withdraw their claims. Then the judge could dispose of the case as a "dropped case." Using the medium of language and of time (delaying a decision), the judge achieved a case resolution. Although the judge's first attempts at persuasion failed, the delayed verdict and the courtroom "psychodrama" the judge staged—an important officer testifying on the alleged weapon—eventually resulted in a dropped case. (I do not know whether the parties ever reconciled; ten months later when I interviewed them, they, although living next door to each other, were still not on speaking terms.)

The invitation to the director of the Bodrum Draft to be an expert witness brought psychodrama into the courtroom. (In fact, a serious investigation would obligate the court to view the place where the wounding occurred.) By hearing all the principals and their children, sometimes twice (as in the case of the eleven year old daughter), the judge strung-out the process in an attempt to allay the hostility between the parties. That the judge felt the best solution was for the litigants to reconcile and drop charges is indicated by his repetition of "Aren't you ready to make up yet? You are all guilty." Because they continued to be angry, he delayed verdict by inviting more witnesses.

When a case was in court, parties did not seek revenge, fearing further interaction would jeopardize their claims. The delay in decision allowed tempers to cool and friends, relatives, and other neighbors to intervene and point out the consequences if they persisted in seeking their opponent's punishment. The judge had said, "Everyone will go to jail, including the eleven year old girl."

In situations like this, the disposition represented the best solution from everyone's standpoint, even if the neighbors failed to comprehend the justice in the decision. It took six months and seven court appearances for the judge to get the parties to agree to drop charges against each other. Dropped cases cannot be sent to appellate court.

Evidence

Other cases, collected at the Bodrum court, demonstrate that eyewitness testimony is considered more reliable than hearsay evidence. For example, in a wounding case in a village, a verdict of guilty was given on the basis of one eyewitness, a Bodrum man who was willing to testify that he saw the defendant strike the other. Three witnesses, who lived in the same village as the principals, had testified that they saw the plaintiff and defendant together on the road, and later they saw the wound, but they would not say there was a connection. One witness had candidly said, "I heard fighting, but I didn't look back. I didn't want to be a witness" (Starr 1985a: Case 1).

In Turkey, as in all civil law countries, a judicial decision is based on evidence presented by witnesses and official agents whose expert testimony on a particular matter is sought by the presiding judge. As the evidence flows in at the fact-finding stage, the judge makes distinctions between legal norms that have been violated and legal rights that may have been denied. After the fact-finding stage is completed, the decision-making stage follows quickly. In preparing to make a decision, a judge relies on a "constructed" dossier, which constitutes for him a carefully reconstructed account of the events under scrutiny. It is upon this written record, consisting primarily of linguistic testimony, along with other official documents from the case, such as summonses, police reports, photographs of wounds, and surveys of property, that he bases his verdict.

Bodrum judges told me that legally correct decisions may not be the best outcome of a case (see Starr 1985b:123), but because their decisions might be scrutinized by the appellate court, they feel obliged to offer a verdict in accord with legal rules, unless social relationship factors are overwhelmingly convincing, as in the second (type B) case cited in this chapter.

One of the ways a judge searches for the truth of a situation is to invite more, and then more, witnesses to come to court to give their accounts of events. In this way, he can give the appearance of sorting out truth from falsehood. Unlike the civil law system unfolding model of Thibaut and Walker (1975) or the building block model of Caesar-Wolf (1984), I suggest an alternative model based on the Turkish district courts, a "net-casting" model. If a fishing analogy might be allowed, first the judge casts a legal net, and if that doesn't bring in a legal principle or the violation of a legal principle, then he casts a social relationship net. By law, he could have sent all the litigants in the second case to jail. Instead, he avoided such a harsh verdict by obtaining a dropped decision.

In this way a Bodrum judge can avoid the Scylla and Charybdis inherent in the instructions about judicial decision-making in the Turkish civil code. If a judge too literally interprets the legal norms when neighbors fight, he would send to jail misguided but essentially harmless citizens, creating a miscarriage of justice. If he ventures into the murky waters of local customs concerning local fights, he might hear many opinions without coming closer to a solution. Although local customs are referred to and used in land distribution, tenant farmer/ land owner relations, and inheritance cases involving a remaining widow, for most conflicts Bodrum judges either follow existing laws or act as mediator by cajoling litigants to drop essentially unsound lawsuits.

Alternative models of how decisions are reached in the civil law system of justice share in common the necessity of the judge's reconstruction of a consistent version of events from the multiple and broken fragments offered him in litigants' and witnesses' testimonies. Competing versions of events must be sorted through, some validated, others discarded. Lying testimony, refusing to tell what one knows, elaborating on the truth—all are aspects of testimony that a Turkish judge must ponder. A Bodrum proverb says, "For one who understands the buzzing of a mosquito is music. For one without understanding, fifes and drums are not enough."[15] Although the messages of the Bodrum courts are neither obscure nor loud, they convey clear symbols of the new norms of interaction, civility, and gender relationships.

Conclusion

In building a new national identity for Turkey, the secular legal system became the foundation of the modern Turkish Republic. Elite judges, carefully trained in rational legal reasoning, based on European models, were charged with the task of promoting the new norms of justice and compassion toward all citizens. These included populism and equality, regardless of class, gender, religion, or ethnicity. The two cases analyzed in this chapter demonstrate the attempt to resolve issues through a method of secular decision-making.

Judges are members of the Turkish elite, and the ones I knew were tolerant, understanding, patient, and sympathetic toward the local peasantry. Judges were treated with great respect. I never heard disparaging remarks about their character, nor about the character of judges in general. Nor did people criticize the legal system. Bodrum courts were busy, active places, in which all classes of citizens sought justice. It never occurred to me in the year and a half I studied disputes in Bodrum courts to ask if there were a misfit between the legal system and the values of the local population. What problems existed were social problems (e.g., male alcoholism), problems occurring from older traditional methods that were being regularized (e.g., informal land arrangements being converted to "legal" deeds), and problems relating to male ideologies of gender superiority (e.g., girl stealing). The high status of judges meant they could, in their nation-building role, invoke an image of a just, nonbiased secular state.

The pre-1920s dualistic Ottoman legal system, with criminal, commercial, and administrative law based on European models, and family law governed by the *Şeriat*, created a splintered image of the state, one side veiled and Islamic, the other European. In the post-1926 Republic of Turkey, the bureaucratic elite hoped, through the secular legal system, to have a monopoly on legitimate power.

The Ataturkian state attempted to present one consistent image of justice and one unified legal system. Islam fell under the control of the modern state through laicism (*lâiklik*), which intended that no Islamic competition could again challenge the secular state's monopoly over law. No rival Islamic courts existed for the more religious to use for family law. Islamic criminal and commercial law had not existed in Asia Minor since 1858 and 1840 respectively, while separate *Şeriat* courts had been abolished in 1924, although judges and lawyers in the secular courts still were skilled in the *Şeriat* in the fields of family and personal law, until the next generation was trained in the Turkish civil code (Lewis 1966:266). By the mid-1960s the ordinary Turkish citizen in western Anatolia had no knowledge of Islamic law, and what advantages and disadvantages it would give him. The modern secular legal system was the only state-sanctioned system they knew, and they used it.

In Bodrum town, the only state-recognized justice existed in rural secular courts, in the provincial director's office (*kaymakan*), and in the mayor's office, which brought violations of health and of standards of measurement to court. The ability of the director's office and the courts to promote norms of fairness and of even-handed justice coupled with the patience, tact, humor, and understanding of the judges and public prosecutor suggest good reasons why the ordinary people of Bodrum district accepted the secular law and made no attempt to fight for the return of an Islamic system.

Notes

1. The data come from my field notes of courtroom trials, made in over a year and a half of courtroom study, and from written dossiers, prepared by the court recorder on a manual typewriter, as the judge reduced and dictated to him testimony that witnesses had just given.

2. For an overview of the field, see Danet (1980). For a critique of eyewitness testimony, see Loftus (1979). For examples of the analysis of language use in trial courts, see Dunstan (1980), O'Barr (1982), and Gumperz (1982b). For sociolinguistic analysis in general, see Gumperz (1982a, 1982b, 1982c) and

Tannen (1982a, 1982b). For examples of conversational analysis in trials, see Atkinson and Drew (1979), Drew (1982), Dunstan (1980), Hayden (1987), and O'Barr (1982). For interesting studies of Islamic law in practice, see Rosen (1989a) and Messick (1983a, 1983b).

3. See Culler (1982) and Derrida (1974).

4. I would like to express thanks to Max Atkinson and Donald Harris for making it possible for me to become a visiting Fellow at the Socio-Legal Centre in Oxford in 1981-82 where I learned some of the techniques that conversational analysts use.

5. The theoretical framework is provided by sociolinguistic analysis of communicative behavior in the courtroom and elsewhere. The latter research strategies were pioneered by Atkinson and Drew (1979), Drew (1982), Caesar-Wolf (1984), Danet (1984), Dunstan (1980), Gumperz (1982a, 1982b), O'Barr (1982), and Tannen (1982a, 1982b).

6. Some empirical trial court research in the United States and Britain has described ways the adversary system has *moved from* a combative, oppositional model *to* one which involves negotiation and plea bargaining. In the United States these informal, customary aspects of reaching a case disposition *are* important aspects of developing a total view of the legal system as it is practiced.

7. In the 1960s it was possible to obtain a law degree from a joint program, sponsored by the faculties of Political Service and Law at Ankara University (see p. 181). The law faculty in Izmir opened in 1978.

8. It is also true that juries, which are made up of lay persons, sometimes are overly impressed by impassioned summations of the prosecution, and may reach a decision of guilty that goes way beyond the facts presented at trial. The trial court judge may then "set aside" the verdict. This recently happened in a New York state court in a murder trial and the judge's decision was subsequently upheld by the Appellate court (Feron 1984:p. B2, col. 3–6).

9. Fieldwork techniques: I sat on one side in the rear of the courtroom, while a male field assistant sat on the other. We kept records in Turkish of as much of each case as we could. Cases which had several witnesses or one long interview with a witness were singled out by us each day for special attention. After court we usually were invited by the judge into his office for coffee (sometimes with attorneys), and when possible, we would inquire about different cases. If the judge was not available, we spoke to the court recorder who had been transcribing that case in the courtroom. As we gained information and understanding of a case, we were careful to follow it the next time, keeping our own case records and dossiers. Sometimes we were able to interview one or both litigants before or after court. When a house lot or piece of land was in dispute, the court needed to visit the site. Sometimes we accompanied the court staff on these trips. Gradually, we built up a corpus of finished cases in which there were enough details known to us for the case to qualify as an "extended

case" (see Gulliver, 1969:11–14). Within three months of daily observations I felt some familiarity with the courtroom and its practices, especially since I had been following village cases to court during four previous months. I turned to the court docket for statistics. I then turned to dossiers. I felt I needed to know how specific types of cases (such as elopement, divorce, and inheritance) were handled through time and across a range of litigants. When, much later, I had won the confidence of the court personnel, they allowed me to hand-copy the divorce case dossiers and the elopement cases which appeared before the court.

10. Research methods included empirical study of the four law courts in the Bodrum district for over a year and a half in the period between 1966 and fall 1968. While living for six months in an outlying village in the Bodrum region, I followed village cases to court. Thus, the court study began within two months of my stay and continued throughout my time in Turkey. Publications about the court data include analyzing whether "folk law" played a role in district courts (Starr 1985b), a study of the legal and social position of rural Turkish women (1984, 1989b), and an analysis of the statistical flows of case-types through these district courts forty years after the new Turkish Republic set aside a millennium of Islamic law (Starr and Pool 1974).

11. I sometimes use *disposition* rather than *decision* because it is a more general word and thus might refer to a decision, a settlement, or dropped charge.

12. I borrow the contrast between *legal* and *social* from the provocative title of an unpublished paper by Merry and Silbey from their mediation research, entitled "Social Disputes or Legal Disputes: Dispute Dimensions and the Convergence of Legal Forms."

13. For other examples of kin or co-villagers lying for each other, see Starr (1978a:249, 268).

14. Note that grounds for judicial decision are the basis for classification, not case type or type of disputes. Social relationship issues also may exist in Type A disputes, but the judicial decision is based on legal norms. Legal norms may also be present in Type B disputes, but the judge based his decision on the social rather than the legal factors involved.

15. "Anlıyana a sivrisinek saz, anamayana davul zurna az."

Chapter Eight

The Continuing Dialectic

A hungry bear will not dance.

Turkish Proverbs (1880)

In addressing the uses of history in anthropological study, Marshall Sahlins, a cultural anthropologist, wrote: "The great challenge to an historical anthropology is not merely to know how events are ordered by culture, but how, in that process, the culture is reordered" (1981:8). I take Sahlins's terse comment to imply a theory by which to study cultural change.

I believe Sahlins is suggesting, first, that a society is shaped through its social agents who have their own diversified cultures. Each person learns a culture that he or she was socialized into as a child, in a household through family members, neighbors, and kin. Later, values and ideas come to that person's ideology through education, the army, the street—that is, life experiences *writ large* that expand or shrink cultural perceptions.

Second, at the societal level, social agents bring their "cultures" to their interactions with institutional structures. The new culture of these structures where people work, or within which they interact as clients, is added to what a person already knows and believes, which is his or her cultural repertoire. A social agent is affected by a structure's culture that impinges and shapes that agent's values, and in turn, the agent reshapes the structure through interaction with it (Giddens 1983:66).

Third, culture change also occurs when persons of different cultures interact within a structure, forging new normative values. Different agents, interacting at the margins of their convergent cultures, can create new perceptives, quasi-autonomous fields, arenas of conflict, and sometimes inchoate understandings.

Fourth, social change takes place through *events and resources*. Present events impinge on formal and informal structures that are daily modified by the small actions of their personnel and clients. Expanding and shrinking resources impinge on decision-making. I differ with Giddens (1983:66) because I consider "rules" not as "independent and generative," but only as another kind of resource—a resource like knowledge of how the system works and can be manipulated, or like political influence, or money. I hold this view because rules may be disregarded or suspended by leading or senior personnel, or subverted by juniors. When rules are ignored by any of the above agents, rules may be no longer controlling. Also, old, usually ignored rules may be reinvoked to support a political argument, to help an ally, to delay a decision, and so forth.

Fifth, a culture changes when we add *time* to our view of the culture. In normal times, change is comparatively slow, although new laws, the response to new technology, to new communication systems, to new social ideas, to new forms of social action, the formation of new groups, and diverse events may speed up change. Analysis of the sequential change in power relations among groups over time unites a social science perspective with an historical one (see Starr and Collier 1989a, 1989b).

Sixth, now add *crisis*. Crisis can be within a structure (or nation-state) or external to it. It can engender quick decision-making or cause structural breakdown, breakup, or paralysis. Add crisis, in combination with younger agents with new ideas, and quick decision-making patterns (perhaps what occurred at the end of the Ottoman Empire) and conflations of quickly changing cultural values occur. The above has been more succinctly said by Sahlins.

In this book I have described some of the logic of change underlying the Ottoman-Turkish legal system, change caused by smaller, orderly changes within the system and as responses to external events. The story I have told is far from complete, and I am well aware of certain breaks in the narrative. Nevertheless, the picture is becoming clearer of how a modern nation-state's law emerged over, above, and through the previous Ottoman state law and the local legal practices of rural people.

Law, in this book has been conceptualized as enduring ideas, structures, processes, and practices (written and unwritten, formal and informal, legalistic and less legalistic, local and national). I have shown some of state law's effects on an outlying region I studied in my first field research in Turkey in the 1960s. I sought the enduring practices of the villagers as they attempted to resolve their own disputes locally, and as they interacted with state legal culture, present in official and unofficial law. I also looked for "fixed forms" of Turkish state legal structures and processes, although, to my astonishment, a decade later some of what I had taken as fixed had been challenged and had undergone radical change at the top (the parliament, public stability, the Constitution). Much later I had an epiphany when I read Karl Marx's astute observation in the *Grundrisse*: "Everything social that has a fixed form merely is a vanishing moment in the movement of society" (1857–1858:149).

Popular Legal Culture

In the rural villages and in the state courts at the district level in Bodrum, Islamic sentiments were not perceptible in the 1960s. The informal processes villagers followed in making a claim, in pursuing justice and/or the resolution of conflict are described in detail (chapter 6). Villagers and judges never cited Islamic maxims or *Sura*s from the *Kur'an* concerning appropriate solutions, as happens among Palestinians in the West Bank (Bisharat 1989:32, 41). Nor did villagers seek out the opinion of an Islamic scholar, as sometimes happens in Morocco (Rosen 1989:46). Instead, they used informal village processes or applied to state officials or the state courts. Popular legal culture was not greatly removed from the official law of the land in western Anatolian villages.

Contrast these Turkish villagers' willingness to use the courts for serious offenses and for property disputes with Bisharat's statement concerning West Bank Palestinians:

> What the juxtaposition of the lawyer's view and the prior disposition suggests . . . is that the public's intense interest in disputation does not translate into awareness and involvement in the law of the lawyers and the state. State law, or *ganun* [*sic*] [i.e., *kanun*], especially concerning civil matters, is not a general reference point that serves to orient and guide normal transactions among individuals. (1989:33)

When the legal consciousness I found among Turkish villagers and elite judges in rural courts is placed in historical perspective, it reveals longer, more widely shared "oppositional" cultural values that give shape to and continually transform many Turkish state structures—from the formation of elite groups to political parties, from educational to military institutions. This cultural dialogue had its roots in the Ottoman Empire, and it continued to evolve in the Turkish state as a persistent competition (between adherents of Islam and adherents of secularism) over state structures that continuously reorders the culture. During my field work in 1966–68, secular elites were more powerful and appeared to have won the competition in the legal arena. But twenty years later, Islamic elites had gained considerable ground in other structures, such as educational institutions (Aksit 1986; Reed 1980, 1986; Heyd 1968) and mobilization of the masses through political parties (Landau 1974; Mardin 1971; Toprak 1981).

Islam

In contrast to some anthropologists who suggest the increasing visibility of Islamic sentiments and Islamic Sufi orders in Turkey in the 1980s is a new phenomenon (Gilsenan 1982:261), I have approached the situation as a cultural dialectic between secularizing and Islamicizing elites, each group seeking—now for over a hundred and fifty years—to establish their discourse and vision of society. In this sense, the new visibility of Islamic adherents and their success in bringing Islamic education into regular public schools and creating a number of state-supported Islamic, *Imam Hatip* secondary schools (Aksit 1986) is merely another swing in the pendulum toward more complexity in the dialogue.

In the first several chapters, I described how Islam and the Ottoman state were interwoven, a seemingly completed tapestry in which other religions, ethnic groups, cultures, and languages combined to create a pluralistic society. Yet, gradually and unevenly, secular ideas were adopted and woven into the policies of a segment of the Ottoman bureaucratic elite. But even the most extreme reformers in the nineteenth century never dreamed of severing Islam from its paramount position as the twin ruling power (with the Sultan) of the Empire.

Revolutionary though Ataturk's changes of the legal system were, they were changes to structures that already were firmly rooted in Turkish society. The first secular Turkish courts had been introduced seventy-five years earlier to hear and resolve conflicts between non-Islamic merchants, trading in Constantinople. Attempts to create secular educational structures and then secular courts were the first challenges by reforming Ottoman bureaucrats to the hegemony of the Ottoman Islamic elites.

In subsequent chapters, I followed the law's effects on and interaction with land, family, and gender relationships, using historical sources and my ethnographic materials from Bodrum town and her villages as an anchor of "place." I was guided in this endeavor by E. P. Thompson's recognition that law has a tendency to intrude into all types of relationships, interacting with them, and changing itself until both become altered (1978:96). Not only did I find law at every level of society, but it entered into the self-identities of the Turkish administrators and those they ruled. Thompson's idea that law has afforded an arena for class struggle, within which alternative notions of law were fought out was used in this book to show how secularizing elites use law to develop ideas of populism, rewarding the small farmer with land ownership and women with legal status equal to men.

In the final chapters, I went into an outlying district, typical in those days of most Anatolian areas, and in Bodrum's villages and Bodrum's courtroom of the 1960s I examined, in cases women brought against men, and in judicial decision-making practices, how much remained of Islamic notions of law and Islamic values. I found not much at all.[1]

Continuity Between Islamic and Republican Turkish Rural Legal Institutions

In Bodrum, I found no knowledge among villagers of Islamic law or of Islamic solutions to conflicts. Three Ottoman legal functionaries did continue into modern times and were used by villagers: the notary, the *vekil*, and the cadestre surveyors. The notary witnessed and wrote up all kinds of business transactions from title deeds to wills. Poorer villagers sometimes transferred land through notary sale, but compared to a title (*tapu*) obtained at court, it had less legal standing. *Vekil*s were legal personnel without law degrees who functioned in civil matters only, and who could represent clients in civil disputes at court. (Of course, they could and did give informal advice about criminal matters also, but could not represent a client in criminal court.) *Vekil*s were the letter writers of a community; they drew up all kinds of documents, searched out titles in the land record office, and gave advice about court and how to write a legal letter, but their abilities, standing, and pay scale were lower than a lawyer's. (A Turkish lawyer had a law degree from one of Turkey's law schools, had undergone an apprenticeship both at court and in a law firm, had taken a Bar course, and was affiliated with the Bar Association in the community where he or she would practice.)

The cadestre survey team was a land titling team, working under state jurisdiction that went village to village. It proceeded as the court would, using the same methods of establishing ownership and working under the same laws. It took statements from witnesses, viewed the site of disputed boundaries, and heard family members and village land experts describe earlier land divisions and ad hoc assignments of houses and fields. By the time it left a village, it had settled a number of land disputes, awarded title (*tapu*) to a number of villagers, and had drawn up (through a professional surveyor who was part of the team) a map of all of village land ownership rights.

A "quasi-legal" role continuing from the older Ottoman Islamic order still was recognized in Bodrum's villages—the expert witness to land transfers. In oral and court-sanctioned land transfers that occurred in a village, this resident adult male was present and remembered all land transactions. At a patriarch's death land could not be divided without this man's presence, for if land was disputed it was his knowledge of generations of transfers that prevailed. This oral history of land transfers was taught to one of his sons, who literally followed in his father's footsteps during his father's life, watching and learning the oral history of land transfers in order to take on the job after his father's death. Like other oral traditions in which rights are maintained and established through the testimony of witnesses, this oral land transfer witness was definitive in establishing land claims. Witnesses are found in other *kadı* justice systems today (Rosen 1989a:21–23), and witnessing of transfers of property were also present under early Roman law (Starr 1989a).

In sum, with the exception of the *vekil*s, the notaries, and the cadestre survey teams, I could find no remnants of earlier Islamic conflict resolution structures.

Islamic Religion

When strong Islamic feelings invest the lives of people, Islam can be found in many daily practices, in addition to the saying of prayers five times each day. *Kur'an*ic verses may adorn their homes. Islamic dramas of life and death may be performed (Gilsenan 1982:17–18, 88–89). Village mosques may become places of frequent visits and festivals; saints' days may mark the calendar; saints' tombs may repose on the landscape. Village women or men may make trips to sacred tombs or graves, a shrine, a tree, and Mecca. Most noticeable among devout Islamic communities is the directness of their oral tradition. Reciting *Kur'an*ic verses is but one manifestation of this. Among devout Muslims there is a *practical readiness* to quote the *Kur'an*, its sayings, and cautionary tales of great prophets and Islamic teachers (cf. Nader 1965b and 1965c). Devout Turkish Muslims are fond of quoting from the *Kur'an*, often in Arabic, the language of the prophet.

No *Kur'an*ic verses decorated the walls of Bodrum or her villagers. No sacred graves or saint tombs marked the countryside. Sacred hot springs could be found on an island, *Kara ada*, off Bodrum's shoreline. Sometimes pilgrims visited these springs, seeking the mystical powers to cure disease or give sight to a blind child. But no one, neither locals nor pilgrims, ever suggested these sacred springs were Islamic. No mosque or Islamic shrine adorned the island. No Islamic prayers were said as parents bathed blind or lame children in the waters.

In the Bodrum district, Islamic sayings were not quoted in support of a discussion. In a conflict, no sayings of the Prophet were invoked to push a position. It is the lack of all such *practical signs* among the villagers and Bodrumites that I point to when I suggest that Islamic tenets of conflict resolution were not a part of daily consciousness. No one knew the customs, rules, and ideas of customary Islamic law. Nor did anyone know if Islamic structures had actually functioned to resolve disputes in this region during the nineteenth century. In Bodrum, no reference to Islamic sentiments or maxims occurred in the courtroom, as happens in Arab Islamic law countries (Rosen 1980–81, 1984, 1989a, 1989b); Eickelman 1985; Messick 1983a, 1983b, 1987; Gilsenan 1982:30–32; Nader 1965a, 1965b). Therefore, in western Turkey, I had to conclude knowledge of Islamic conflict resolution was nonexistent. This finding was less startling because I already knew that many of the rural agricultural households were only one or two generations removed from their migratory past,[2] and nomadism has not gone hand in hand with Islamic observances (Barth 1964).

Customary Law

Turkey did not develop a customary law system, similar to those described among the Bedouin in Saudi Arabia, the Palestinians, or African tribal groups.[3] Customary law, once considered the "pure" law of particular ethnic groups by anthropologists and administrators, has undergone much closer scrutiny now that African history and Middle Eastern history has become known and important in anthropological studies. As we gain understanding of the relationship between foreign administrators and tribal groups, anthropologists recognized that customary law was, in fact, a "residual category." That is to say, customary law is that law which native groups were able to preserve as their own jurisdiction in juxtaposition to the law brought to them by the foreign (usually European) rulers (cf. Chanock 1985; Moore 1989; Vincent 1989; Starr and Collier 1987, 1989a). Chanock, a law professor, has taken the reconceptualization a step further, suggesting that African customary law was "part of a process of legalization, of a transformation in African institutions rather than a continuity" (p. 61).

Western Turkey fits the model of this brief synopsis of colonial history in a different way. Because Turkey was never colonized, local actors never had to maneuver to safeguard their leadership positions, and no localized "law-ways" developed as a preserve of local leaders that paralleled the preserve of African local leaders, namely customary law. Western Turkey did not become a region enclosed and encapsulated within the nation-state, like African tribal groups or American Indian reservations.

But the ways African rural society was transformed through the interaction between the colonized and colonial institutions of control to some extent does parallel the ways that the Turkish rural landscape and its social relations were transformed, first by the Ottoman, and later by the Turkish Republican ruling elites. In Ottoman times the Islamic bureaucracy and the secular bureaucrats shared a common Osmanlı culture, a common language both written and oral (Ottoman-Turkish), and a common cultural heritage. The culture of the bureaucrats and intelligentsia differed from the Turkish-speaking farmers, the nomads of the Anatolian plateau, and the other smaller ethnic groups present in Asia Minor then. The Ottoman administrators were as foreign in language and culture from the Turks of Anatolia as the British administrators were in Africa. But unlike the British in Africa, the Ottomans shared with rural Anatolians a common religion and a common law, which were Islamic and Ottoman.

Although the state created by Ataturk and his coterie brought a new legal system and a new culture to the rural villages, it used "Turkishness" as a symbol of fatherland and adopted the language of the Anatolian Turks as the language of the nation, which created a fierce patriotism. Another reason why Ataturk and his secular elites met little opposition in western and central Anatolia (as they transformed the landscape, the social relationships, and the administrative structures of the former Ottoman cities and countryside) was the earlier state had collapsed and the countryside was devastated by war.

Courts, Judges, and Legal Education

A court and a court system are constituted at a particular historic time and evolve in relationship to other historical events, structures, and changes in the power rankings of social groups. Courts can be seen as foci of power, contextualized within other circles of power, both ejecting powerful outcomes and subjected to constraints.

When we view particular legal forums in wider social and historical contexts, studies of trial courts at a specific time express local, regional, and national values. This happens through the interaction of localized litigants and the judges who, as part of the Turkish elite, in courtroom talk and in legal decisions reflect knowledge gained at national law faculties, as well as accommodation to local values. In the mid-1960s only two law faculties existed in Turkey—one at Istanbul University, the other at Ankara University. A third source for a law degree was a joint program existing between the faculties of Political Science and Law at Ankara University. (The program was ended in the early 1970s.)

Law faculties, legal education, and hierarchically organized court systems are institutions for training and sustaining law that emerged at specific historical moments. They evolved subject to influences and molding; they also shape and nurture attitudes and partial ideologies. Since the 1920s, when Turkey's legal system became entirely secular, and even before in commercial, criminal, administrative, and maritime law, Turkey's law lay squarely within the European Civil Law tradition. This legal tradition affords a prominent role for law professors who draft legislation and legal codes (Merryman 1985:59–60), and Turkey is no exception. Turkish judges as students were taught law by the very professors who drafted legislation, or at least who had studied with those who drafted legislation a generation before. Thus begins the circle of justice.

When law students complete their four years of study, they decide whether to become lawyers or career civil servants (e.g., judges or public prosecutors). For any choice, an apprenticeship (Turkish: *staj*) is necessary. After law school, a new lawyer serves an apprenticeship at court and in law firms. Beginning judges and prosecutors serve apprenticeships under the tutelage of experienced judges and prosecutors. This required system of apprenticeship and the institutional framework of supervision of all judges by the highest council of judges (*Yüksek Hâkimler Kurulu*) protect the system from infusions of influence and also act to constrain radical legal change in process and in deciding cases.

In courtroom discussions and in case decisions, judges move rural litigants from their particularistic, localized attitudes towards more national cultural values. The legal training of judges is important in other ways as well. Future trial court judges are taught in law school and on their apprenticeship to narrow the issues in dispute, to extract information, turning it into facts relevant to legal norms, how to establish who has the burden of proof, and when to shift this burden of proof from plaintiff to defendant. Court decisions need to reflect the types of remedies courts can give. In many instances the training of judges acts to define the nature of elite/commoner conflict when it reaches the courts, because by placing "a conflict" in a legal environment, the dispute itself becomes subject to the laws written by law professors, who are part of the legal elite and who have trained these judges.

Thus, the circle of legitimation of justice is complete. Law professors write the law. These same law professors train the judges and lawyers who will use the law. In the courtrooms, solving conflicts is a process of establishing "facts" and finding the appropriate law. Conflicts are placed into a "legal environment," where the ideologies of the legal elite are carried out in the practices of the judge's decision.

The State

Studying the circle of justice allowed me to move toward a more general theory of how law works and reflects changes within Turkish society, both being modified by and shaping the state.

Although I found few remnants of Islamic law at the lowest levels of village, small district town, and district courts, what I did find was quite unexpected. Taking a longer historical view of social change, a continuing preoccupation of the Ottoman-Turkish state with the problem of controlling the periphery was apparent. It appeared in prior centuries in the Ottoman attempts to break up and disperse "tribal confederacies." It appeared in the twentieth century under the guise of raising women's status—this not only undermined the power of the patriarch of multiple household units, it also undercut the age-old rights of Islam to define Moslem women as inferior to men and as needing male supervision. The new secular law denied the customary, localized, cultural privileges accorded to men to use force to make women submissive and to divorce at will through renunciation. By undercutting male superiority enshrined in law, the new Republic broke the power of rural male lineages. By creating the nuclear family as the domestic unit, the state assured a rural population unable to be mobilized as a fighting kin group.

Revolution and Change

In the western and central Anatolian countryside, the Ataturkian revolution broke up existing class and status relations, changed existing agrarian relations, and redefined domestic relations. As an anthropologist, I found that, to understand how the legal system I thought I knew in 1960s could evolve so quickly into new structures of the 1980s—for example, under the 1983 Constitution, two new Supreme Courts were created, now totaling eight Supreme Courts—it was necessary to know something of political events that put the Turkish state into crisis. I needed to know the legal ideas and practices of earlier state legal structures and how they had conceptualized individuals and groups, first in the empire and later in the Turkish state.

The *dispute resolution paradigm* that I had used in my first field research of regional social control systems now places law courts in a wider historical framework.

Summary and Finale

In tracing the ways a secular legal consciousness developed among the Turkish governing elite and was brought to rural villagers in western Anatolia, I have pointed to the decline of the omniscient sacred community of Islam in Turkey; the change in the language of administration from Osmanlı Turkish to the popular Turkish of the Anatolian farmers; the diminishing importance of kinship structures, especially of the "tribal confederacy"; the male lineage; male control of women; and the growth of Turkish identity, increasingly defined in nationalistic and patriotic terms (see Anderson 1983:28). While the Ottoman-Turkish administrator was linked to the illiterate Turkish farmer through Islam in both its official and popular forms, the modern Turkish administrator is linked to the Turkish farmer through nationalistic pride in country and through political party participation.

Creating a nation of Turks from a decaying empire was a long slow process, still incomplete as the twentieth century ends. Indeed, the attempt to define everyone within the Turkish state as a Turk has created its own problems. Yet when faced with the urgent need to save the country from being carved up by European powers in 1919, Turkish nationalism became an important symbol and brought forth the largest numbers of soldiers who identified themselves as Turks. Ataturk's attempts to save the nation were supported by the urban intellectuals, the youth, most of the Turkish bureaucracy (whose source of identity and loyalty was only the state), and almost all the soldiers.

The proverb at the opening of this chapter cites the hungry Turkish bear who only dances when fed, and one might ask: Who is the bear? Perhaps, he is the controlling secular elite who not only dominates in the contested arenas that is "the state," but also has reduced Islam—the omnipresent system of law, state, and religion—to only its religious sphere in western Anatolia. These secular elites have also erased from the written law much of the gender-based inequality inherent in Islam. Thus, in the mid-1960s under the most liberal Constitution Turkey has yet known, the Constitution of 1961, secular elites seemed to have won the contest in the western Anatolian countryside. Now in the last decade of this century, the bears continue to dance, being fed on the expanding Turkish trade with Europe and the Islamic Middle East.

The contest between Turkish Islam and Turkish secularism apparently will, however, continue well into the next century. Thus, perhaps the dancing bears are the Islamic elites who have gained considerable ground during the last twenty-five years. After Ataturk's death, the Turkish state moved to a multiparty electoral system, which brought more democratic processes to Turkey in the form of free elections, but which also provided fertile ground for Islamic groups to organize and enter the national political arena. Although the problems of national politics of 1971 to autumn 1980 have sometimes been cast as a struggle between leftist and rightist groups, Islamic groups of several persuasions also have played major roles. It was, after all, the concessions of Demirel to Erbakan's Islamic party (the National Salvation Party) that led to the military takeover of 1980, although to bring off a bloodless coup must have taken several years of negotiation and planning.

Since 1974, Islamic elites have gained considerable ground in setting the agendas and programs of several contemporary political parties,[4] and in mobilizing the support of some of the peasantry and town dwellers. Islamic elites also have made considerable headway in bringing Islamic education into secular classrooms. Before 1951 there were no *Imam Hatip* schools in Turkey (Akşit 1986:29). By 1984 state-supported *Imam Hatip*, Islamic schools had increased to 341; and twenty more were built during the early 1980s (*Türkiye İstatistik* 1985:136). Furthermore, Islamic elites have secured the establishment of a conservative Higher Institute for Islamic Studies. Established at Istanbul and Konya in 1952, graduates of *Imam Hatip* high schools can pursue further studies. In addition, students from the Islamic high schools, the *Imam Hatip* schools, are entering and graduating in increasing numbers from the Ankara Political Science Faculty, the primary faculty for training most of the middle- and high-level officials of the extensive Turkish administration system.

Although law schools have increased in Turkey—six law faculties, since the Educational Reorganization Act of 1983[5]—Islamic elites have not succeeded in adding Islamic law as a regular course to the law school curriculum. Islamic law is only taught at Law Faculties as Ottoman legal history. But at Ankara University, the home of the law faculty that trained the first generation of new Republican lawyers and judges, law students may take a number of contemporary courses in Islamic law at the nearby Faculty of Religion of Ankara University.

Few ardent supporters of Islam have entered the Law School at Ankara University as students, although about ten women were visibly wearing the Islamic headscarf, the *türban*, during spring semester 1989. However, current procedures of selecting and supervising judges and public prosecutors will prevent Islamic fundamentalist students from using Islamic principles in Turkish secular legal structures, and should they try, they would be dismissed from service.

Nor have Islamic students penetrated the military academy to any great extent, although each year some are accepted. Students of ardent

Islamic persuasion are expelled every few years, a procedure that allows students to enter, change their views and continue, rather than being prohibited at the beginning of a career. So it is doubtful if, at this time, Islamic groups will focus much energy on gaining access to legal or military structures in order to rise through the ranks and control from within.

Given the nature of the conflict between secularizing and Islamic elites in Turkey, there is no need for Islamic groups and their children to penetrate legal or military institutions. Considering the emphasis during Ataturk's one-party rule in suppressing Islamic values, it is remarkable that militant Muslims have gained so much political party visibility and so many concessions toward their values within fifty years. For example, a huge half-completed mosque, built at government expense, stands opposite and rivals the newly built, national university in Diyarbakır (now an outpost of eastern Turkey; under the Ottomans, an important town, known as "the Paris of the East"). The university at Diyarbakır was established to bring health care, medical services, and enlightenment to the neglected eastern provinces, because ruling elites hoped that education and development might curb the eastern separatist desires. And even in Ankara (once a small city that was chosen for Turkey's Republican capital), a new mosque (taking twenty years to build) has finally been completed. Called *Kocatepe* mosque, it rivals in prominence Ataturk's own tomb and is lighted as brightly at night. It is the largest mosque in Turkey. Thus, in a time of scarce government resources, it is remarkable that government mosque-building parallels government construction of secular universities.

Yet in Ankara, a third symbol of power is also visible, a power that rivals the *Kocatepe* mosque and the mausoleum of Ataturk. On the Cankaya hill, where the burgeoning class of secular business elites now lives, atop a completed elegant shopping center stands the third symbol of Ankara—the *donné kule*—a long thin needle-tower with a "turning restaurant" at the top, a symbol that heralds the new capitalism of the urban upper classes.

Turkish business elites are both Islamic and secularist, although those living in Cankaya are mostly secular. Like the urban traders and the rural *ayan*s of the nineteenth century, a strong capitalist class is demanding new laws and institutions to facilitate its interests. Perhaps these business elites, who are trading with the Islamic east and secular west, will become the third and mediating force amidst the dramatic struggles within the governing elites concerning the direction of national values.

Notes

1. Elsewhere I have discussed remnants of Islamic legal concepts apparent in current law and courtroom practices especially visible in marriage and divorce cases (Starr 1985b).

2. *Transhumance* is the practice of migrating from winter campgrounds to summer pastures with flocks, making the trip up and back during the yearly cycle.

3. See Kennett (1925); Steward (n.d.); Gulliver (1963, 1969, 1971); Bohannan (1957); Gluckman (1955); Comaroff and Roberts (1981); Chanock (1985).

4. Colonel Türkeş and his grey wolves were a secret military organization committed to Islamic values in a pan-Islamic world. Erbakan's NSP (in Turkish, *Milli Selâmet Partesi*) had an important following. For a more comprehensive view, see Toprak (1981) and Landau (1974). For interest-group politics in Turkey, see Bianchi (1984).

5. Marmara University in Istanbul, and at universities in Izmir, Konya, and Diyarbakır.

Appendix I[1]

Chronology of Uprisings Against the Ottoman Empire and Significant Events in the Formation of the New Republic

1804 and 1815
: Serbian uprisings.

1821
: Beginning of Greek War of Independence.

1829
: Serbian Independence at Treaty of Andrinople.
: Greek Independence.

1840
: Egypt became quasi-independent under Muhammad Ali.

1875
: Rebellions in Bosnia, Herzegovina, and Bulgaria.

1877
: 24th April: Russia invades Turkey.
: May: Abdülhamid suspends constitution and dissolves parliament.

1878
: 3 March: Treaty of San Stephano with Russia.
: 13 June–13 July Congress and Treaty of Berlin:
   - Gave Bosnia and Herzegovina to Austria.
   - Independence of Serbia, Rumania, and Montenegro.
   - Gave Tunis to France.
   - Gave Cyprus to the British.
   - Gave city of Batum with part of Transcaucia to Russia.

1896

Revolt by students of Military Medical School in Constantinople suppressed.

1897

17 April: Turkey declares war on Greece, following a Greek threat to annex Crete. Peace settlement by intervention of the European Powers.

1906

October: Kemal (Ataturk) helps to found Fatherland (*Vatan*) Society in Damascus.

1908

24 July: "Young Turk" Revolution in Salonika. Committee of Union and Progress forces Abdülhamid to restore constitution of 1876 and recall parliament.

5 October: Bulgaria proclaims independence.

7 October: Austria-Hungary annexes Bosnia and Herzegovina.

12 October: Crete votes for union with Greece.

Kemal (Ataturk) sent to Tripolitania on mission for Committee of Union and Progress.

1909

13 April: Counterrevolution in Constantinople. Union and Progress striking force, with Kemal (Ataturk) as divisional chief of staff, marches on the city from Salonika.

1910

Kemal (Ataturk) serves as chief of staff in suppression of revolt in Albania.

Kemal (Ataturk) sent to Paris with military mission to attend French army maneuvers.

1911

13 September: Kemal (Ataturk) posted to general staff in Constantinople.

5 October: Italian invasion of Tripoli.

1912

8 October–3 December: First Balkan War. Montenegro, Serbia, Bulgaria, and Greece invade Turkey. Severe Turkish defeats. Loss of Salonika. Armistice agreed before Constantinople.

Coup d'etat against Government by Union and Progress officers.

25 November: Kemal (Ataturk) appointed Director of Operations for relief of Adrianople.

Fall of Adrianople.

1913

30 May: Treaty of London between Turkey and Balkan states.

30 June–20 July: Second Balkan War.

27 September: Treaty of Bucharest restores territory to Turkey.

27 October: Kemal (Ataturk) appointed military attache in Sofia.

1914

28 June: Assassination of Archduke Franz Ferdinand at Sarajevo.

2 August: Turkey signs secret alliance with Germany.

11 August: Turkey purchases German warships *Goeben* and *Breslau* on arrival in the Bosporus.

28 October: Turkey shells Russian Black Sea ports.

3 November: Russia declares war on Turkey.

5 November: Britain and France declare war on Turkey.

1915

2 February: Kemal (Ataturk) appointed to reorganize and command Nineteenth Division, in Thrace.

19 February: Unsuccessful Allied naval attack on Dardanelles.

25 April: Allied military landings at Ariburnu (Anzac) on Gallipoli Peninsula. Advance checked by Kemal (Ataturk), with Nineteenth Division.

1916

9 January: Allied evacuation of Gallipoli Peninsula.

27 June: Şerif of Mecca proclaims independence of Arabia.

11 March: British forces capture Baghdad.

5 July: Kemal (Ataturk) appointed commander of Seventh Army in Syria.

October: Kemal (Ataturk) returns to Constantinople.

11 December: British forces capture Jerusalem.

1918

3 July: Death of Sultan Mehmed V; Vahid-ed-Din succeeds him as Mehmed VI.

7 August: Kemal (Ataturk) reappointed commander of Seventh Army, in Palestine.

19–30 September: Brtitish forces, under General Allenby, drive Turkish forces out of Palestine and Syria. Kemal defends frontier north of Aleppo.

30 October: Armistice signed between Turkey and Britain at Mudros.
31 October: Kemal (Ataturk) takes over command of Army Group at Adana, which was dissolved by 7 November.
13 November: Kemal (Ataturk) returns to Constantinople. Allied fleets enter Constantinople.
21 November: Dissolution of parliament.

1919

18 January: Opening of peace conference at Versailles.
15 May: Greek forces land in Smyrna, with Allied approval.
19 May: Kemal (Ataturk) lands in Samsun.
21 June: Kemal (Ataturk) issues "Declaration of Independence" at Amasya. Summons Nationalist Congress at Sivas.
23 June: Kemal (Ataturk) ordered by government to return to Constantinople.
8 July: Kemal (Ataturk) resigns from the army and is dismissed by government.
23 July–6 August: Nationalist Congress at Erzurum, under presidency of Kemal (Ataturk). Issue of National Pact.
4–13 September: Nationalist Congress at Sivas under presidency of Kemal (Ataturk). Confirmation of National Pact. Establishment of Representative Committee.
5 October: Resignation of government.
7 November: New parliament elected in Constantinople with nationalist representation.
27 December: Kemal (Ataturk) establishes headquarters at Angora, with Representative Committee.

1920

28 January: National Pact adopted by Constantinople parliament.
16 March: Military occupation of Constantinople by Allies.
11 April: Dissolution of Constantinople parliament.
23 April: First Grand National Assembly meets at Angora.
10 June: Treaty of Sevres presented by Allies to sultan's government.
22 June–9 July: Greek army advances to Anatolia and captures Bursa.
10 August: Treaty of Sevres signed by sultan's government.
24 August: Draft treaty initialed in Moscow between Soviet Union and nationalist government.
28 September–2 November: Nationalist forces invade Armenia and capture Kars.
2 December: Soviet Union establishes Armenian Republic at Erivan.
3 December: Treaty of Gumru settles Turco-Armenian frontiers.

1921

20 January: Grand National Assembly at Angora adopts Constitution Act, based on popular sovereignty.

16 March: Treaty of Moscow between nationalist government and Soviet Union.

23 March–1 April: Greeks resume offensive in Anatolia, and are checked at Second Battle of Inonu.

10 July: Greeks resume offensive and capture Eskişehir.

5 August: Kemal (Ataturk) given full powers as commander in chief by Grand National Assembly.

23 August–13 September: Battle of the Sakarya. Turks check Greek advance before Angora (Ankara).

13 October: Treaty of Kars between nationalist government and Transcaucasian Soviet Republics.

20 October: Treaty of Angora between nationalist government and France.

1922

26 August–9 September: Nationalist forces defeat Greeks in counteroffensive and capture Smyrna, which is destroyed by fire.

23 September: Nationalist forces enter neutral zone at Chanak, threatening Constantinople.

3–11 October: Conference at Mudanya agrees on armistice between Allies and nationalist government.

1 November: Kemal (Ataturk) proclaims abolition of sultanate.

17 November: Flight of Sultan Mehmed VI from Constantinople.

1923

24 July: Signing of the Treaty of Lausanne at the peace conference.

9 August: Foundation of People's Party.

11 August: Second Grand National Assembly.

2 October: Turkish forces occupy Constantinople, following Allied evacuation.

9 October: Angora (Ankara) becomes capital of Turkey.

29 October: Proclamation of the Turkish Republic, with Kemal (Ataturk) as president.

1924

3 March: Abolition of caliphate, Ministry of Religious Affairs, and religious schools.

8 April: Abolition of religious courts.

1925

11 February–12 April: Revolt in Kurdistan.

4 March: Law for Maintenance of Public Order gives government exceptional powers.

30 August–2 September: Kemal (Ataturk) tours Kastamonu province, announcing abolition of fez, suppression of religious brotherhoods, and closing of sacred tombs as places of worship.

1926

17 February: Adoption of new Civil Law code.

15 June–13 July: Plot against life of Kemal (Ataturk) in Izmir (Smyrna). Trial and execution of ringleaders.

1–26 August: Trial and execution of "Young Turk" leaders and others in Ankara.

1927

15–20 October: Kemal (Ataturk) makes historic speech to Congress of People's Party.

1 November: Third Grand National Assembly. Kemal (Ataturk) reelected president of the republic.

1928

3 November: Introduction of Latin alphabet.

1930

23 December: Religious riot at Menemen. Trials and executions.

1931

15 April: Foundation of Turkish Historical Society.

4 May: Fourth Grand National Assembly. Kemal (Ataturk) reelected president of the republic.

1932

12 July. Foundation of Turkish Linguistic Society.

12 August: Turkey becomes member of League of Nations.

1934

9 January: First five-year plan for industrial development.

9 February: Balkan Pact concluded between Turkey, Greece, Rumania, and Yugoslavia.

29 November: Kemal takes name of Ataturk, in terms of new law requiring Turks to adopt surnames.

8 December: Women made eligible to vote in parliamentary elections and to become members of parliament.

1935

1 March: Fifth Grand National Assembly. Ataturk reelected president of the republic.

1938

11 March: Illness of Ataturk officially announced.

18 September: Second five-year plan for industrial development.

10 November: Death of Ataturk.

11 November: Succession of Ismet Inönü as president of the republic.

Notes

1. Chronology based mostly on Kinross (1964:523–30), with reference to Garraty and Gay (1972:616–19).

Appendix II

Turkish Rural Law Enforcement Agents

Village-based Gendarmes. A gendarme station has been maintained in the village since about 1900. In the 1960s its ostensible purpose was to prevent smuggling between nearby Greek islands and the Turkish mainland. Gendarmes were never stationed in the region of their birth, and thus they were outsiders to the village social system. A characteristic of the sergeant and two soldiers stationed in Mandalinci was their interpretation of their mandate to intervene in situations that they classified as "potentially violent." Since there was not much for the gendarmes to do, they tended to strictly enforce the Turkish gun laws, which state that every person carrying a gun must have a gun permit. In the past, it had been village custom to shoot off guns at weddings and other celebrations. A few villagers used old guns to hunt small game, and villagers have been known to shoot off guns in a gleeful mood, all of which led the gendarmes to investigate, and sometimes to make arrests, which involved interviews by the district prosecutor in Bodrum, and sometimes trial for criminal activities in the Bodrum court.

On five occasions during my fieldwork, four different villagers asked a gendarme to intervene in a dispute on their behalf. And when a serious wounding occurred in a fight between two village youths, the gendarmes were quickly informed, as they controlled the only village telephone, and the parents of one youth needed to summon a vehicle to take their son to the Bodrum hospital. In this dispute, the intervention of village gendarmes clearly acted to prevent retaliation and the spread of violence to larger kin or friendship units. But in another village dispute, the intervention of the gendarmes escalated the dispute into the Bodrum court, where only the judge's careful sifting of events and claims eventually straightened out the underlying issues and so resolved the dispute (see pp. 133–34).

District Gendarme Officers. On several different occasions during my fieldwork, district gendarme officers came to Mandalinci on business. In two cases, they came to investigate claims made in letters about alleged misconduct on the part of a local gendarme. On a third, a captain was merely spending a leisurely off-duty day at a "scenic seaside" village. But his visit coincided with an erupting dispute between a man and his wife's young lover. The officer was able to successfully negotiate an unofficial resolution. All interactions between villagers and gendarmes do not have such beneficial outcomes, however.

Gendarmes play a complex role in keeping village peace. Their presence in the village clearly allays certain kinds of violence, but gendarmes also interact with villagers in ways which create new disputes between villagers, and between the gendarmes and certain villagers. Thus, integration into larger social units has both benefits and drawbacks for Mandalinci people. Benefits accrue from undercutting a value system which suggests that a man *ought* to actively retaliate within an eighteen-hour period against another adult male who has committed an offense against his honor. Disadvantages accrue from giving gendarmes "authoritative positions of power over villagers" (Starr 1978c). Villagers are virtually defenseless when gendarme behavior affronts their values. The only redress open to them is to make written complaints to a gendarme's superior officer, and hope that that officer will feel responsible for the behavior of his subordinate.

Discretionary Powers of the Gendarmes. Village gendarmes exercise a degree of discretion in filing reports. I recorded at least three instances in which, after carrying out a village investigation, the gendarme did not make a written report, meaning the matter was dropped. On the other hand, the subdistrict gendarmes, being unfamiliar with village personalities, are more likely to make a written report immediately, which then leads directly to the public prosecutor's office.

The Turkish Legal System. When a villager takes a grievance out of the village context, he has a number of arenas in which to seek justice, but some arenas are determined by the type of grievance. For instance, if he or she has a grievance over land he can take the case to be heard at the administrative office of the district director in Bodrum (the *Kaymakam*), or he can open a case directly at the lower or higher Bodrum Civil Law court, depending on whether the disputed land is over or under 1,000 liras ($100) in value. If he feels some type of crime has been committed against him or his property, he can report the alleged behavior directly to the village gendarme, to the subdistrict gendarme (stationed in a large nearby village), or directly to the public prosecutor. (See Figure 1, p. 135, for a diagram of the chain of jurisdiction pertaining to civil and criminal cases that occur in the village.)

The Public Prosecutor. The public prosecutor (whose office was located in the Bodrum courthouse rather than in the police station) was required to carry out his own investigation. He read the earlier reports, interviewed the principals, and interrogated witnesses to attempt to establish (1) whether lawbreaking activity occurred, and (2) whether evidence existed that would stand up in court of the "alleged criminal activity." Thus, the public prosecutor also had considerable discretion in deciding which cases to prosecute. His high salary, his training (which involved four years' study at one of Turkey's two law schools), his sense of professionalism, and the fact that his "record-keeping" was subjected to official scrutiny at least once a year, all acted to keep him accountable to standards set by the national government and to the national codes of criminal procedure and criminal law.

Selected Glossary

Adliye Sarayı: Courthouse (Literally: the palace of justice).

Adliye: Courthouse, court system.

Ağır Ceza Mahkemesi: Criminal court of first instance for major felony cases. In some jurisdictions a court of Appeal. Found only in the provincial capitals and cities.

Askeriye: The armed forces.

Asliye Ceza Mahkemesi: Criminal court of first instance, located in district towns, and in all the larger centers of population. Does not handle major felony cases.

Asliye Hukuk Mahkemesi: Civil Court of first instance.

Avrupa Tüccarı: European merchants.

Avukat: Attorney.

Ayan: A notable in Ottoman times, often important rural landholders who formed a status group.

Başlık: Brideprice.

Belediye: Municipality.

Berat: Patent, warrant, tile of privilege. European traders obtained trading franchises by purchasing these.

Ceza Kararnamesi: Court decision in a criminal case.

Ceza Kanunu: The Crimnal Code.

Çifthane: A family farm.

Çiftlik: A big farm.

Dar-ı Surayı Bab-ı Ali: Legislative council of the Grand *Vizier.*

Defterhane: Land Registry office.

Derebey: A feudal lord.

Diyanet İsleri Müdürlüğü: Department of Religious Affairs, established March 3, 1924.

Divan-ı Ahkâm-ı Adliye: The highest Ottoman Court of Appeals for all *nizamiye* courts. It was established in 1868.

Divan-ı Humayun: Imperial Chancery of State or Imperial Council.

Dolmuş: Taxi that only starts when it is filled up and drives along a set route; jitney taxi.

Dönüm: A land measure of about 920 square meters that has been standardized to equal about one-quarter of an acre.

Encümen-i Âli: A legislative High Council created from the merging of two earlier councils in 1839.

Esham: A tax-farming system introduced into Anatolia by the Ottomans in the middle of the eighteenth century. This system fixed the profit of a title holder at 5% yearly for periods of eight to ten years.

Fıkıh (Arabic: *fiqk*): Muslim canonical jurisprudence.

Gülhane Proclamation of 1839, also called *Gülhane Hatt-ı Hümayunu*: Firman read by the Foreign Minister Mustafa Resid Pasa on Oct. 3, 1839 in Gülhane Park, declaring the political reforms of Sultan Abdülmejid.

Had: Limit; boundary.

Hadith: Narrative relating the deeds and utterances of the Prophet, Muhammed and his companions.

Hanefi (Arabic: *Ḥanafī*): One of the four classical schools of Islamic law of the Sunni Muslims. Founded by Abu Hanifah.

Hambelî (Arabic: *Ḥanbalī*): One of the four classical schools of Islamic law of the Sunni Muslims. Founded by Ahmad ibn Hanbal.

Hatt-ı Hümayun: The name of the legislation introducing the Tanzimat reforms. Also called the *Gülhane Rescript*.

Hayriye Tüccarı: The Muslim merchants' guild in Ottoman times.

Hisar: Castle; fort.

Hukuk Fakultesi: Law school.

Hurriyet: Freedom; liberty.

Iç güvey: A groom who lives with his wife's family.

Il: Administrative province, formerly called *vilayet*.

Ilçe: Administrative district within an *il*, formerly called *kaza*.

Ilk Okul: Elementary school.

Ilim: Science, knowledge.

İlmiye: The Ulema class in Ottoman society; Muslim theologians.

Iltizam: A land-holding system of the Ottomans.

İmam Hatip schools: Religious high schools in Turkey, established 1952.

Ittihatcilar as in *Ittihati ve Terakki Cemeyeti*: Committee of Union and Progress, a political party in power after the revolution of 1908.

Jeunes Turcs: The Young Turks, a revolutionary party active in the second half of the nineteenth and beginning of the twentieth centuries.

Kadı: A judge of Islamic canon law, and in Ottoman history, governor of a *kaza*.

Kanun: Law; Code of Laws. Historically refers to secular rather than religious laws. Also used to refer to pronouncements of the Sultan.

Kâtip: A clerk, scribe or secretary.

Karar: A judgment or decree or order pronounced by a court in settlement of a controversy submitted to it.

Kaymakam: A district director.

Kaza: Formerly, a district town, now known as *ilçe*.

Keşif: Legal investigation by a judge at a site either subject to a civil dispute or the scene of an alleged crime.

Kişla: The winter pastures of transhumant groups.

Kutadgu Bilik: Famous Turkish political writings of the eleventh century.

Mahkeme: A law court.

Mal Müdürü: The Director of the Land Office.

Mâlikâme: State lands held in fief by a private person for life, with fixed yearly taxes payable to the state treasury. These leases were often renewable (but at a higher rate) by the senior title holder's male or female heirs.

Maliki (Arabic: *Mālıkī*): One of four schools of law of the Sunni Muslims. Founded by Imam Malik.

Maliye: The financial office in Ottoman times.

Mecelle (also called *Mecelle-i Ahkâm-ı Adliye*): The Ottoman code of Civil Law issued between 1869 and 1876.

Meclis-i Âyan: Chamber of Notables, in the first Ottoman parliament, established in 1876 under the first Ottoman Constitution.

Meclis-i Hass-ı Vükelâ: Council of Ministers or cabinet, formed during the Tanzimat and composed of the heads of executive councils and departments.

Meclis-i Meb' usan: Chamber of Deputies, in the first Ottoman parliament established in 1876 under the first Ottoman Constitution. Much more representative than the *Meclis-i Âyan*.

Meclis-i Vâlâ: High Council, created in 1838–39. This was the first and most important legislative council of the Tanzimat reformers. In 1867 it was divided into a Council for Judicial Regulations and a council of State.

Medrese: School of Islamic theology and sciences in Ottoman period.

Mektep: Secular school.

Merat: A type of state-owned land, consisting of uncultivated areas lying outside the boundaries of existing communities, usually available for clearing and cultivation.

Metruk: Landed property that at death escheated to the state.

Mevlûd: A poem written by Süleyman Celebi depicting the birth of the Prophet Muhammad. (The word also refers to a religious gathering held in memory of a deceased person, in which the *Mevlûd* is chanted.)

Millet: A religious community, living in a Muslim country that in return for paying the capital tax, enjoyed protection and safety. Based on the *Zimmi* concept.

Mîrî: Farm land owned by the state, and leased to tax farmers.
Müftü (Arabic: *Mufti*): Official expounder of Islamic law; Islamic judge.
Muhtar: Village headman.
Mülk: Freehold land; real property.
Mülkiye: The Civil service in Ottoman times.
Nahiye: An administrative sub-district within an *ilçe*.
Nizamiye (or *Adliye-i Nizamiye*): A law court in the first secular system of courts, introduced after 1850 as part of the Tanzimat reforms.
Noter Senedi: Any legal document prepared by a Civil law notary. It serves as proof of a business transaction; of a negotiable instrument; of a security; a promissary note; a title document (but not a title deed, *tapu*).
Porte (French: door): The building, housing the central governmental bureaucracy of the Ottomans.
Rüşdiye: Secular secondary schools, introduced as part of the educational reforms in the nineteenth century.
Sancak: An administrative unit under the Ottomans, about the size of a province.
Şeriat (Arabic: *Shari^c^a*): The canonical law of Islam. The body of sacred law of Islam, embodied in the *Ku'ran*, the *Hadith*, and the *fıkıh*. As secular law and secular courts developed among the Ottomans in the nineteenth century, the actually body of laws referred to by the term *Şeriat* changed, becoming more limited.
Şeyhülislâm: The highest Islamic legal authority, came next to the Grand Vizier in governmental importance.
Şeybender: Head of the market; consul in a foreign country.
Sulh Ceza Mahkemesi: Lower Criminal Court for minor offenses.
Sulh Hukuk Mahkemesi: Lower Civil court.
Talâk (Arabic: *talaq*): Divorce of a wife by her husband through renunciation under Islamic law.
Tapu: Title deed.
Tapu Temessükü: A type of deed to land in the nineteenth century that provided a right to the revenue from the land, without conferring freehold ownership.
Taxim: Division, portion (as in *toprak taksimi*, division of land).
Türban: A long headscarf, convering hair, neck, and top of shoulders worn by religious Turkish Muslim women to convey deference to Islamic values.
Tanzimat: Name of the period of nineteenth century Ottoman reforms begun in 1839 and extending to the enactment of the first Ottoman Constitution in 1876.

Tımar: A tax farming system widely in use in the early and Medieval periods of Ottoman rule. The leaseholder had to feed and maintain a certain numbers of cavalry soldiers (*sipahyan*) and their horses.
Türk Medenî Kanunu: The Turkish Civil Code, issued in 1926, based on the Swiss Civil Code.
Ulema (Arabic: ulamā) Doctors of Islamic theology, who formed the corps of the Islamic legal structure.
Ulûm (the plural form of *ilim*): Science.
Umumi Nüfus Sayımı: The Census (now *Genel Nüfus Sayımı*).
Vali: The Director of a province.
Veraset: Inheritance.
Vezir (Arabic: *watana*): Minister, and *Vezir-i azam*, the grand minister.
Vatan: Fatherland; nation.
Vekil: Agent, representative. Agents granted certain powers by contractual agreement who can work in Civil courts. *Vekil*s also write various legal letters, search out documents in different record bureaus and are especially active in land cases.
Vakıf (sing.), *evkaf* (plural): Pious foundation.
Vilayet: A province, now known as *il*.
Yargıtay: The Supremen Court of Turkey, located in Ankara.
Yayla: High plateau; summer pastures.
Yeni Osmanlılar: The Young Ottomans, a political group seeking reforms who often expressed their ideas through literary works. They were active in the second half of the nineteenth century.
Yesideés (Turkish: *Yezidis*): A religious group from Kurdistan, often called devil worshippers, who followed a religion based on Zoroastrianism. Their rituals include "fire worship."
Yıldız: Star.
Yüksek Hâkimler Kurulu: The highest Judiciary Committee, responsible for supervising the judiciary.
Yüksek Islam Enstitüsi: Higher Institute for Islamic Studies, established at Istanbul and Konya in 1952 for graduates of the *Imam Hatip* schools.
Zimmi (Arabic: *dhimmīs*): A free non-Muslim subject living in a Muslim country who, in return for paying a fixed poll and a land tax, enjoyed protection and safety. Belonged to a specific *millet*.

timar: Ottoman system in which [illegible] periods of Ottoman rule. The possessor had to recruit and maintain a certain number of cavalry soldiers (sipahi) and their horses.

Türk Medeni Kanunu: The Turkish Civil Code, passed 1926. It is based on the Swiss Civil Code.

ulema (Arabic, ulamā): Doctors of Islamic theology who formulated the rules of the Islamic legal structure.

ulum: the plural form of ilm, science.

[illegible]: The [illegible] of [illegible].

vali: The Director of a province.

[illegible]

[illegible] and [illegible] the [illegible]

[illegible]

[illegible] representative who can work in civil cases. [illegible] legal letters, [illegible] documents [illegible] and [illegible] especially active in land cases.

[illegible]

[illegible]

Yargıtay: The Supreme Court of Turkey, located in Ankara.

yayla: [illegible] summer pastures.

Yeni Osmanlılar (The Young Ottomans): political group seeking reforms who often expressed their ideas through literary works. They were active in the second half of the nineteenth century.

[illegible] A religious group [illegible] often called devil worshippers, who followed a religion based on Zoroastrianism. Their ritual [illegible]

[illegible]

Yüksek Hâkimler Kurulu: The High Council of Judges; Committee responsible for supervising the judges.

[illegible]

[illegible]

Laws, Statutes, and Codes

Code Civil Turc [du 1926], loi No. 743, du 17 Février 1926.
Journal Official, No. 339 du Avril 1926.

Mejelle

Cevdet, Ahmed

1967 "Report of the *Mejelle* Commission." Trans. B. A. L. Tyser. *The Mejelle*. Being an English Translation of *Majallahel-Ahkam-i Adliya* and a Complete Code on Islamic Civil Law. Lahore: All Pakistan Legal Decision, Nabha Road.

Rahman, S. A.

1967a "Foreword" to The *Mejelle*. Being an English Translation of *Majallahel-Ahkam-i-Adliya* and a Complete Code on Islamic Civil Law. Trans. B. A. L. Tyser. Lahore: All Pakistan Legal Decisions, Nabha Road, pp. i–ii.

1967b [The *Mejelle*.] A translation of *Majallahel-Ahkam-i-Adliya* and a Complete Code on Islamic Civil Law. Trans. B. A. L. Tyser. Lahore: All Pakistan Legal Decisions, Nabha Road, pp. i–ii.

Tyser, B. A. L.

1967 *The Mejelle*. Being an English Translation of *Majallahel-Ahkam-i Adliya* and a Complete Code on Islamic Civil Law. Lahore: All Pakistan Legal Decision, Nabha Road.

Sudanese Mohamedan Law Courts Organization and Procedure Regulations
Section 53.

Türk Kanunu Medenîsi [known as *Türk Medenî Kanunu*]

1926 Kanun No. 743, Yayin Tarihi [date of publication] 4 April 1926, Yururluk Tarihi [date effective] 4 October 1926 Resmi Gazete [Official Gazette] No. 339.

Türk Medenî Kanunu Şerhi Istanbul: İsmail Akgün Matbaası
1967

Ottoman Family Law of 1917.

Williams, Ivy, ed.
1925 *The Swiss Civil Code.* English Version. Oxford: Oxford University Press.

Bibliography

Abadan-Unat, Nermin

1977 "Implications of Migration on Emancipation and Pseudo-Emancipation of Turkish Women." *International Migration Review* 2(1):54–55.

1981a "Social Change and Turkish Women." In *Women in Turkish Society*, ed. N. Abadan-Unat. Leiden, Netherlands: E. J. Brill, pp. 5–39.

1981b *Women in Turkish Society* (ed.). Leiden, Netherlands: E. J. Brill.

1986 "Turkish Migration to Europe and the Middle East: Its Impact on Social Structure and Social Legislation." In *Social Legislation in the Contemporary Middle East*, ed. L. O. Michalak and J. W. Salacuse. University of California, Berkeley, Institute of International Studies.

Abel, Richard

1973 "Why Go to Court: A Historical and Comparative Study of Patterns of Local Court Use in Kenya." Unpublished working draft.

1974 "A Comparative Theory of Dispute Institutions in Society." *Law and Society Review* 8(2):217–347.

1979a "The Rise of Capitalism and the Transformation of Disputing: From Confrontation over Honor to Competition for Property." [Review of *Dispute and Settlement in Rural Turkey*, by J. Starr.] *UCLA Law Review* 28(3):233–55.

1979b "Western Courts in Non-Western Settings: Patterns of Court Use in Colonial and Neo-Colonial Africa." In *The Imposition of Law*, ed. S. B. Burman and B. E. Harrell-Bond. New York: Academic Press, pp. 167–200.

Ahmad, Feroz

1977 *The Turkish Experiment in Democracy, 1950–1975*. Boulder, CO: Westview Press.

Aktan, Reşat

1966 "Problems of Land Reform in Turkey. *Middle East Journal* 20:317–333.

Akşit, Bahattin

1986 "*Imam-Hatip* and Other Secondary Schools in the Context of Political and Cultural Modernization of Turkey." *Journal of Human Sciences* 5(1):25–41.

Allen, Henry E.

1935 *The Turkish Transformation*. Chicago: University of Chicago Press.

Anderson, Benedict

1983 *Imagined Communities: Reflections on the Origin and Spread of Nationalism*. London: Verso Editions.

Ansay, Tuğrul

1983 *Review of Mary Zwahlen's Le Divorce en Turquie*. (Contribution à létude de la réception du code civil Suisse). *The American Journal of Comparative Law* 31:751–53.

Ansay, Tuğrul and Don Wallace, Jr.

1966 *Introduction to Turkish Law*. Ankara, Turkey: Güzel İstanbul Matbaası.

Antoun, Richard T.

1979 *Low-Keyed Politics: Local-Level Leadership and Change in the Middle East*. Albany, NY: State University of New York Press.

1990 "Litigant Strategies in an Islamic Court in Jordan." In *Law and Islam in the Middle East*, ed. D. Dwyer, Westport, CT: Bergin and Garvey, pp. 35–60.

Atkinson, J. Maxwell and Paul Drew

1979 *Order in Court. The Organization of Verbal Interaction in Judicial Settings*. London: Macmillan.

Barnes, J. A.

1961 "Law as Politically Active: An Anthropological View." In *Studies in the Sociology of Law*, ed. G. Sawer. Canberra, Australia: Australian National University, pp. 167–96.

Barth, Frederik

1964 *Nomads of South Persia. The Basseri Tribe of the Khamseh Confederacy*. New York: Humanities Press.

Barton, R. F.

1919 *Ifugao Law*. Berkeley, CA: University of California Press.

Berkes, Niyazi

1959 "Translator's Introduction" to *Turkish Nationalism and Western Civilization: Selected Essays of Ziya Gökalp*. Westport, CT: Greenwood, pp. 13–31.

1964 *The Development of Secularism in Turkey*. Montréal: McGill University Press.

Bianchi, Robert
1984 *Interest Groups and Political Development in Turkey.* Princeton, NJ: Princeton University Press.

Bisharat, George
1989 *Palestinian Lawyers and Israeli Rule. Law and Disorder in the West Bank.* Austin, TX: University of Texas Press.

Blok, Anton
1974 *The Mafia of a Sicilian Village, 1860–1960: A Study of Violent Peasant Entrepreneurs.* New York: Harper and Row.

1989 "Symbolic Vocabulary of Public Executions." In *History and Power in the Study of Law: New Directions in Legal Anthropology,* ed. June Starr and Jane F. Collier. Ithaca, NY: Cornell University Press, pp. 31–54.

Bodrum
1966 Printed pamphlet. Published by the Turkish Tourist Bureau. On file with the author.

Bodrum Ilçesinin 1965 Yılına ait Genel Nüfus Sayımı.
1965 [Census of Bodrum district.] Document in Bodrum Census Bureau. Copy on file with the author.

Bohannan, Paul
1957 *Justice and Judgment Among the Tiv.* London: Oxford University Press.

Boissevain, Jeremy
1968 "The Place of Non-Groups in the Social Sciences." *Man* 3(4):542–56.

1974 *Friends of Friends: Networks, Manipulators and Coalitions.* Oxford: Basil Blackwell.

Bosserup, Ester
1970 *Woman's Role in Economic Development.* New York: St. Martin's Press.

Bracken, Katherine W.
1954 "Legal Reform in Turkey, 1839–1953." Unpublished manuscript, Princeton University Library, dated May 15, 1954.

Braudel, Fernand
1966 *The Mediterranean and the Mediterranean World in the Age of Philip II.* Vol. I. New York: Harper and Row.

Caesar-Wolf, Beatrice
1984 "The Construction of 'Adjucable' Evidence in a Witness Hearing." *Text* (special issue, ed. Brenda Danet). 4(1–3):193–223.

Census of Turkey, 1927
1929 *Ümumi Nüfus Tahriri*. Türkiye Cumhuriyeti Başvekalet. İstatistik Ümum Müdürlüğü 28 Oct. 1927. Ankara: Husnutabiat Mabaası.

Census of Turkey, 1950
1950 *Ümumi Nüfus Sayımı*. Recensement Général de la Population (Du 22 Octobre 1950). Nesriyat Publication, No. 359, Ankara: Türkiye Cumhuriyeti Başvekalet İstatistik Ümum Mürdürlüğü. Présidence du conceil office central de statistique. Ankara.

Census of Turkey, 1965
1965 *Genel Nüfus Sayımı*. İdari Bolunus. 24.10.1965. Republic of Turkey. Prime Ministry State Institute of Statistics. Ankara.

Chanock, Martin
1983 "Signposts or Tombstones? Reflections on Recent Works on the Anthropology of Law." *Law in Context* I:107–25.
1985 *Law, Custom and Social Order: The Colonial Experience in Malawi and Zambia*. Cambridge: Cambridge University Press.

Chartier, Roger
1985 "Text, Symbols, and Frenchness." *Journal of Modern History* 57(4):682–95.

Cohen, Abner
1969 *Custom and Politics in Urban Africa: A Study of Hausa Migrants in Yoruba Towns*. Berkeley, CA: University of California Press.
1981 *The Politics of Elite Culture*. Berkeley, CA: University of California Press.

Cohn, Bernard S.
1981 "Anthropology and History in the 1980s." *Journal of Interdisciplinary History* 12(2):227–52.
1983 "Representing Authority in Victorian India." In *The Invention of Tradition*, ed. E. Hobsbawm and T. Ranger. Cambridge: Cambridge University Press.
1989 "Law and the Colonial State in India." In *History and Power in the Study of Law: New Directions in Legal Anthropology*, ed. J. Starr and J. F. Collier. Ithaca, NY: Cornell University Press, pp. 131–52.

Collier, Jane F.
1973 Law and Social Change in Zinacantan. Palo Alto, CA: Stanford University Press.
1974 "Women in Politics." In *Women, Culture and Society*, ed M. Rosaldo and L. Lamphere. Palo Alto, CA: Stanford University Press.

Colson, E.

1953 Social Control and Vengeance in Plateau Tonga Society. *Africa* 23:199–212.

Comaroff, John and Simon Roberts

1981 *Rules and Processes: The Cultural Logic of Disputes in an African Context*. Chicago: University of Chicago Press.

Coşar, Fatma Mansur

1978 "Women in Turkish Society." In *Women in the Muslim World*, ed. L. Beck and N. Keddie, Cambridge, MA: Harvard University Press, pp. 124–40.

Coulson, J.

1964 *A History of Islamic Law*. Edinburgh: Edinburgh University Press.

Culler, J.

1982 *On Deconstruction*. Ithaca, NY: Cornell University Press.

Cuniet, Vital

1894 *Histoire de l'Asie Mineure*. Book III. Paris.

Damaska, Mirjan

1975 "Presentation of Evidence and Fact-Finding Precision." *University of Pennsylvania Law Review* 1083–1106.

Danet, Brenda

1980 "Language in the Legal Process." *Law and Society Review* 14(3):445–565.

1984 "Studies of Legal Discourse." (ed.). *Text* (Special Issue) 4:(1–3):1–275.

Davison, Roderic H.

1963 *Reform in the Ottoman Empire, 1856–1876*. Princeton, NJ: Princeton University Press.

de Planhol, Xavier

1958 "Geography, Politics, and Nomadism in Anatolia." *International Social Science Bulletin* 11(4):525–31.

Degler, Carl N.

1980 *At Odds. Women and the Family in America from the Revolution to the Present*. New York: Oxford University Press.

Derrida J.

1974 "White Mythology: Metaphor in the Text of Philosophy." *New Literary History* 6(1):5–74.

Dobash, R. E. and R. Dobash

1979 *Violence Against Wives. A Case Against the Patriarchy.* New York: The Free Press.

Drew, Paul

1982 "Analyzing the Use of Language in Courtroom Interaction." In *Handbook of Discourse Analysis*, ed. T. A. van Dijk. London: Academic Press.

Duben, Alan

1985 "Turkish Families and Households in Historical Perspective." *Journal of Family History* 10:75–97.

Dunstan, R.

1980 "Context for Coercion: Analyzing Properties of Courtroom 'Questions.' " *British Journal of Law and Society* (summer):61–77.

Dwyer, Daisy

1990 *Law and Islam in the Middle East*. Westport, CT: Bergin and Garvey.

1979 "Law Actual and Perceived: The Sexual Politics of Law in Morocco." *Law and Society Review* 13(3):739–56.

in press "Litigant's Law and Judicial Tensions in Morocco: Westermarck's Ethnography of Law in a Contemporary Context." *Papers for Edward Westermarck.* ed. Timothy Stroup, Holland: Acta Philosophica Fennica.

Eickelman, Dale

1985 *Knowledge and Power in Morocco*. Princeton, NJ: Princeton University Press.

Elias, Norbert

1972 "Process of State Formation and Nation Building." Paper read at the 7th World Congress of Sociology, Varna, Bulgaria, September 1970. *Transactions of the 7th World Congress of Sociology,* International Sociological Association. Geneva.

Elliott, C. B.

1838 *Travels in the Three Great Empires of Austria, Russia, and Turkey.* Vol. II. London: Richard Bently.

Engel, David M.

1978 *Code and Custom in a Thai Provincial Court: The Interaction of Formal and Informal Systems of Justice*. Tucson, AZ: University of Arizona Press.

Epstein, A. L.

1954 *Juridical Techniques and the Judicial Process*. Manchester: published for the Rhodes-Livingstone Institute by Manchester University Press.

1967 "The Case Method in the Field of Law." In *The Craft of Social Anthropology.* ed. A. L. Epstein. London: Tavistock, pp. 205–30.

Epstein, T. S. and D. Jackson (eds.)
1977 *The Feasibility of Fertility Planning: Microperspectives.* Oxford and New York: Pergamon Press.

Ermarth, Michael
1985 "Mindful Matters: The Empire's New Codes and the Plight of Modern European Intellectual History." *Journal of Modern History* 57(4):506–27.

Erder, Leila
1981 "The Women of Turkey: A Demographic Overview." In *Women in Turkish Society,* ed. N. Abadan-Unat. Leiden, Netherlands: E.J. Brill, pp. 41–58.

Esposito, John L.
1982 *Women in Muslim Family Law.* Syracuse, NY: University Press.

Fallers, Lloyd A.
1974 *The Social Anthropology of the Nation-State.* Chicago: Aldine.

Fallers, L. A. and M. Fallers
1976 "Sex Roles in Edremit" in *Mediterranean Family Structures,* ed. J. G. Peristiany. London: Cambridge University Press, pp. 243–60.

Feron, James
1984 "Judge is Upheld in Setting Aside Stouffer Verdict." *New York Times* (May 30), p. B2, col. 3–6.

Feroze, Muhammad Rashid
1962 "Family Laws of the Turkish Republic." *Islamic Studies* 1:131–47.

Field, Henry
[1885] *The Greek Islands and Turkey After the War.* London: Sampson, Law, Marston, Searle, and Rivington.

Findley, Carter
1980 *Bureaucratic Reform in the Ottoman Empire.* Princeton, NJ: Princeton University Press.

1986 "Mahkama." *Encyclopedia of Islam* (new edition), Vol. 6 (Fascicules 99–100). Leiden, Netherlands: E.J. Brill, pp. 5–11.

Fitzpatrick, Peter
1985 "Is it simple to be a Marxist in Legal Anthropology?" *Modern Law Review* (July):1–32.

Frangakis-Syrett, Elena
1988 "Izmir's Trade with Western Europe in the Eighteenth and Early Nineteenth Centuries." Lecture presented at Turkish Seminar, Columbia University, Sept. 16, 1988.

Friedman, Lawrence M.

1990 *The Republic of Choice. Law, Authority and Culture.* Cambridge, MA: Harvard University Press.

Friedman, Lawrence M. and R. V. Percival

1976 "A Tale of Two Courts: Litigation in Alameda and San Benito Counties." *Law and Society Review* 10(2):267–301.

Fuller, Lon

1978 "The Forms and Limits of Adjudication." *Harvard Law Review* 92:353–409.

Galanter, Marc

1974 "Why the 'Haves' Come out Ahead: Speculations on the Limits of Legal Change." *Law and Society Review* 9(1):95–160.

Galantı, Avram

1946 *Bodrum Tarihine* Ek. [An Addition to Bodrum's History]. Book I and II. Istanbul: Basımevi.

Garbett, C. K.

1973 "The Analysis of Social Situations." *Man* (New Series) 8:214–27.

Garcia Marquez, Gabriel

1970 *One Hundred Years of Solitude*. New York: Harper and Row.

Garfinkel, H.

1967 *Studies in Ethnomethodology.* Englewood Cliffs, NJ: Prentice-Hall.

Garnett, Lucy M. J.

1909 *The Turkish People: Their Social Life, Religious Beliefs and Institutions, and Domestic Life*. London: Methuen & Co.

Garraty, John A. and Peter Gay

1972 *The Columbia History of the World.* New York: Harper and Row.

Gazetteer of Turkey.

1960 Official Standards Names, Approved by United States Board on Geographic Names. 2 vols. Office of Geography, Dept. of Interior, Washington DC.

1984 Defense Mapping Agency. Washington DC.

Geertz, Clifford

1968 *Islam Observed*. New Haven, CT: Yale University Press.

1973 *Interpretation of Cultures*. New York: Basic Books.

1983 "Local Knowledge: Fact and Law in Comparative Perspective." In C. Geertz, ed. *Local Knowledge: Further Essays in Interpretive Anthropology.* New York: Basic Books.

Gibb, H. A. R. and H. Bowen

1967 *Islamic Society and the West.* Vol. I. Islamic Society in the Eighteenth Century. Pt. 1. London: Oxford University Press.

Giddens, A.

1983 *Central Problems in Social Theory: Action, Structure and Contradiction in Social Analysis.* Berkeley, CA: University of California Press.

Gilsenan, Michael

1982 *Recognizing Islam: Religion and Society in the Modern Arab World.* New York: Pantheon Books.

Gluckman, Max

1955 *The Judicial Process Among the Barotse of Northern Rhodesia.* Manchester: Manchester University Press.

1961 "Ethnographic Data in British Social Anthropology." *The Sociological Review* (New Series) 9:5–17.

Goffman, E

1961 *Encounters.* Indianapolis: Bobbs-Merrill.

Gökalp, Zina

1913 "*Halk Medeniyeti.*" In *Halka Doğru* 1(14–15), published in Istanbul. [Civilization of the People.] Trans. Niyazi Berkes. In *Turkish Nationalism and Western Civilization.* Westport, CT: Greenwood: 1959, 89–92.

Gordon, Robert

1988 "Law and Ideology." *Tikkun* 3(1):14–18, 83–86.

Greenhouse, Carol

1986 *Praying for Justice.* Ithaca, NY: Cornell University Press.

Grønhaug, Reidar

1974 *Micro-Macro Relations: Nomadic Adaptations in Antalya.* Bergen, Norway: Dept. Social Anthropology, Occasional Papers.

Gulliver, P. H.

1963 *Social Control in an African Society.* London: Routledge and Kegan Paul.

1969a "Introduction to Case Studies of Law in non-Western Societies." In *Law in Culture and Society,* ed. L. Nader. Chicago: Aldine, pp. 11–23.

1969b "Dispute Settlement Without Courts." In *Law in Culture and Society,* ed. L. Nader. Chicago: Aldine, pp. 24–68.

1971 *Neighbors and Networks: The Idiom of Kinship Among the Ndendeuli of Tanzania*. Berkeley, CA: University of California Press.

1973 "Negotiations as a Mode of Dispute Settlement: Towards A General Model." *Law and Society Review* 7:667–92.

Gumperz, John

1982a *Discourse Strategies*. Cambridge: Cambridge University Press.

1982b "Fact and Inference in Courtroom Testimony." In *Language and Social Identity*, ed. J. Gumperz. Cambridge: Cambridge University Press, pp. 163–95.

1982c *Language and Social Identity.* (ed.) Cambridge: Cambridge University Press.

Güriz, Adnan

1966 "Sources of Turkish Law." In *Introduction to Turkish Law*, ed. T. Ansay and D. Wallace, Jr. Ankara, Turkey: Güzel Istanbul Matbaası, pp. 1–22.

Hale, William

1981 *The Political and Economic Development of Modern Turkey.* London: Croom Helm.

Hansen, Edward and Timothy C. Parrish

1983 "Elites Versus the State. Toward an Anthropological Contribution to the Study of Hegemonic Power in Capitalist Society." In *Elites*. ed. G. Marcus, pp. 257–77.

Hayden, Robert

1987 "Turn-Taking, Overlap, and the Task at Hand: Ordering Speaking Turns in Legal Settings." *American Anthropologist* 14(2):251–70.

Heidborn, A.

1908 *Manuel de Droit Public et Administratif de l'Empire Ottoman*. Vol. 1. Viènne: C. W. Stern.

Henry, J.

1987 "Turkish Woman Judge Visits U.S.A. and Describes Women's Status."

Heper, Metin

1976 "Political Modernization as Reflected in Bureaucratic Change: The Turkish Bureaucracy and a 'Historical Bureaucratic Empire' Tradition." *International Journal Middle East Studies* 7:507–21.

1985 *The State Tradition in Turkey.* Hull, England: The Eothen Press.

Heyd, Uriel

1954 *Language Reform in Modern Turkey.* Jerusalem: Israel Oriental Society, No. 5.

1968 *Revival of Islam in Modern Turkey: A Lecture.* Jerusalem: Magnes Press.

Hirst, Paul
1979 *On Law and Ideology.* London: Oxford University Press.

Hobsbawm, E. J.
1959 *Primitive Rebels. Studies in Archaic Forms of Social Movements in the Nineteenth and Twentieth Centuries.* New York: Norton.

Hoebel, E. A.
1954 *The Law of Primitive Man.* Cambridge, MA: Harvard University Press.

Hourani, Albert
1968 "Ottoman Reform and the Politics of Notables." In *Beginnings of Modernization in the Middle East*, ed. William R. Polk and Richard L. Chambers. University of Chicago Press, pp. 41–68.

Inalcık, Halil
1964 "Turkey: The Nature of Traditional Society." In *Political Modernization in Japan and Turkey,* ed. E. Ward and D. A. Rustow. Princeton, NJ: Princeton University Press, pp. 42–63.
1977 "Centralization and Decentralization in Ottoman Administration." In *Studies in Eighteenth Century Islamic History* ed. T. Naff and R. Owens. Carbondale, IL: Southern Illinois University Press, pp. 27–52.
1984 "The Emergence of Big Farms, *Çiftliks*: State, Landlords, and Tenants." In *Contributions à l'Histoire Economique et Sociale de l'Empire Ottoman, Collection Turcica III,* ed. J. L. Bacque-Grammont and P. Dumont. Leuven, France: Peeters, pp. 105–26.

Kâğıtçıbaşı, Ciğdem
1982 "Introduction." In *Sex Roles, Family, and Community in Turkey,* ed. C. Kâğıtçıbaşı. Bloomington, IN: Indiana University Press.

Kandiyoti, Deniz
1976 "Social Change and Family Structure in a Turkish Village (Bachelors and Maidens: A Turkish Case Study)." In *Kinship and Modernization in Mediterranean Society,* ed. J. G. Peristiany. Hanover, NH: Center for Mediterranean Studies, pp. 61–71.

Karal, Enver Ziya, ed.
1945 *Atatürk'ün Söylev ve Demeçleri* [The Speeches and Statements of Ataturk]. 3 vols. Istanbul.

Karpat, Kemal H.
1968 "The Land Regime, Social Structure, and Modernization in the Ottoman Empire." In *Beginnings of Modernization in the Middle East,* ed. W. R. Polk and R. L. Chambers, pp. 69–90.

Kasaba, Resat
1988 *The Ottoman Empire and the World Economy. The Nineteenth Century.* Albany, NY: State University of New York Press.

Kazamias, Andreas M.
1966 *Education and the Quest for Modernity in Turkey.* Chicago: University of Chicago Press.

Kazgan, Gulten
1981 "Labour Force Participation, Occupational Distribution, Educational Attainment and the Socio-Economic Status of Women in the Turkish Economy." In *Women in Turkish Society,* ed. N. Abadan-Unat. Leiden, Netherlands: E.J. Brill, pp. 131–59.

Kennett, Austin
1925 *Bedouin Justice.* Cambridge: Cambridge University Press.

Kidder, R.
1979 "Toward an Integrated Theory of Imposed Law." In *The Imposition of Law,* eds. S. Burman and B. Harrell–Bond. NY: Academic Press, pp. 289–306.

Kili, Suna
1969 *Kemalism.* Istanbul: Robert College, School of Business Administration and Economics, Occasional papers.

Kinross, Lord
1964 *Ataturk: The Rebirth of a Nation.* London: Weidenfeld and Nicolson.

Kiray, Mübeccel
1976 "The Family of the Immigrant Worker." In *Turkish Workers in Europe, 1960–1975,* ed. N. Abadan-Unat. Leiden, Netherlands: E. J. Brill, pp. 214–16.

Kolars, John F.
1963 *Tradition, Season, and Change in a Turkish Village.* Department of Geography, Research Paper No. 82. Chicago: University of Chicago Press.

Kuran, Ercumend
1968 "The Impact of Nationalism on the Turkish Elite in the Nineteenth Century." In *Beginning of Modernization in the Middle East: The Nineteenth Century,* ed. W. R. Polk and R. L. Chambers. Chicago: University of Chicago Press.

Kushner, David
1977 *The Rise of Turkish Nationalism, 1876–1908.* London: Frank Cass.

Ladas, Stephen P.
1932 *The Exchange of Minorities: Bulgaria, Greece, and Turkey.* New York: Macmillan.

Lakoff, George and Mark Johnson
1980 *Metaphors We Live By.* Chicago: University of Chicago Press.

Lamar, J. V. and Sam Allis
1987 "Turkey: The Hot New Tourist Draw." *Time Magazine* (June 13): 66–7.

Landau, J. M.
1974 *Radical Politics in Modern Turkey.* Leiden, Netherlands: E.J. Brill.

Lewis, Bernard
1960 *The Arabs in History,* 2nd ed. New York: Harper and Row.
1966 *The Emergence of Modern Turkey.* London: Oxford University Press.

Llewellyn, K. and E. A. Hoebel
1941 *The Cheyenne Way. Conflict and Case Law in Primitive Jurisprudence.* Norman, OK: University of Oklahoma Press.

Loftus, Elizabeth
1979 *Eyewitness Testimony.* Cambridge, MA: Harvard University Press.

Magnarella, Paul J.
1988 *Kanun ve Aile* [Law and Family]. Assessing the Effects of Ataturk's Efforts to Transform the Moral Basis of Turkish Life Through the Implementation of European Legal Codes. *The World and I* (June):502–13.

Malinowski, Bronislaw
1926 *Crime and Custom in Savage Society.* London: Routledge and Kegan Paul.
1942 "A New Instrument for the Interpretation of Law — especially Primitive." *Yale Law Journal* 51:1237–1254.

Mansur, Fatma
1972 *Bodrum. A Town on the Aegean.* Leiden, Netherlands: E.J. Brill.

Marcus, George, ed.
1983 *Elites: Ethnographic Issues.* Albuquerque, NM: University of New Mexico Press.

Mardin, Şerif
1961 "Some Explanatory Notes of the Origins of the 'Mecelle' (Mejelle)." *The Muslim World* 189–96; 274–79.
1962 *The Genesis of Young Ottoman Thought. A Study in the Modernization of Turkish Political Ideas.* Princeton, NJ: Princeton University Press.
1969 "Power, Civil Society, and Culture in the Ottoman Empire." *Comparative Studies in Society and History* (June):258–81.
1971 "Ideology and Religion in the Turkish Revolution." *International Journal of Middle Eastern Studies* 2:197–211.

1973 "Center-Periphery Relations: A Key to Turkish Politics?" *Daedalus* 102(1):169–90.

Marx, K.

1857–1858 *Grundrisse der Kritik der politischen Ökonomie, Rohentwurf.* Edited and trans. by D. McLellan. New York: Harper and Row, 1971.

Mayer, Adrian

1966 "Quasi-Groups in the Study of Complex Societies." In *The Anthropology of Complex Societies*, ed. M. Banton. Association of Social Anthropologists, Monograph 4. London: Tavistock.

McGowan, Bruce

1981 *Economic Life in Ottoman Europe: Taxation, Trade, and the Struggle for Land, 1600–1800.* Cambridge: Cambridge University Press.

Merry, Sally E.

1990 *Getting Justice and Getting Even.* Chicago, IL: University of Chicago Press.

Merry, Sally E. and Susan Silbey

n.d. "Social Disputes or Legal Disputes: Dispute Dimensions and the Convergence of Legal Forms."

Merryman, John Henry

1985 *The Civil Law Tradition: An Introduction to the Legal Systems of Western Europe and Latin America.* 2nd ed. Palo Alto, CA: Stanford University Press.

Messick, Brinkley

1983a "Legal Documents and the Concept of 'Restricted Literacy' in a Traditional Society." *International Journal of Society and Language* 42:41–52.

1983b "Prosecution in Yeman: The Introduction of the *Niyaba.*" *International Journal of Middle East Studies.* 15:507–18.

1986 "The Mufti, the Text, and the World: Legal Interpretation in Yemen." *Man* (New Series) 21:102–19.

Miller, William

1966 *The Ottoman Empire and its Successors, 1801–1927.* New York: Octagon. First published 1936, Cambridge: The University Press.

Mizzi, Sibil

1981 "Women in Senglea—The Changing Role of Urban Working Class Women in Malta." Unpublished Ph.D. dissertation, Department of Anthropology, SUNY Stony Brook.

Moore, Sally Falk

1972 "Legal Liability and Evolutionary Interpretations." In *The Allocation of Responsibility*, ed. M. Gluckman. Manchester, England: Manchester University Press.

1973 "Law and Social Change: The Semi-Autonomous Social Field as an Appropriate Subject of Study." *Law and Society Review* 7(4):719–46.

1978 *Law as Process. An Anthropological Approach.* London: Routledge and Kegan Paul.

1986 *Social Facts and Fabrications: Customary Law on Kilimanjaro, 1880–1980.* Cambridge: Cambridge University Press.

1989 "History and the Reformation of Custom on Kilimanjaro." In *History and Power in the Study of Law,* ed. J. Starr and J. Collier. Ithaca, NY: Cornell University Press, pp. 277–301.

Nader, Laura

1965a "The Anthropological Study of Law." In *The Ethnography of Law,* ed. L. Nader. *American Anthropologist* (special issue) 67(6)(2):1–32.

1965b "Choices in Legal Procedure: Shia Moslem and Mexican Zapotec." *American Anthropologist* 67(2):394–99.

1965c "Communication between Village and City in the Modern Middle East." *Human Organization* 24(1):18–24.

1965d *The Ethnography of Law.* (ed.) *American Anthropologist* (special issue) 67(6)(2).

1969a *Law in Culture and Society.* (ed.) Chicago: Aldine.

1969b "Styles of Court Procedure: To Make the Balance." In *Law in Culture and Society,* ed. L. Nader. Chicago: Aldine, pp. 69–91.

1974 "Up the Anthropologist—Perspectives Gained from Studying Up." In *Reinventing Anthropology,* ed. D. Hymes. New York: Vintage Books, pp. 284–311.

1990 *Harmony Ideology.* Stanford, CA: Stanford University Press.

Nader, Laura and Harry Todd, Jr.

1978 "Introduction." In *The Disputing Process—Law in Ten Societies,* ed. L. Nader and H. Todd. New York: Columbia University Press, pp. 1–40.

Nagata, Yuzo

1976 *Some Documents on the Big Farms (çiftliks) of the Notables in Western Anatolia.* Tokyo: Institute for the Study of Languages and Cultures of Asia and Africa. Studia Culturae Islamicae, No. 4.

Nansen, Dr.

1922a "Reciprocal Exchange of Racial Minorities Between Greece and Turkey." Report to the League of Nations. Geneva (c.736. N447).

1922b "Relief Measures for Refugees in Greece and Asia Minor." Report by Dr. Nansen, High Commissioner of the League of Nations. Geneva (mimeo) (12 pp. C736(a). M447(a).

1923 "Report" by Dr. Nansen. Official Journal. League of Nations. (January):133–36.

Netting, R. McC., R. R. Wilk, and E. J. Arnould
1984 "Introduction." In *Households. Comparative and Historical Studies of the Domestic Group,* ed. R. McC. Netting, R. R. Wilk, and E. J. Arnould. Berkeley, CA: University of California Press, pp. xiii–xxxviii.

Newton, C. T. Sir
1862 *A History of Discoveries at Halicarnassus, Cnidus, and Branchidae.* Vol. II. London: Cox and Wyman.

Nicholson, M. E. R.
1987 "The Basque Notary: An Intercultural Mediator." *International Journal of Sociology* 15:85–103.

O'Barr, Wm.
1982 *Linguistic Evidence.* New York: Academic Press.

Olson, Emelie A.
1982 "Duofocal Family Structure and an Alternative Model of Husband-Wife Relationships." In *Sex Roles, Family and Community in Turkey.* ed. C. Kâğıtçıbaşı. Bloomington, IN: Indiana University Press, pp. 33–72.

Onar, S. S.
1955 "The *Majalla.*" In *Law in the Middle East.* Vol. I. Origin and Development of Islamic Law. Ed., Majid Khadduri and Herbert J. Liebesny. Washington, DC: The Middle East Institute, pp. 292–308.

Ostrorog, Count Leon
1927 *The Angora Reform: Three Lectures Delivered at the Centenary Celebrations of University College on June 27, 28, and 29, 1927.* London: University of London Press.

Pearl, David
1979 *A Textbook on Muslim Law.* London: Croom Helm.

Polk, William R. and R. Chambers
1968 "Editor's Introduction." In *Beginnings of Modernization in the Middle East.* Chicago: University of Chicago Press, pp. 1–25.

Pospisil, Leo
1958 *Kapauku Papuans and Their Law.* New Haven, CT: Yale University Publications in Anthropology, No. 34.
1967 "Legal Levels and Multiplicity of Legal Systems in Human Societies." *Journal of Conflict Resolution* 2(1):2–26.

1971 *Anthropology of Law: A Comparative Theory.* New York: Harper and Row.

Quataert, Donald
1983 *Social Disintegration and Popular Resistance in the Ottoman Empire, 1881–1908. Reactions to European Economic Penetration.* New York: New York University Press.

Radcliffe-Brown, A. R.
1933 "Primitive Law." In *Encyclopedia of the Social Sciences*, Vol. 9:202. New York: McMillan.

Raḥmān, A. Abdul and Y. Nagata
1977 "The *Iltizām* System in Egypt and Turkey." *Journal of Asian and African Studies* [Tokyo] 14:169–94.

Ramsaur, E. E.
1957 *The Young Turks: Prelude to the Revolution of 1908.* Princeton, NJ: Princeton University Press.

Ramsay, Sir William M.
1897 *Impressions of Turkey During Twelve Years' Wanderings.* London: Hodder & Stoughton.

1916 "The Intermixture of Races in Asia Minor: Some of its Causes and Effects." *Proceedings of British Academy,* 7:359–422.

Redhouse, Sir James
1968 *Redhouse Sözlüğü: Türkçe-Ingilizce.* [New Redhouse Turkish-English Dictionary.] Istanbul: Redhouse Press.

Reed, Howard
1980 "Ataturk's Secularizing Legacy and the Continuing Vitality of Islam in Republican Turkey." In *Islam in the Contemporary World*, ed. C. K. Pullapilly. Notre Dame, IN: Cross Roads Press, pp. 316–39.

1986 "Education in Islam: Issues and Priorities." Presented on Panel New Directions in Contemporary Turkish Scholarship, organized by E. Olson and J. Starr. Middle East Studies Association Meetings, Boston, November 22.

Refugee Settlement Commissions' Quarterly Reports to the League of Nations.
1924–1931 Twenty-seven reports. (c524, M. 187).

Refugee Settlement, General Survey on the Work Accomplished up to the Year 1926 (Ser. L.O.N.P. 1926.II.32).

Roberts, Simon
1979 *An Introduction to Legal Anthropology.* Harmondsworth, Eng: Penguin.

Rosen, Lawrence
1980–81 "Equity and Discretion in a Modern Islamic Legal System." *Law and Society Review* 15(2):217–45.
1984 *Bargaining for Reality: The Construction of Social Relations in a Muslim Community.* Chicago: University of Chicago Press.
1989a *The Anthropology of Justice: Law as Culture in Islamic Society.* Cambridge: Cambridge University Press.
1989b "Case Law and the Logic of Consequence." In *History and Power in the Study of Law: New Directions in the Anthropology of Law,* ed. June Starr and Jane Collier. Ithaca, NY: Cornell University Press, pp. 302–19.

Rothenberger, John E.
1978 "The Social Dynamics of Dispute Settlement in a Sunni Muslim Village in Lebanon." In *The Disputing Process—Disputing in Ten Societies.* New York: Columbia University Press, pp. 152–80.

Rudolph, Lloyd D. and Susanne Rudolph
1983 "Oligopolistic Competition Among State Elites in Princely India." In *Elites,* ed. G. Marcus. Albuquerque, NM: University of New Mexico Press, pp. 193–220.

Rustow, Dankwart
1957 "Politics and Islam in Turkey 1920–1955." In *Islam and the West,* ed R. N. Frye. Mouton, pp. 69–107.

Sahlins, Marshall
1981 *Historical Metaphors and Mythical Realities.* Ann Arbor, MI: University of Michigan Press.

Schacht, Joseph
1955 "The Law." In *Unity and Variety in Muslim Civilization,* ed. Gustave E. von Grunebaum. Chicago: Chicago University Press, pp. 74–87.
1964 *An Introduction to Islamic Law.* Oxford: Clarendon.

Schneider, Jane and Peter Schneider
1983 "The Reproduction of the Ruling Class in Latifundist Sicily, 1860–1920." In *Elites,* ed. Marcus. Albuquerque, NM: University of New Mexico Press, pp. 141–92.

Schneider, Peter, Jane Schneider, and Edward Hansen
1972 "Modernization and Development: The Role of Regional Elites and Noncorporate Groups in the European Mediterranean." *Comparative Studies in Society and History*:328–50.

Schutz, A.

1967 *The Phenomenology of the Social World.* Evanston, IL: Northwestern University Press.

Scott, Joan Wallach

1988 *Gender and the Politics of History.* New York: Columbia University Press.

Scott, Richard B.

1968 "The Village Headman in Turkey. A case study." Institute of Public Administration for Turkey and the Middle East. Ankara: Sevinc Matbaası.

Shaw, Stanford J.

1968 "Some Aspects of the Aims and Achievements of the Nineteenth-Century Ottoman Reformers." In *Beginning of Modernization in the Middle East,* ed. W. R. Polk and R. Chambers, pp. 29–39.

1969 "The Origins of Representative Government in the Ottoman Empire: An Introduction to the Provincial Councils, 1839–1876." Near East Roundtable, ed. R. Bayley Winder. New York: Near East Center, Center for International Studies, New York University.

1970 "The Central Legislative Councils in the Nineteenth-Century Ottoman Reform Movement Before 1876." *International Journal of Middle Eastern Studies* I:51–84.

1971 "The Editor's Desk." *Journal of Middle Eastern Studies* 2:195–96.

Shaw, Stanford J. and Ezel Kural Shaw

1977 "Reform, Revolution, and Republic: The Rise of Modern Turkey, 1808–1975." *History of the Ottoman Empire and Modern Turkey,* Vol. II. Cambridge: Cambridge University Press.

Skocpol, Theda

1979 *States and Social Revolutions: A Comparative Analysis of France, Russia and China.* Cambridge: Cambridge University Press.

Snyder, F.G.

1981 "Anthropology, Dispute Processes and Law: A Critical Introduction." *British Journal of Law and Society* 8(2):141–80.

Soteriadis, George

1918 *An Ethnological Map Illustrating Hellenism in the Balkan Peninsula and Asia Minor.* London: Edward Stanford.

Starr, June

1968 "The Ecological Basis of Residence in Bodrum, Turkey: Some Contrastive Examples." Presented at Middle East Studies Meetings, Austin, TX, November 15–16.

1978a *Dispute and Settlement in Rural Turkey: An Ethnography of Law.* Leiden, Netherlands: E.J. Brill.

1978b "Negotiations: A Pre-Law Stage in Rural Turkish Disputes." In *Cross-Examinations: Essays in Memory of Max Gluckman*, ed. P. H. Gulliver. Leiden, Netherlands: E.J. Brill, pp. 110–32.

1978c "Turkish Village Disputing Behavior." In *The Disputing Process*, ed. L. Nader and H. Todd. New York: Columbia University Press, pp. 122–51.

1980 "First Thoughts on Western Law in Islam: Its Effect on Family Life in Aegean Turkey." *American Legal Studies Forum* (April):23–31.

1981 "Strengths of the Anthropological Method in the Study of Law." *UCLA Law Review* 28(3):591–604.

1982 "Sociolegal Approaches to India's Land Reform Policies, 1948–1979." Presented at University of Warwick, Coventry, England, Seminar in Law and Society, Spring.

1984 "The Social and Legal Transformation of Rural Women in Aegean Turkey." In *Women and Property/Women as Property,* ed. Renée Hirschon. London: Croom Helm, pp. 92–116.

1985a *Adliye: The Ethnography of a Rural Turkish Law Court*. Color Video, Film Script, and Teacher's Guide. 30 minutes, sound. Available from author.

1985b "Folk Law in Official Courts in Turkey." In *People's Law and State Law: The Bellagio Papers,* ed. A. Allott and G. R. Woodman. Dordrecht, Netherlands: Foris, pp. 123–41.

1989a "The 'Invention' of Early Legal Ideas: Sir Henry Maine and the Perpetual Tutelage of Women." In *History and Power in the Study of Law: New Directions in Anthropology of Law,* ed. June Starr and Jane Collier. Ithaca, NY: Cornell University Press, pp. 345–68.

1989b "The Role of Turkish Secular Law in Changing the Lives of Rural Muslim Women, 1950–1970." *Law and Society Review* 23(3):497–523.

1990 "Islam and the Struggle Over State Law in Turkey." In *Law and Islam in the Middle East*, ed. D. Dwyer. Westport, CT: Bergin and Garvey.

1991 "Foreign Merchants and Ottoman Notable Farmers: A Nexus for Understanding Historical Legal Change." Presented at Law and Society Meetings, Amsterdam, Holland, June.

Starr, June and Jane F. Collier

1987 "Historical Studies of Legal Change." *Current Anthropology* 28(3):367–72.

1989a "Dialogues in Legal Anthropology." In *History and Power in the Study of Law: New Directions in Anthropology of Law,* ed. J. Starr and J. F. Collier. Ithaca, NY: Cornell University Press.

1989b *History and Power in the Study of Law: New Directions in the Anthropology of Law.* Ithaca: Cornell University Press.

Starr, June and Jonathan Pool
1974 "The Impact of a Legal Revolution in Rural Turkey." *Law and Society Review* 8(4)533–60.

Starr, June and Barbara Yngvesson
1975 "Scarcity and Disputing: Zeroing-in on Compromise Decisions." *American Ethnologist* 2(3):553–66.

Stewart, Frank
n.d. *Bedouin "Tribal" Law Cases.* Manuscript on file with the author.

Stirling, Paul
1957 "Land, Marriage, and the Law in Turkish Villages." In *The Reception of Foreign Law in Turkey. International Social Science Bulletin* 9:21–33.
1960 "A Death and a Youth Club: Feuding in a Turkish Village." *Anthropological Quarterly* 33:51–75.
1965 *Turkish Village.* London: Weidenfeld and Nicolson.

Sunar, Ilkay
n.d. "The Political Rationality of Ottoman Economics: Formation and Transformation." In *Polity, Economy, and Society in Ottoman Turkey and North Africa*, ed. Ş. Mardin and W. I. Zartman. Princeton, NJ: Princeton University Press.

Szyliowicz, Joseph S.
1966 *Political Change in Rural Turkey: Erdemli.* The Hague: Mouton.
1971 "The Mülkiye and Elite Recruitment in Turkey." *World Politics* (April):371–98.

Tannen, Deborah
1982a *Analyzing Discourse: Text and Talk.* ed. D. Tannen. Georgetown University Roundtable on Language and Linguistics, 1981. Washington, DC: Georgetown University Press.
1982b *Conversational Style.* New Jersey, Ablex, Norword.

Tekeki, Sirin
1981 "Women in Turkish Politics." In *Women in Turkish Society,* ed. N. Abadan-Unat. Leiden, Netherlands: E.J. Brill, pp. 293–310.

Thibaut, John and Laurens Walker
1975 *Procedural Justice. A Psychological Analysis.* New York: John Wiley & Sons.

Thompson, E. P.
1975 *Whigs and Hunters: The Origin of the Black Act.* New York: Pantheon.
1978 *The Poverty of Theory.* New York: Monthly Review Press.

Tigar, Michael E. and Madeleine R. Levy
1977 *Law and the Rise of Capitalism*. New York: Monthly Review Press.

Timur, Serim
1981 "Determinants of Family Structure in Turkey." In *Women in Turkish Society*, ed. N. Abadan-Unat. E.J. Brill, Leiden, Netherlands: pp. 59–73.

Toprak, Binnaz
1981 *Islam and Political Development in Turkey*. Leiden, Netherlands: E.J. Brill.

Trimberger, Ellen Kay
1978 *Revolution from Above: Military Bureaucrats and Development in Japan, Turkey, Egypt, and Peru*. New Brunswick, NJ: Transaction Books.

Turan, İlter
1984 "Cyclical Democracy: The Turkish Case." Paper Presented at the Annual Meeting of the Midwest Political Science Association, Chicago, April 11–14.

Turkish Proverbs.
1880 [Translated into English.] Venice: Armenian Monastery of St. Lazarus.

Türkiye Itatistik Yıllığı.
1985 Ankara: Basbakanlık Devlet Istatistik Enstitusu.

Turner, Victor
1957 *Schism and Continuity in an African Society. A Study of Ndembu Village Life*. Manchester: Manchester University Press.

Tute, Richard C., Sir
1927 *The Ottoman Land Laws. With a Commentary on the Ottoman Land Code of the Seventh Ramadan 1274*. [Jerusalem].

Ümumi Nüfus Tahriri. [1927 Census of Turkey].
1929 Türkiye Cumhuriyeti Başvekalet. Istatistik Ümum Müdürlüğü. 28 October 1927. Ankara: Husnutabıat Mabaası.

Van Velsen, J.
1964 *The Politics of Kinship*. Manchester: Manchester University Press.
1967 "The Extended-Case Method and Situational Analysis." In *The Craft of Social Anthropology*, ed. A. L. Epstein. London: Tavistock Press, pp. 129–49.

Veinstein, Gilles
1976 "Ayan de la Région d'Izmir et Commerce du Levant (Deuxième Moitie du XVIIIe Siècle)." *Études Balkaniques XII*:3, 71–83.

Velidedeoğlu, H. V.

1957 "The Reception of the Swiss Civil Code in Turkey." In *The Reception of Foreign Law in Turkey. International Social Science Bulletin* 9:60–65.

Verdery, Katherine

1983 *Transylvanian Villagers: Three Centuries of Political, Economic, and Ethnic Change*. Berkeley, CA: University of California Press.

Vincent, Joan

1989 "Contours of Change. Agrarian Law in Colonial Uganda, 1895–1962." In *History and Power in the Study of Law: New Directions in Legal Anthropology*, ed. J. Starr and J. F. Collier. Ithaca, NY: Cornell University Press, pp. 153–67.

von Grunebaum, E.

1962 *Medieval Islam: A Study in Cultural Orientation*, 2nd ed. Chicago: Chicago University Press.

Wallerstein, Immanuel

1980 "The Ottoman Empire and the Capitalist World-Economy: Some Questions for Research." In *Türkiyenin Sosyal ve Ekonomik Tarihi* (1071–1920):[Social and Economic History of Turkey (1071–1920)]. Papers presented to the First International Congress on the Social and Economic History of Turkey, Hacettepe University, Ankara, 1977. Ankara: Meteksan Sirketi, pp. 117–22.

Weber, Eugen

1976 *Peasants into Frenchmen. The Modernization of Rural France*. Palo Alto, CA: Stanford University Press.

Witty, Cathie

1978 "Disputing Issues in Shehaam, a Multi-Religious Village in Lebanon." In *The Disputing Process—Law in Ten Societies*, ed. L. Nader and H. Todd, Jr. New York: Columbia University Press, pp. 281–314.

1980 *Mediation and Society*. New York: Academic Press.

Wolf, Eric R.

1966 "Kinship, Friendship and Patron-Client Relations in Complex Societies." In *The Social Anthropology of Complex Societies*, ed. M. Banton. London: Tavistock, pp. 1–22.

Yalman, Nur

1973 "Some Observations on Secularism in Islam." *Daedalus* 102(1):139–68.

1979 "On Land Disputes in Eastern Turkey." *Research in Economic Anthropology* 2:269–302.

Yasa, Ibrahim
1957 *Hasanoğlan: Socio-Economic Structure of a Turkish Village*. Ankara, Public Administration Institute.

Yener, S.
1973 *Beş Yıllık Planada Nüfus Projeksiyonları için Kullanılan Yontem.* Ankara, State Planning Organization.

Yngvesson, Barbara
1988 "Making Law at the Doorway: The Clerk, the Court, and the Construction of Community in a New England Town." *Law and Society Review* 22: 410–48.

Young, George
1905–1906 *Corps de Droit Ottoman: Récueil des Codes, Lois, Règlements, Ordonnances et Actes les Plus Importants du Droit Intérieur, et d'Études sur le Droit Coutumier de l'Empire Ottoman.* 7 vols. Oxford: Clarendon.

Zwahlen, Mary
1981 *Le Divorce en Turquie:* Contribution a l'étude de la réception du Code Civil Suisse. Genève: Librairie Droz.

Index

Abadan-Unat, Nermin, 91, 94, 112
Abdülaziz, Sultan, 121, 122
Abdülhamid II, Sultan, 11, 22, 36, 37
Abdülmecid, Sultan, 24
Abel, Richard, 148n, 151, 159
Adjudication, defined, 148n
Adliye (term), xix
Administrative director. *See* Kaymakam
Administrative law
  in Ottoman Empire, 7–8
  in Turkish Republic, 55–57, 152
Adversary system of justice. *See* Common law tradition
African customary law, 179–80
Agaoğlu, Ms. Surreya, 42n
Agricultural *(Mîrî)* land, 45, 47, 48
Ahmad, Feroz, 57
Aksit, Bahattin, 176, 184
Aktan, Resat, 65
Alexander the Great, 70
Allen, Henry E., 39
Allis, Sam, 88n
Anderson, Benedict, 183
Ankara University, 154, 181, 184
Ansay, Tuğrul, 68n, 97, 100, 101, 108, 111
Anthropology, and history, xxxv–xxxvii
Antoun, Richard T., xxi
Appellate court, 155, 167, 168
Araz-i memleket. See Mîrî land
Arnould, E. J., 113n
Artemisia (queen of Caria), 70
Askeriye (military institution). *See* Military
Ataturk (Mustafa Kemal)
  emergence of, 11, 12–13
  legal models and, 152
  reconstruction of Turkish society and, 12–17, 180
  Turkish national identity and, 13–15, 55, 89–90
  view of women, 94–95
Atkinson, J. Maxwell, 171n
Avrupa Tüccarı (foreign merchants), 52
Ayans (notables)
  business elites and, 185
  development of, 47, 48
  growth of power of, 49–51, 73
  nineteenth century trade and, 6
  Ottoman agrarian production and, 49–51
  peasants and, 6, 8, 50, 51
  power of, 8

Bad debts
  court disputes and, 143–46
  village negotiations and, 133–36
Barnes, J. A., xli
Barth, Frederik, 179
Barton, R. F., 124
Bass, George, 83
Begazit I (Ottoman emperor), 70
Berats (licenses for traders), 52–53
Berkes, Niyazi, 8, 12, 21
Bey, Mahmut Es'ad, 16

Bey, Selahattin, 42n
Bianchi, Robert, 186n
Bilgin, Osman Nuri, 87n
Birth control techniques, 109–10. *See also* Family size
Bisharat, George, 123, 147, 175
Blok, Anton, 65
Boats, 76, 84
Bodrum District
 after creation of Turkish Republic, 74–77
 boats in, 76, 84
 change in, xxxix, 86–87
 composition of, 77–79
 destruction of church building in, 75–76
 historical background on, 69–70
 land cases in, 60–66
 land relations in (1950-1970), 57–60
 map of (1968), 46
 modern reference to Islamic sentiments and, 175, 177–79
 in nineteenth-century, 70–73, 120–23
 population by religion (1927), 75
 in relation to major cities, 4
 roads in, 76, 77, 82, 83, 147n
 tourist industry in, 77, 82–86
Bodrum district courts
 chain of jurisdiction in, 135
 disputes in, 143–46
 evidence in, 167–69
 fieldwork method in study of, 171n
 in 1960s, 80–81
 in 1980s, 84
 setting of, 157
 types of cases in, 158–59
Bodrum town
 as administrative center in 1960s, 77–82
 growth of, 82–86
 neighborhoods in, 78
 professional population in, 82–83
Bohannan, Paul, xxv, 127, 186n
Boissevain, Jeremy, 148n
Bracken, Katherine W., 30, 32, 37
Bridewealth, 107
Business activity, and religion, 52–53, 64

Cadestre surveys, 59, 66, 177
Caesar-Wolf, Beatrice, 155, 168, 171n
Cam, Mrs. Emine, 71, 88n
Camels, 85
Carpet-weaving, 72, 73
Cases. *See* Law cases, or Topic, e.g. divorce
Castle of Christian Knights of St. John, 70
Celebi, Evliya, 70
Celebrities, 83–84
Centralization, early attempts toward, 30
Certified note (*noter senedi*), 59
Cevdet, Ahmed (Ahmed Cevdet Pasa), 33, 34, 37
Chanock, Martin, xxxvii, 179, 186n
Chartier, Roger, xxxvi
Children, in divorce cases, 97
Christian community, in twentieth-century Bodrum, 75
Çiftliks (big farms), 49–51
Circle of justice, 22, 181
Circumcision rituals, 110
Civil cases, 135, 158. *See also* Land cases
Civil law, imperial (*Kanun*), 22, 27, 40
Civil law tradition, 33, 151–55, 168–69. *See also Mecelle-i Ahkam-i Adliye*
Cohen, Abner, xli
Cohn, Bernard S., xxxv, xli
Collier, Jane F., xxxvii, 95, 103, 146, 174, 179
Colson, E., 127
Comaroff, John, xvii, 186n
Commercial law, 27–28, 29, 169. *See also Mecelle-i Ahkâm-i Adliye;* Trade

Committee of Union and Progress, 11–12
Common law tradition vs. civil law tradition, 151–55
Conflict resolution. *See also* Dispute negotiation
  disputes in court and, 143–46
  Islamic law and, 147, 175, 177–79
  in unstructured situations, 128–42
  village councils and, 125–26
  village methods of, 127–47
Constitution of 1961, 183
Constitution of 1876 (*Kanun-ı Esasî*), 36–37
Cosar, Fatma Mansur, 91, 113n
Coulson, J., 5, 34, 42n
Council of Ministers (*Meclis-i Vükelâ*), 27
Council of State (*Surayı Devlet*), 32
Coup d'états, and Young Turks, 11–12
Court docket, xli, 96–97, 157
Court hearings
  disputing processes and, 143–46
  length of, 81–82, 154, 158
Court of appeal (*Divan-i Ahkâm-ı Adliye*), 32–33. *See also* Appellate court
Court of appeal (Nezareti-i Ahkâm-ı Adliye), 33
Court of Maritime Commerce, 29
Courts
  cultural change and, 180–82
  status of women and, 89–92, 95–103, 112
Court stenographer, 80–81
Crafts guilds, 6
Criminal cases
  brought by women, 101–3
  land cases, 63, 64–66
  village chain of jurisdiction in, 135
Criminal law
  Ataturk and, 152
  penal code of 1858 and, 29, 31–32
  secular courts and, 29
Crisis, and cultural change, 174
Cross-examination, 153, 154
Culler, J., 170n
Cultural change. *See* Social change
Culture. *See* European culture; Ottoman Empire; Tanzimat Period; Turkish national identity
  definition of, xxxvi
Cuniet, Vital, 68n, 114n
Customary law ('urf), 123, 179–80
  and state law, 149, 156
"Cyclical democracy," 15

Damaska, Mirjan, 155
Danet, Brenda, 170n, 171n
Dar-ı Şurayı Bab-ı Âli (legislative council), 25–26
Davison, Roderic H., 24, 25, 29, 31, 33, 41n
Debt. *See* Bad debts
Defterhane (Land Registry Bureau), 55, 57–58
Degler, Carl N., 115n
Demirel, Süleyman (Turkish prime minister), 184
Democracy, 94. *See also* Multiparty system
De Planhol, Xavier, 53, 72, 87n
Derebeys, 48, 56
Derrida, J., 170n
Dervish orders, 5
Disposition, as term, 172n. *See also* Legal disposition cases
Dispute, defined, 148n
Dispute and Settlement in Rural Turkey (Starr), xx–xxi
Dispute negotiations
  dyadic, 128–31
  nature of, in unstructured situations, 128, 147
  rank and status effects in, 138–43
  strategies used in, 138–43
  triadic, 132–38
Dispute resolution paradigm, xl, 28, 182

Divan-i Ahkâm-i Adliye
(court of appeal), 32–33.
See also Appellate court
Divorce. *See also* Family law; Women
cases, 60, 96–98, 99
grounds for, and patriarchy, 98, 100, 108, 111
Ottoman reform and, 39
secular civil law and, 91, 96–98
Diyarbakır, university at, 185
Dobash, R., 111
Dobash, R. E., 111
Domestic unit
household as, 96, 113n
nuclear family as, 182
Donné kule, 185
Dönüm, 57, 68
Drew, Paul, 171n
Duben, Alan, 105
Dunstan, R., 171n
Dwyer, Daisy, xxi
Dyadic dispute negotiation, 128–31, 141

Economic prosperity, and dispute resolution, 65
Education. *See also* Legal education
Ataturk-led revolution and, 14, 15
Imam Hatip schools and, 18, 176
Islamic, in modern Turkey, 176
reform during Ottoman Empire and, 8–10
secular, 176
Eickelman, Dale, 59, 81, 124, 179
Elias, Norbert, xl
Elites
conflict over change in empire, 12–13
judges as among, 156, 169
in nineteenth century, 6–7
non-Islamic values and, 15, 17, 18
secularizing vs. Islamicizing, 176
transformation in rural Anatolia and, 179–80
Elliott, C. B., 119
Empirical method, and sociolegal research, 150, 171n
Employment disputes, village negotiations and, 130–33
Encümen-i Âli
(legislative council), 26
Enforcement, 141–42
Engel, David M., xxv, 159
Enlightenment, xxiii
Entrepreneur, status of, 138
Epstein, A. L., xxv, 127, 148n
Epstein, T. S., 109
Erbakan, Neçemittin, 186n
Erder, Leila, 105
Ermarth, Michael, xxxvi
Ertegun, Ahmet, 83
Esham system, 48
Esposito, John L., 39
Estatism, as term, 93
Ethnicity. *See also* Population exchange
in nineteenth-century Anatolia, 51–52, 55
in nineteenth-century Ottoman Empire, 70–73
European culture, 7–10, 16–17, 23
Events, and cultural change, 173
Evidence, 167–69. *See also* Testimony; Third parties
Evkaf (pious endowments), 5
landownership and, 45, 47
Extended patriarchal household, 107–8, 113n

Fallers, Lloyd A., xxiii, 91, 94
Fallers, M., 91
Family *evkaf*, 47
Family law. *See also* Divorce; Women
Islamic law and, 38, 40, 169
Ottoman secular courts and, 17
in Tanzimat Period, 24, 33, 38–40
Turkish civil code and, 90–91, 152

Family size, limitation of, 92, 103, 105, 108–11, 115n
Fazil, Mustafa, 10
Feron, James, 171n
Field, Henry, 52, 54, 68n, 87n
Fieldwork methods, 171n
    learning Turkish, xxviii, xxxv, xxxix
Findley, Carter, 8, 21, 31, 33, 35, 40, 41n, 42n
Fishing, 77
Fitzpatrick, Peter, xxxvii
Fixed forms, 174–75
Foreign merchants (*Avrupa Tüccarı*), 52
Foreign trade. *See* Commercial law; Trade
Forest cases, 60–63
France, 8, 30
Frangakis-Syrett, Elena, 68n
Freehold *(mülk)* land, 45, 47
Friedman, Laurence M., 159
Friedman, Lawrence M., xli
Fuller, Lon, 148n

Galanter, Marc, 143
Galantı, Avram, 68n, 70, 71, 75, 76, 77, 87n, 114n
Garbett, C. K., 148n
Garcia Marquez, Gabriel, 69
Garfinkel, H., 148n
Garnett, Lucy M. J., 38
Geertz, Clifford, xxi, xxxvi
Gendarmes
    in chain of jurisdiction, 135
    discretionary power of, 196
    district, 196
    in triadic negotiations, 132, 136–38
    village-based, 195–96
Gender relationships, 15, 111. *See also* Divorce; Family law; Women
Giddens, A., xxiii, 173, 174
Gilsenan, Michael, 176, 178, 179
Gluckman, Max, xxv, 127, 148n, 186n
Goffman, E., 148n
Gordon, Robert, xxxv
Government headquarters (*Porte*), 8, 21, 26
Great Britain, 52
Greco-Turkish War, 55, 74–76
Greeks
    in nineteenth-century Ottoman Empire, 71–73
    in Ottoman Bodrum, 120–22
    Ottoman trade and, 52
    in rural Anatolia, 53
Greenhouse, Carol, xli
Grønhaug, Reidar, 68n
Gülhane Rescript of 1839, 22
Gulliver, P. H., xxv, 127, 172n, 186n
Gumperz, John, 150, 170n, 171n
Güriz, Adnan, 149

Had (boundary) concept, 7–8
Hansen, Edward, xli
Harris, Donald, 171n
Hatt-ı Hümayun (Imperial Rescript), 22–25
Hayden, Robert, xli, 171n
Hayriye Tüccarı (Muslim guild), 53
Heidborn, A., 31, 32, 33, 41n
Heper, Metin, 14, 22
Herodotus, 69, 86
Heyd, Uriel, 14, 18, 19n, 176
High Council of the Tanzimat, 27
Historical framework, anthopology and, 173–74, 182
History, anthropology and, xxxv–xxxvii
Hobsbawm, E. J., 65
Hocas (Islamic teachers), 6
Hoebel, E. A., xviii, xxiv, xxv, 127, 142
Household
    forms of, 106–7
    patriarchal, 107–8
    separateness of, and women's rights, 98, 99–100, 108, 111
    size of, 103–7
    as unit, 96, 113n

Household head, in dispute negotiation, 132–33, 138

Iç güvey model, 74, 107
Ideology, secular vs. Muslim, xxxiii–xxxiv
İlmiye (Ottoman cultural /religious institution), 7, 9
Iltizam land system, 47–49
İmam, 18, 123–24, 125, 148n
İmam Hatip schools, 18, 176, 184
Imperial Rescript. *See Hatt-ı Hümayun*
Inalcik, Halil, 3, 6, 7, 8, 22, 49, 50, 81
Incompatibility, as grounds for divorce, 101
Infant neglect, 108–9
Inheritance cases, 58, 60, 61. *See also* Land cases; Property redistribution
Inönü, Ismet (Turkish president), 57
Institutional structures
  and cultural change, 173
  rural conflict resolution and, 127
Intelligensia, 10–12. *See also* Young Ottomans; Young Turks
Intermediaries. *See* Third parties
Iran, secular ideologies and, xxxviii
Islam. *See also* Islamic fundamentalism
  business and, 52–53, 64
  in culture of Turkish Republic, 14–15, 178–79
  educational system and, 8, 9, 94
  in modern Turkey, 17–19, 87, 94, 176–77, 178–79
  in nineteenth-century Bodrum, 121
  in Ottoman Empire, 3–7, 12, 14, 37
  popular legal culture and, 123–24
  practices of, 5–6, 178–79
  Tanzimat reform and, 23–25
  village conflict resolution and, 126, 146–47
  vs. secularism, 17, 175–76, 183–85
Islamic fundamentalism, persistance of Turkish secular law and, xxxviii
Islamic institutes (*Yüksek Islam Institüleri*), 18
Islamic law (Şeriat). *See also Mecelle-i Ahkâm-i Adliye*
  commercial law and, 27–28, 29
  evkaf lands and, 47
  family law and, 24, 33, 36, 90–91, 169
  Fıkıh and, 34
  freehold property and, 48
  law school curriculum and, 184
  Mecelle and, 33
  origin of, 90
  Ottoman Empire and, 5–7
  state law and, xix, 21, 31
  village conflict resolution and, xl, 175, 177–79
Islamic leaders (*Ulemas*), 8, 25, 28, 31, 34
Istanbul University, 154, 181
Izmir. *See* Smyrna

Jackson, D., 109
Jagger, Mick, 84
Jewish community, 52
Johnson, Mark, xvii
Judges. *See also* Judicial process
  constraints on, 155–57
Judicial process
  in civil vs. common law tradition, 151–55
  decision-making in, 151, 155–57, 159–67
  determination of truth in, 151, 155
  empirical method in study of, 150
  filing of cases and, 157–58
  Turkish legal process and, 149
Jurisdiction, chain of, 135
Jurisprudence, Muslim definition of, 90

Jurisprudence of uncertainty, xxiv
Jury trial, 153, 154, 171n

Kadi courts (Islamic courts), xix, 5, 16
Kadis (Islamic judges), 5
Kagitcibasi, Cigdem, 113n
Kandiyoti, Deniz, 113n
Kanun-i Esasi (constitution of 1876), 36–37
Kanun (imperial civil law), 22, 27, 40
Karal, Enver Ziya, 67n
Karpat, Kemal H., 30, 45, 51, 55, 56, 66
Kasaba, Resat, 68n
Katib Celebi, 22
Kaymakam (administrative director), 59–60, 79, 80, 135, 170, 196
Kaza districts, xxiii, 6, 77
Kazamias, Andreas M., 19n
Kazgan, Gulten, 91
Kemal, Mustafa. *See* Ataturk
Kennett, Austin, 186n
Kidder, Robert, xli
Kili, Suna, 93
Kinross, Lord, 94, 95
Kinship structures, 122, 183
Kiray, Mübeccel, 91
Kolars, John F., 68n
Kur'an
  quoting of, 147, 178–79
  as symbol, 153
Kuran, Ercumend, 19n
Kushner, David, 14, 19n

Ladas, Stephen P., 19n, 87n
"Laicism," concept of, 15
Lakoff, George, xvii
Lamar, J. V., 88n
Land, classes of, in Ottoman Empire, 45, 47
Landau, J. M., 19n, 176, 186n
Land auctions, 48–49
Land cases, in Bodrum District, 60–66, 143–46. *See also* Forest cases; Inheritance cases; Orchard access cases
  in criminal courts, 63, 64–66
  frequency of, 60–61
  by type, 61–64
  types with low frequency, 61, 62, 63–64
Land deed (*Tapu temessükü*), 49
Land-division cases, 58, 61, 65–66
Land ownership, 56–60. *See also* *Mülk* land; Title to land
Land reform, 55–57
Land Reform Law of 1945, 57
Land Registry Bureau (*defterhane*), 55, 57–58
Land transfer, and witnessing, 124–25, 178
Language, 183
  in legal process, 150, 157
Language reform, 13, 90
Law. *See also* Islamic law *(Seriat)*; Secular legal system
  concept of, xxiii, xxxv, 148n, 174
  social interactions and, 176–77
Law and order, in modern Bodrum district, 79–80
Law cases. *See* Civil cases; Criminal cases; Divorce, cases; Inheritance cases; Land cases; Legal disposition cases; Social relationship cases
Law enforcement agents, 195–97
Law faculties, Turkish
  joint degree programs, 171, 181
  number of, in 1960s, 154, 171n, 181
  number of, in 1980s, 181
Law Merchant, 32
Law of Title Deeds of 1876, 56
Lawyers, 81, 152–53, 181
League of Nations, 15, 74
Legal disposition cases (Type A cases), 158, 159–63
Legal education. *See also* Law faculties, Turkish
  constitution of 1876 and, 37–38
  in modern Turkey, 154, 171n, 180–82, 184
  in Ottoman Empire, 32

Legal Education *(Continued)*
secular legal system and, 16
Legal field, defined, 148n
Legal representative (*Vekils*), 66, 81, 124, 177
Legal system. *See* Islamic law; Popular legal culture; Secular legal system
Legislative act, in legal tradition, 152
Legislative councils, 25–27
Lessing, Kurt, 130
Levy, Madeleine R., xviii, xxiii, xxiv, 6
Lewis, Bernard, 8, 9, 11, 13, 16, 19n, 22, 30, 31, 39, 42n, 47, 49, 50, 56, 57, 67n, 68n, 73, 90, 91, 113n, 148n, 170
Llewellyn, K., xviii, xxiv, xxv, 127, 142
Loftus, Elizabeth, 170n
Love, Iris, 83

McGowan, Bruce, 49, 50
Magnarella, Paul J., xxi
Mahkeme (term), 33
Mahmud II, Sultan, 8, 24, 25, 30, 49
Mâlikâme system, 48
Malinowski, Bronislaw, xxiv, xxv
Mandalinci Village
background on, 119–21
map of, 120
Mansur, Fatma, 70, 82, 87n, 88n, 113n
Marcus, George, xli
Mardin, Şerif, xxi, 3, 6, 7, 13, 19n, 23, 33, 36, 41n, 42n, 176
Margaret (princess of England), 83–84
Marriage law
Ottoman reform in, 38, 39–40
secular Turkish civil code and, 90–91
Marriage practices
modern, 85
in nineteenth-century, 72, 73–74, 122
Marx, Karl, 175
Mausolus (king of Caria), 69–70
Mecelle-i Ahkâm-i Adliye (partial codification of Şeriat), 33–36, 40–41
content of, 34–35
mülk lands and, 47
significance of, 35
Meclis-i Hass-ı Umumi (legislative council), 26
Meclis-i Vâlâ-yı Ahkam-ı Adliye (Supreme Council of Judicial Ordinances), 25–27, 32–33
Meclis-i Vükelâ (Council of Ministers), 27
Mektep schools, 8, 9
Mendell, Nancy, 115n
"Men of the Tanzimat," 10
Merchant class, 52–53
Merry, Sally, xli, 172n
Merryman, John Henry, 152, 153, 155, 181
Messick, Brinkley, xxi, 124, 171n, 179
Metrouke land, 45
Mevat land, 45, 47
Military (*Askeriye*), 7, 8, 11–12, 184–85
Miller, William, 51
Millet (religious group), 3, 8, 16–17
Minister (Vezir), 25
Ministry of Commerce (*Ticaret Meclis-i*), 28
Mîrî (*araz-i memleket*) land, 45, 47, 48
Mizzi, Sibil, 115n
Moore, Sally Falk, xvii, xxiv, xxv, xli, 148n, 179
Mosque-building, government, 185
Mourning rituals (mevlûd), 110
Müftü (Islamic judge), 6
Muhtar (village headman), 125–26, 135
Mülkiye (Imperial Office), 7
Mülk land, 45, 47
Mültezim, 48
Multiparty system, xxxiv, 17–18, 92, 95, 96, 183–84
Mustaches, xix

Nader, Laura, xxi, xxv, xli, 148n, 151, 157, 178, 179
Nagata, Yuzo, 47, 48, 49, 50
Nansen, Dr., 19n, 87n
Nationalism, 53. *See also* Turkish national identity
"Net-casting" model of judicial decision-making, 168–69
Netting, R. McC., 113n
Newton, Sir C. T., 70
Nezareti-i Ahkâm-ı Adliye (court of appeal), 33
Nicholson, M. E. R., 59
Nizamiye courts, 33
  civil law and, 32
  penal code and, 31
  written law and, 37
Non-Islamic religious groups (*Zimmi*), 3, 24, 37, 47
Non-Islamic values, 15, 17, 18, 93–94, 111
Notables. *See Ayans*
Notaries, 59, 66, 124, 177
Noter senedi (certified note), 59
Nuclear household, 113n

Oaths of honesty, 153
O'Barr, Wm., xli, 170n, 171n
Olson, Emelie A., 113n
Onar, S. S., 42n
Oral law tradition, 124–25, 178
Orchard access cases, 61
Osmanlı, 72
Ostrorog, Count Leon, 16, 31, 36
Ottoman Empire. *See also* Tanzimat Period
  administrative institutions in, 7–8
  big farms and, 49–51
  chronology of uprisings against, 187–90
  circle of justice and, 22
  classes of land in, 45, 47
  division of, 51
  dualism of legal system in, 169
  educational reform in, 8–10
  evolution of secular courts and, 27–30
  multiethnicity of, 51–52, 55, 70–73
  representative government and, 23
  role of Islam in, 3–7
  rural social control in, 73–74
  uprisings in, 40
  Versailles Treaty and, 13
Ottoman Land Code of 1858, 30–31, 47, 50, 55, 56
Ottoman Law of Family Rights of 1917, 39, 96, 112n
"Ottoman way," 7–8

Pagan religion (*Yesidées*), 54
Palace of justice (term), xix
Palestinians, 123, 175
Parallel systems
  educational reform and, xxi, xxxix, 8–9, 24, 41
  legal reform and, xxi, 41
Pasa, Ahmed Cevdet. *See* Cevdet, Ahmed
Pasa, Mustafa Resid. *See* Resid, Mustafa
Patrons, 132, 136, 138
Pearl, David, 113n
Peasants, and *ayans*, 6, 8, 50, 51
Penal code, 29, 31–32. *See also* Criminal cases; Criminal law
Percival, R. V., 159
Philip V of Macedonia, 70
Plantation farming systems (çiftliks), 49–51
Political parties. *See* Multiparty system
Polygamy, 39–40, 90
Pool, Jonathan, xx, 19n, 88n, 101, 114n, 172n
Popular legal culture, 123–24, 175–76
Population, in Bodrum District in 1927, 75

Population *(continued)*
household size and, 104
modern levels of, 82–84
in 1960s, 87n
by village, 104, 105, 106
Population exchange, 15, 74–75, 87n
Porte (Ottoman government headquarters), 8, 21, 26
Pospisil, Leo, xviii, xxv
Property damage, village negotiations and, 130
Property redistribution, 65
Province (*vilayet* or *ıl*), 79
Public disturbance case, 163–67
Public prosecutor, 197
Public safety, threat to, 154

Rahman, A. Abdul, 47, 48, 49
Railroad, 53–54
Ramsaur, E. E., 10, 11, 12
Ramsay, Sir William M., 14, 51, 53, 54, 55, 72, 87n
Redhouse, Sir James, 22
Reed, Howard, 13, 176
Religion. *See* Ethnicity; Islam
Religious disputes, 37
Representative government, 23
Republican People's Party (RPP), 57
Research methods, 172n
Resid, Mustafa (Mustafa Rasid Pasa), 23, 26, 28, 30, 34
Resources, and cultural change, 173
Roads, 76, 77, 82, 83, 147n
Robert College, 9
Roberts, Simon, xvii, xxxvii, 186n
Rosen, Lawrence, xxi, xli, 59, 81, 124, 171n, 175, 178, 179
Rothenberger, John E., xxi
Routine cases (Type C cases), 159
RPP. *See* Republican People's Party
Rudolph, Lloyd D., xli
Rudolph, Susanne, xli
Rules, as resource, 174
Rural district court. *See* Bodrum district court
Rural economy, 50, 65
Rüşdiye (adolescent) schools, 9
Rustow, Dankwart, 55

Sahlins, Marshall, 173, 174
Schacht, Joseph, 5, 24, 40, 89, 90
Schneider, Jane, xli
Schneider, Peter, xli
School attendance violation case, 159–63
Schutz, A., 148n
Scott, Joan, xxxvi
Secondary education, 9
Secret societies, 12. *See also* Dervish orders
Secular courts
criminal courts and, 29
evolution of, 27–30
introduction of, 176
Secularism
ideals of, 89–90
vs. Islam, 175–76, 183–85
Secular legal system
Ataturk and, xxxviii, 16–17
constitution of 1876 and, 37
emergence of, 32–33, 40–41
endurance of, xxxviii
European Civil Law tradition and, 181
Islamic culture and, 19
status of women and, 90–91, 95–103
type of grievance and, 196–97
Selim III, Sultan, 8
Senno, Richard, 115n
Şeriat. *See* Islamic law
Şeyhülislâm (head of Ottoman Muslims), 33
commercial disputes and, 28, 29
Mecelle and, 34
Shaw, Ezel Kural, 8, 9, 23, 41n, 42n
Shaw, Stanford J., 6, 8, 9, 10, 19n, 23, 29, 41n, 42n, 148n
Silbey, Susan, 172n
Skocpol, Theda, xxiii, xxxiv

Smyrna (modern Izmir), 67n, 83
countryside around, 53–55
in nineteenth-century, 51–52
Social change
interaction at margins and, 173
secular civil law and, 89–90, 93–95
temporal dimension of, 21, 174
Social relationship cases (Type B cases), 159, 163–67. *See also* Divorce, cases
Social status
disputing strategies and, 138–43
positions of, in rural Turkey, 138
Social structure, in nineteenth-century Anatolia, 51–52
Sociolinguistic analysis, 150
Soteriadis, George, 71, 73, 114n
Sponge diving, 76–77
State, the, control of the periphery and, 182
State land. *See Metrouke* land; *Mevat* land
State law. *See also* Secular legal system
meanings of, xxiv
village processes and, 175
vs. Islamic law, in Ottoman Empire, 21
Stirling, Paul, xxi, 65, 91
Stock, David, 115n
Suavi, Ali, 10
Sunar, Ilkay, 67n
Surayı Devlet (Council of State), 32
Szyliowicz, Joseph S., 13, 91

Tangerine orchards, 76
Tannen, Deborah, 171n
Tanzimat Period
circle of justice and, 22
constitution of 1876 and, 36–37
emergence of secular legal system and, 32–33
evolution of secular courts and, 27–31
growth of civil court system in, 32
Hatt and, 22–25
land reform and, 49, 50
legal education and, 37–38
legislative councils and, 25–27
Mecelle and, 33–36
Ministry of Justice and, 37
penal codes and, 31–32
reform beginnings and, 22–25
Tapu temessükü (land deed), 49
Taxation
ayans and, 49
under Islamic law, 24
in modern Turkey, 66
in Ottoman Empire, 3
Turkoman confederacy and, 53
Tax-farming, 30–31, 56. *See also Esham* system; *Iltizam land* system; *Timar* system
Taxim (division of land), 58
Tekeki, Sirin, 95
Testimony
lying in court, 162, 172n
oaths of honesty in Turkey, 153
truth-telling in court, 150–55, 168, 172n
Theft, village negotiations and, 128–30, 133–36
Thibaut, John, 155, 168
Third parties, in dispute negotiation, 132–38, 141, 142
Thompson, E. P., xviii, xxiii, 176
Tigar, Michael E., xviii, xxiii, xxiv, 6
Timar (tax-farming) system, 30–31, 47, 50
defined, 67n
Time, and cultural change, 21, 174
Title to land, 58–60, 66
Tobacco production, 85, 105
Todd, Harry, Jr., xxv, 148n, 151
Toprak, Binnaz, 19n, 176, 186n
Tourist industry, 77, 82–86
Trade. *See also* Commercial law
ayans and, 6, 50

Trade *(continued)*
- concessions to European traders and, 52–53
- nineteenth-century Bodrum District and, 70–73
- Smyrna and, 52
- social control in early Bodrum, 74
- sponge diving and, 77

Traders' Law, 28
Triadic dispute negotiation, 132–38, 141
Trial. *See* Common law tradition vs. civil law tradition; Jury trial; Law cases
Tribal confederacies, 182, 183
Trimberger, Ellen Kay, xxiv
Truth, determination of, 151, 155. *See also* Testimony
Turgot (boat captain), 128–30
Türkeş, Colonel Alparsalan, 186n
Turkish Civil Code (*Türk Mendinî Kanunu*)
- grounds for divorce in, 97
- judicial decision-making and, 156
- legal process and, 153

Turkish national identity, 13–15, 55, 89–90
Turkish Republic. *See also* Ataturk
- creation of, 13
- emergence of, 54
- events in formation of, 190–92
- land administration in, 55–57
- reconstruction of society in, 12–17

Turkoman confederacy, 53–54, 66, 72
Turner, Victor, xxv, 127, 148n
Tute, Richard C., Sir, 45, 48, 58
Type A cases (legal disposition cases), 158, 159–63
Type B cases (social relationship cases), 159, 163–67
Tyser, B. A. L., 34

Ulemas (Islamic leaders), 8, 25, 28, 31, 34
Unstructured situations
- dyadic negotiation in, 128–31
- nature of dispute negotiation in, 128
- patterns of negotiation in, 138–42
- triadic negotiation in, 132–38

Upwardly extended household, 113n
Usufruct rights, 59
Uxorilocal marriage, 115n

Vakıf land. *See Evkaf*
Van Velsen, J., xxv, 127, 148n
Vatan (fatherland) organization, 11
Vatan ve Hürriyet (fatherland and liberty) organization, 11
Veinstein, Gilles, 6, 49, 50
Vekils (legal representatives), 66, 81, 124, 177
Velidedeoğlu, H. V., 91
Veraset (court-decided inheritance cases), 58
Verdery, Katherine, xxv
Vezir (minister), 25
Vilayet (province), 79
Village council, 125–26
Village gendarme. See Gendarmes
Village headman *(Muhtar)*, 125–26, 135
Vincent, Joan, 179
Violence, vs. legal redress, 65
Virilocal marriage, 115n
von Grunebaun, E., 90
Voting rights, 95

Walker, Laurens, 155, 168
Wallace, Don, Jr., 97
Wallerstein, Immanuel, xix, 50
Weber, Eugen, xxv
Weddings, 110
Wife-beating, 111, 113n
Wilk, R. R., 113n
Williams, Ivy, 90, 91
Witnesses
- evidence in Bodrum district court and, 167–68

Witnesses *(continued)*
  oral law tradition and, 124–25, 178
  in Turkish legal process, 153–54
Witty, Cathie, xxi
Wolf, Eric R., xli
Women. *See also* Family law
  Ataturk's view of, 94–95
  courtroom behavior of, 80
  divorces initiated by, 98, 99
  elites, in twentieth century, 91
  under Muslim vs. secular civic law, 90–91
  Ottoman reform and, 39–40
  participation in public events, 115n
  property rights and, 91
  rural, and secular law, 91–93, 95–96, 102–3
  rural, changing consciousness of, 103–8
  Turkoman, 72
  voting rights for, 95
Women's movement, 110, 111

Yalman, Nur, xxi, 14, 65
Yargìtay appellate court, 155
Yasa, Ibrahim, 91
Yesidées (pagan religion), 54
Yngvesson, Barbara, xli, 148n
Young, George, 38, 41n
Young Ottomans (exile movement), 10–11, 33
Young Turks, 11–13, 37
Yürük tribe, 54, 66, 72

Zimmi (Arabic: dhimmīs; recognized non-Muslim *millet*), 3, 24, 37, 47
Zwahlen, Mary, xxi, 100, 101, 111